SAINT DAVID'S PARISH, SOUTH CAROLINA
MINUTES OF THE VESTRY 1768-1832
PARISH REGISTER 1819-1924

by

Brent H. Holcomb, C. A. L. S.

𝕿𝖍𝖊 𝕯𝖎𝖔𝖈𝖊𝖘𝖊 𝖔𝖋
𝕾𝖔𝖚𝖙𝖍 𝕮𝖆𝖗𝖔𝖑𝖎𝖓𝖆

Please direct all correspondence and orders to:

www.southernhistoricalpress.com
or
SOUTHERN HISTORICAL PRESS, Inc.
PO BOX 1267
375 West Broad Street
Greenville, SC   29601
southernhistoricalpress@gmail.com

ISBN #0-89308-144-2

Printed in the United States of America

INTRODUCTION

This book contains transcriptions of two original volumes: the Vestry Minutes and the Parish Register of St. David's Parish (or church), Cheraw, South Carolina.

St. David's parish was created in 1768 by an Act of the Assembly, and was the last colonial parish to be established. In 1769 the District of Cheraws was set up to be co-terminous with St. David's parish. In 1785, Cheraws District was divided into three counties: Chesterfield, Marlboro, and Darlington.

The Vestry was as much a political body (or moreso) as a religious one. It took care of the poor, binding out bastards, voting, etc. and especially collecting taxes. Therefore, persons of all denominations (not merely Anglicans) will appear in the Vestry Minutes. Of course, when the church was disestablished in 1778, the vestry's functions were then mostly religious. The original volume of the vestry minutes is not paginated. Bishop Gregg relied heavily on this source for his History of the Old Cheraws, and of course, the records were in better condition at that time. His voter lists are more complete, and are generally accurate.

The Parish Register was used for over one hundred years. It typically gives baptisms (often with birth dates), marriages, and burials with a few other tidbits of information. The rector often performed baptisms and burials for persons outside his congregation and outside his parish, and entries for those persons can be found as well as the Anglicans. Of interest are the burials of old persons, often giving their ages. There were a number of refugees from Charleston and other coastal areas at the close of the Confederate War, and an occasional baptism, marriage or burial for some of them will be found.

Since the records for Chesterfield County were largely destroyed in 1865, these records are a virtual gold mine, since Cheraw is in that county. Darlington County lost its records by fire in 1806, and some help can be found for this loss as well.

My thanks to St. David's Church in Cheraw for their permission to publish these records, and especially for having the volume of Vestry Minutes restored for posterity.

Brent H. Holcomb, C. A. L. S.
Box 21766
Columbia, S. C. 29221
January 22, 1979

JOURNAL

OF THE PROCEEDINGS

OF THE VESTRY OF THE PARISH OF

ST. DAVID.

The General Assembly of the Province of South Carolina, having Passed an Act, bearing Date the [12th] Day of [April 1768] for making New Parish out of Part of the Parishes of St. Mark, Prince Frederick, and of [Pr]ince George,

The following Gentlemen were by the said Act appointed as [Co]mmissioners for the said Parish, which by the Act is appointed to go by the Name of St. David

Cladius Pegues	Charles Bedingfield
Philip Pledger	James James
Alexander Mackintosh	Robert Weaver
George Hicks	James Thomson
Thomas Ellerbee	Thomas Crawford
Robert Alison	Thomas Porte
Thomas Lide	Benjamin Rogers

.... In all 14

Monday   August   the 1st   1768

[fo]llowing Gentlemen, Commissioners of the Church according to Public Notice   re met at the House of Mr. Charles Bedingfield, viz.

Claudius Pegues	Thomas Lide
Philip Pledger	Charles Bedingfield
Alexander Mackintosh	James James
George Hicks	Benjamin Rogers
Robert Alison	

In all... 9

following Gentlemen declined acting as Commissioners in the affairs of the church... viz.

Alexander Mackintosh   James James   Robert Alison   3

Election for Vestry Men and Church Wardens for the Parish of St. David came. Then the following Gentlemen were duly Elected as Church Officers, viz.

Claudius Pegues	Alexander Gordon
Philip Pledger	Benjamin Rogers,
William Godfrey Vestry-Men	Church-Wardens.
Charles Bedingfield	
Thomas Lide	
Thomas Ellerbee	
Thomas Bingham	

Durham Hitts was this Day appointed Clerk of the Vestry, and Parish of St. David.

1

The following is the Number of Votes which Each of the Vestry-Men and Church-Wardens had at the Election

Claudius Pegues had of Votes	18
Philip Pledger	18
William Godfrey.............	17
Charles Bedingfield........	17
Thomas Lide	17
Thomas Ellerbee had of Votes	18
Thomas Bingham	18
Alexander Gordon...........	18
Benjamin Rogers............	18

The Electors of the Church Officers, were

William Hardwick	Thomas Bootright, Senr.	James Knight
Duke Glen	Jesse Counsell	Samuel Wise
John Mackintosh	John Pledger	James Thursby
John Jenkins	Robert Clary	Thomas Williams
Edward Ellerbee	Robert Anderson	Thomas Wade
John Husbands	Benjamin Jackson	Leonard Dozier

In al....

At. Mr. Charles Bedingfield's, on Tuesday, August 2nd, 1768.
The following Persons were duly sworn into their Offices for the Parish of St. David   viz.

Claudius Pegues
Philip Pledger
William Godfrey
Charles Bedingfield
Thomas Lide
Thomas Ellerbee
Thomas Bingham,
          Vestry-Men.

Alexander Gordon
Benjamin Rogers,
          Church-Wardens.

Durham Hitts, Clerk of the
Vestry and Parish

Monday   September 26th   1768

    The Writs of Election of a Member of Assembly for the Parish of St. David having been up from Charles Town; Twenty six Advertisements were sent to the different P   the Parish; Requiring the Appearance of the Inhabitants of the said Parish at Mr. Mackintosh's on Tuesday, and at Mr. Charles Bedingfield's on Wednesday, the   Fifth Days of October Ensuing; Being the Days appointed for the Election of a [mem]ber to Represent the Parish in the Common's House of Assembly. Likewise Circular Letters were writ to the Captains James Knight, James Thom[son], Thomas Connor, and Benjamin Jackson; and to Messrs. John Kimbrough, Wil[liam] Watkins, Robert Lide, and Gideon Gibson, With two or three Advertisements of Election Enclosed in Each to Put up at the most Public Places in their respect[ive] Districts, and a Desire to bring their Companies under their proper Leaders to Place of Election to prevent Confusion.

Journal of St. Davids

The Advertisement was as follows.

    The Inhabitants of the Parish of St. David are required to meet on Tuesday, the Fourth Day of October Ensuing, and at the House of Mr. John Mackintosh, and on Wednesday the Fifth Day of

the same Month, at the House of Mr. Charles Bedingfield, in
Order to Elect a Member of Assembly for the said Parish. The
Hours of Election to be from Ten in the Forenoon to Four in the
Afternoon.

By Order of the Church Wardens.
September 26th, 1768.   Durham Hitts, C. P.

The Circular Letter was as follows.

Sir.

You have Enclosed Advertisements for Electing a Member of
Assembly for this Parish. Please to Circulate them to the most
convenient Places. You are desired by the Captains Pledger,
Hicks, Lide &c. for the Honour of the Parish to bring as many
Voters as you possibly can to the Place of Election where they
will meet You with each of their Companies. They also desire,
that you will keep and bring up the People under their Proper
Leaders, in order to prevent Confusion. They hope that you will
on this Occasion Exort yourself to the utmost of Your Power.

I am, Sir,

Your humble Servant.

[Sept]ember 26th, 1768.   Durham Hitts, C. P.

The foregoing Circular Letters were directed for forwarding to
Mr. John Kimbrough, as follows,

Kimbrough,

As the Time is so short between our receiving the writs
of Election and the Time for Electing of a Member for this Parish
as You will see in the Letter directed to you You will do a good
piece of Service to the Public in causing the Letters Enclosed,
directed to the Captains Thomson and Knight, and to Mr. Watkins
and Mr. Gibson to be Conveyed to them as speedily as possible.

I am, Sir,

Your humble Servant,
[Septem]ber 26th 1768.   Durham Hitts, C. P.

October the Fourth, 1768, The Poll for Election of a Member
of Assembly for the [Parish] of St. David in Craven County, South
Carolina, was opened at the House of Mr. Mackintosh, and the
following Persons Voted, viz.

[Bart]holomew Bell	Lewis Rowan	Thomas Harry
[Simo]n Holmes	Charles Lowther	John Mackintosh
[John] Reynolds	Charles Lizonby	Charles McCall
[William]Reeves	John Davis	Roderick McIver
[John] Holley	John Courtney	John Evans
----- Lucas	Malachi Newberry	Daniel Devonald
-----[J]amieson	Thomas Evans	Thomas James
[Richard McD]------	------------	------------
Edward Lowther	John Knight	Abel Wilds
Francis McCall	Philip Pledger	Edward Jones
Gideon Parish	James James	Walter Downes
William Edwards	Daniel Man	Aaron Daniel
John McCall	Magnus Cargill	Robert Blair

John Cheeseborough   William James   Lewis Blalock
John Prothero   John Dyer   Daniel Luke
Evan Prothero   John Marshe   Benjamin Wright
James Knight   Thomas Lay   Gilbert Moody
James Rogers   Richard Blizard   Thomas Lane
Joseph Dabbs   Nathaniel Douglas   William Megee
Peter Kolb   Thomas Davidson   Samuel Evans
John Kimbrough   David Harry   Martin Kolb
John Cooper   Joshua Douglas   Robert Lide
David Harry   Jacob Lampleigh   Joseph Alison
William Dewitt   Howel James   John Alran
[W]illiam Allen   Joseph Barker   John Brown
Andrew Hunter   Isam Ellis   John Flennagan
[J]ohn McCall   William Tyrell   Job Edwards
[C]hristopher Teal   Abel Edwards   Richard McLaMore
[Ge]orge King   James Bruce   Anthony Pouncey
[Jo]siah Evans   William Pouncey   Duke Glen
[Sa]muel Wilds   Joshua Edwards   David Evans
John Rowell   John Brown   John Bruce
[D]ennis Gelphis   Enoch Luke   James Dozer
[B]enjamin Orrick [Oniel?] Jenkin David   Martin Dewitt
Thomas Edwards   Richard Allen   John Darby
[Jo]hn Griffith   Philip Robland

          Number of Voters this Day   [113]

     Day, October 5th, 1769. The Poll for Electing of a Member
of Assembly   of St. David in Craven County, South Carolina, was Opened at the House of   Bedingfield, and the following Persons Voted, viz.

-------- Bootright   Peter Heathey   William Johnson
----- ---dner   John Frazier   Thomas Williams
----- Carter   Thomas Sommerlin   William Hicks
---- James   John Williams   John Beverley
---- --vis   William Hardwicke   George Hicks
---- --edingfield   Thomas Lide   John Lyons
--------------   John Husbands   John Pledger
--------------   Jonathan Williams   ----------------
---- -ardiner
William Ellerbee   Thomas Bingham   Jonathan Wise
---mas Ellerbee   William Jones   John Shumake
--och Thomson   Thomas Connor   John Hicks
Edward Ellerbee   Kader Keaton   Thomas Rogers
Charles Irby   William Godfrey   Samuel Williams
John Sutton   George Sweeting   John Powe
Edward Bryan   John Moffatt   William Hempworth
Benjamin Rogers   John Westfield

          Number of Voters this Day 53

Claudius Pegues, Esq., was Unanimously Elected a Member of Assembly for the Parish of St. David ... All the Votes for both Days
being for him.

          The Votes the First Day were   113
                    the second Day   53
          The Full Number of Votes were   166

                    ANNO DOMINI 1769

                         4

February 4th, 1769

An Advertisement for the Meeting of the Freeholders in the Parish
of St. David, to Elect Church Officers.
    The Freeholders of St. David's Parish are required to meet
at Mr. Charles Bedingfield's, on Easter Monday (being the Ensuing 27th of March), in Order to Elect Church Officers. The
Election to begin precisely at Ten of the Clock in the Forenoon.

[Fe]bruary 4th, 1769.   Durham Hitts, C. P.

The last Assembly having been dissolved by his Excellency the
Governor of South Carolina almost as soon as called, New Writs
for an Election were sent up to the Church Wardens of St. David's
Parish, on Saturday, February 25th, 1769, [----ione]d the following Advertisement.
    The Freeholders of St. David's Parish, are required to give
their Attendance at Mr. John Mackintosh's on Tuesday the Ensuing
7th of March, and at Mr. Charles Bedingfield's on Wednesday the
8th of March in Order to Elect a Member of Assembly for the said
Parish. The Hours of Election to ... Ten in the Forenoon to
Four in the Afternoon.
            By Order of the Church Wardens.
            Durham Hitts
February 27th, 1769

... Tuesday, March 7th, 1769. The Poll was Opened at Mr. John
Mackintosh's ... of a Member of Assembly for the Parish of St.
David in Craven County, ... The following Persons voted, viz.

Philip Pledger	Claudius Pegues	Gideon Gibson
Benjamin Rogers	John Rothmahler	Alexander Mac.....
---------------	Nicholas Bedgegood	Thomas Davis
---------------	[John Mackintosh]	James Bruce
Richard Ponder	Samuel Hasleton	Robert Moody
Robert Alison	Walter Owens	Moses Bass
John Crawford	Harrison Lucas	Peter Keatley
Jordan Gibson, Sen'r	Charles Lizonby	John Davis
William Lucas	Robert Clary	David Evans
Reuben Gibson	Gideon Parish	William Edwards
Abel Edwards	Thomas Ellerbee	John Evans
Samuel Evans	John Hitchcock	Robert Lide
John Williams	Thomas Harry	John Prothero
Jacob Lampleigh	John Marshe	John McCall
James James	James Knight	Thomas James
Thomas Edwards	Thomas Avery	John Flennagan
James Rogers	Daniel Man	William Dewitt
Samuel Wilds	John Jamieson	Joshua Lucas
John Bruce	Charles Sparkes	Roderick McIver
Thomas Davidson	Isam Ellis	John Darby
William Babcock	Thomas Lane	Josiah Evans
Nathaniel Hunt	Thomas Lide	John Crews
Charles Bedingfield	John Jackson	Blundall Curtis
Daniel Sparkes	Benjamin James	John Mikell
Malachi Murphy	Walter Downes	William Floyd
Arthur Hart	James Mikell	William Tyrrell
William McTierre	David Harry	George Booth
Stephen Sebastian	John Kimbrough	Jacob Buxton
Jonathan Wise	Edward Lowther	Evan Prothero
Peter Kolb	Jordan Gibson	James Thomson
Edward Owens	Solomon Staples	

            Number of Voters this Day, were ....

Wednesday, March 8th, 1769. The Poll was Opened at Mr. Charles Bedingfield ... Election of a Member of Assembly for the Parish of St. David, in Craven County, [South Caro]lina. The following Persons Voted, viz.

...becca Lide	John Perkins	Jacob Johnson	Thomas Wade
... nes Griffith	William Hicks	Richard George	William Prestwoo[d]
[Cather]ine Little	Thomas Bootright	Daniel Lundy	Solomon Holmes
[J]ohn Sutton	Elizabeth Counsell	Benjamin Ladd	William Hayes
William Boatright	Michael Griffith	William Lankford	John Westfield
John Jones	Jesse Counsell	Edward Bryan	Benjamin Jackson
William Gardner, Senr.	William Godfrey	Enoch James	Frederick Kimbrell
[F]rancis Burton	John Knight	William Hardwicke	Joel Yarborough
... David	Samuel Windes	Sarah Booth	William Johnson
... Blizard	Willm. Gardner Junr.	George Hicks	William Jackson
... Lundy	Silas Harendine	Charles Irby	Thomas Tomkins
...am Hempworth	Philip Howell	Abel Wilds	David David[son]

Colonel George Gabriel Powell, Esq. was Elected a Member from the Parish of St. David's by a Majority of 154 Votes.

Easter Monday   March 27th   1769

Meeting of the Church Officers and Freeholders of the Parish of St. David Pee Dee River. The following Gentlemen were duly Elected at the House of Charles Bedingfield by Balloting to serve as Church Officers the ensuing ... viz.

[Cla]udius Pegues   Alexander Gordon
[Phi]lip Pledger   Benjamin Rogers
[Wi]lliam Godfrey   Church Wardens
[Char]les Bedingfield
[Tho]mas Lide
[Tho]mas Ellerbee   Vestry Men
[Tho]mas Bingham

Monday, May the 1st, 1769. The Church Wardens and Vestry Men of St. David's Parish, were duly qualified by taking the Oath appointed for ... Purpose.

Inacting of the Commissioners for the Parish of St. David in Craven County, the Province of South Carolina, at the House of Mr. Thomas Lide on Pee-Dee River on Saturday, September 23rd, 1769.
...ent

[Cla]udius Pegues   Philip Pledger   Thomas Ellerbee
[Rob]ert Alison   Thomas Lide   Charles Bedingfield
Benjamin Rogers   In all 7   Durham Hitts, Clerk.

[ORDE]RED ... That as the Clerk of the Parish did not receive the Letter, convening the present Meeting, to advertise it properly, till too late, thereby another Meeting appointed to be held at the House of Mr. Charles Bedingfield, on Wednesday the Ensuing 25th of October, and that advertisements be writ, and put up in every public Place in the Parish to give Notice to all the Parish Commissioners to give their Attendance at the above-said Time and Place in Order to lay off the Place for building a Church in the said Parish.

6

AN ACT for Establishing a Parish in Craven Coun-
[ty] by the Name of St. David, And for appointing Com[mis]sioners
of the High Roads in the said Parish, WHEREAS, Inhabitants resi-
ding on Pedee River, in the Par[ishes of St.] Mark's, Prince
George in Craven County, have represented [many inconveniences
which they are under for want of having] a Parish laid out in
[the said county, and prayed that a law may be passed for that
purpose,] WE THEREFORE pray his Most Sacred Majesty that it may
be Enacted. And Enacted by his Excellency the right Noble Lord
Charles Grevi[lle Montagu,] Captain General, Governor and Com-
mander in Chief, in and over [his] Majesty's Province of South
Carolina by and with the Advice and Con[sent of his] Majesty's
Council and the Commons House of Assembly of the [said] Province
and by the Authority of the same. THAT immediately [from and]
after the passing of this Act, a Parish shall be laid out and
Established in [Craven] County aforesaid. Bounded in the Following Manner, that is to [say, by a] Northwest Line to be run from
the Northward Corner of Wi[lliamsburgh] township to Lynches'
Creek, and from thence by that Creek to th[e provincial] line,
and that the Line, dividing St. Mark's from Prince Fred[erick's
parish] be carried on in the same Course from Great Pee Dee where
it [now ends to the pro]vincial line aforesaid, by which together
the Lines afore[said and] Lynches' Creek, the new Parish shall
be bounded, and that[the said] parish shall hereafter be called
and known by the name of Saint [David.]
    BE IT FURTHER ENACTED, by the Authority aforesaid, THAT
[a church] Chapel and a Parsonage House shall be built at such
Places [within the b]ounds of the said Parish as the Major part
of the Comm[issioners hereafter na]med, shall order and direct.
    AND BE IT FURTHER E[NACTED by the au]thority aforesaid,
THAT the Rector of Minister of the said [parish for the] Time
being shall Officiate in the said Church and Chap[el alternately
and] shall be Elected and Chosen in the same manner as the[rec-
tors or ministers] of the several other Parishes in this Province
are Elec[ted and chosen, and] Shall have Yearly paid to him and
his Successors fore[ver, the same salary as is a]ppointed for the
Rector or Minister of any other Par[ish in this Province, the
pa]rishes of St. Philip and St. Michael Excepted, out [of the
fund] to be appropriated for Payment of the Salary [of the Clergy
of this Province] and the Public Treasurer for the Time being
[is hereby authorized to pay the same under] the like penalties
[and forfeitures as for not paying the salaries due to the other]
Rectors....
    AND BE IT FURTHER ENACTED BY THE Authority aforesaid, That
Claudius [Pegu]es, Philip Pledger, Alexander McKintosh, George
Hicks, Thomas Elle[rbee, Rob]ert Allison, Thomas Lide, Charles
Bedingfield, James James, Robert [Weaver,] Thomas Crawford, James
Thompson, Thomas Port, and Benjamin Rogers, be, and they are
hereby appointed Commissioners or Super[visors for the] building
of the new Church, and Chapel and Parsonage House [in the par]-
ish of St. David, and they, or a major part of them are fully
autho[rized and impowere]d to Purchase a Glebe for the said
Parish and to take [subscriptions], and to receive and gather,
Collect and sue for all such sum[or sums of] Money as any pious
and well directed Person or Persons shall [give and co]ntribute
for the Purposes aforesaid. And in the Case of the Death, Ab-
scense (sic),[or refusing to] Act of any of the Said Commissioners, the Church Wardens and [vestry] of the Parish of Saint David
for the time being, shall and may[nominate a]nd appoint another
Person or Persons to be Commissioner or Com[missioners] in the
room or place of such so Dead, Absent, or refusing to Act, [as
to the said] Church Wardens and Vestry shall seem meet, which

7

Commission[er or Com]missioners so to be nominated and appointed,
shall have the same[powers a]nd Authority for putting this Act
in Execution to all intents [and purposes, as] the Commissioners
herein named.
     AND BE IT ALSO ENACTED by the Authority[aforesaid, That from
and] after the Dissolution of the present General Assembly,[the
inhabitants of] the Parish of St. Mark's which heretofore chose
two members [of Assembly, and]the Inhabitants of the Parish of
St. David, Qualified by [law for that purpose] shall chose and
elect One Member each and no [mor]e,[to represent the sa]id
Parishes respectively in General Assembly any [law, usage, or
custom to] the Contrary Notwithstanding. And that Writs[for
electing Members] to serve in General Assembly for the said
Parish[es, shall be issued at the same] time and in the same
manner as [for the several others parishes in this] Province,
accord ing to the directions of the Act of the General Assembly
in that case made and provided.
[apparently several lines missing or omitted here]
...Parish of Saint David. And the Said Commissioners or a Majority of them shall have the same Powers 'and Authorities for laying
out, making and keeping in repair the Roads in the said Parish,
and shall be subject and liable to the like Penalties and forfeitures as the Commissioners for the High Roads in the other
Parts of this Province have or are subject and liable unto by
the Laws of this Province. And in case any of the Commissioners
appointed by this Act shall happen to die, depart the Province,
or refuse to Act, it shall and may be lawful for the remainder
of the Commissioners or a major part of them to nominate and
appoint another Commissioner or Commissioners in the room of
him or them so dying, departing the Province, or refusing to
Act. And the Commissioner or Commissioners so nominated and
appointed shall have the same Powers and Authorities and be subject to the same Penalties and forfeitures as the Commissioners
appointed by this Act.
Certified a true copy.
Tho's. Farr, Jun.

Thursday, February 1st, 1770.
At a meeting of the Church Officer, of the Parish of St. David,
at the House of Mr. Charles Bedingfield.
Agreed: By the Church Wardens and Vestry, That Mr. Ely Kershaw
be appointed a Commissioner for Building the Parish Church of
St. David, in the room of Robert Alison, Deceased.

          Monday, April 30th, 1770.
At a Meeting of the Freeholders of the Parish of St. David, at
the House of Mr. Charles Bedingfield, the following Gentlemen
were unanimously Elected to serve as Church Officers for the
Ensuing Year, viz,

John Kimbrough   William Godfrey
Eli Kershaw   William Pegues, Church Wardens
Jesse Counsell
Samuel Wise
Henry William Harrington
John Pledger
William Ellerbee, Vestry
Monday the Ensuing 14th of Ma.. is the Day appointed for the
Afore... Gentlemen to meet at Mr. Bed[ingfields] to take the
usual Oaths.

MEMORANDUM OF AGREEMENT made concluded, and agreed Upon the
Twenty second day of February in the Year of our Lord One thou-
sand seven hundred and seventy BETWEEN Thomas Bingham of St.
Davids Parish in the Province of South Carolina House Carpenter
of the One part, and Ely Kershaw, Philip Pledger, George Hicks,
Thomas Lide, Benjamin Rogers, Charles Bedingfield, Thomas
Ellerbee and Claudius Pegues Commissioners for Building the Par-
ish Church of St. David of the Other part. WITNESSETH that for
And in consideration hereafter Mentioned the said Thomas Bingham
doth hereby Undertake and promise to build the Said Parish Church
Agreeable to a Plan by him delivered to be Erected in the South
West side of Peedee River Upon Land Granted for that Purpose by
Ely Kershaw on such part ... As shall be shown by the said Commissioners and be such Dimension and different kind of work as
follows, The H[ouse] To be fifty three feet long and Thirty feet
wide Sixteen feet high From the foundation to the plate; to be
rased upon a good and Sufficient Brick and Lime foundation two
feet high above The surface of the Ground; The Roof to be kept
from the Upper Coller Beam at both ends and to be covered with
[N]ineteen inch Juniper Shing[les] ends drawn and [j]ointed
the House Arched Over [the] Joists as Low as the slops of the
wind[ows?] With good pine featheredg Boards plained Jointed and
Beeded Two folding pannelled Doors one on the side and the Other
At the West end Four feet wide seven feet high with Brick steps
to Each; Five windows on One side and six on the Other and two
at the East end and these thirteen windows are to be Sashed and
contain eighteen lights each of a glass twelve by ten pannelled
folding shutters Three windows on the West End above the Gallery
are also to be sashed and Contain Eighteen lights each of glass
eight by ten; The Doors and all the Windows to be Arched a Gallery
at the West End from side to side Eight feet wide with three rows
of seats raised one above another with backsto each a passage in
the middle of four feet wide the Breast work of the said Gallery
to be Three feet pannelled work With a Neat stair case bannistered
the Main Isle to be eight feet wide from the west door to the
Altar the cross Isle six feet wide; The Alter to be Ten feet long
and six feet wide rased One step above the flor bannistered Door
and a neat Communion Table Two Rows of Pews ... Each side as near
five feet in wedth as the Bredth of the H[ouse] will Admit of and
three feet and an half high pannelled w... And panelled doors;
[si]des and ends of the Church to be Pannelled work as hig[h as
the] tops of the pews the remain... Of the sides and ends ... ..
...er with the whole Arch to be Neatly ... rabeted and beaded
Boards The whole House to be floored with ¼ Inch Boards Quarter
Stuff; The Pulpit and Sounding Board of polished black walnut
To be built together with the Clerks Desk staircase and Bannister
After the model of George Town Pulpit as near as possible It can
be done by the Workman All the sashes agreeable To the Lights
before mentioned and to be glazed. The whole House To be painted
inside and out of such colours as the Commissioners Shall think
proper All plain Colours and the said Thomas Bingham, doth promise and Oblige himself to find at his own Proper cost and expence and to transport the same to the spot All the Bricks Lime
Timber Plank Boards Shingles and all Materials whatsoever for
Building and fully compleating the said Church; excepting Locks,
Hinges, Nails Iron and Iron work Glass Paint Oyl and putty and
that the Timber Plank and boards shall be of good sound and Last-
ing Wood and that The same shall be inspected and must be Approved
of by any of The Commissioners who shall be Appointed by the rest
for ... Purpose. LASTLY, that the said Thomas Bingham Doth hereby
Oblige himself that the whole Church shall be fully Compleated in
a Neat and Workman Like manner According to rule Order and Pro-
portion and agreeable to the ...n by him delivered on or before

...st day of March which will be in the year One [thousand]seven
hundred and Seventy two, and for and in Conse... ..n of the said
premises The said Ely Kershaw, Philip Ple[dger],[George] Hicks,
Thomas Lide, Benjamin Rogers, Charles Bedingfield, Thomas Ellerbee and Claudius Pegues doth hereby Promise and Oblige themselves
or their Successors to pay Unto the said Thomas Bingham by Orders
on the Public Treasurer of this Province the sum of Two Thousand
six hundred Pounds Currency One half of the said Sum when The
Church is raised enclosed and Covered the remainder when it is
Fully compleated, AND for the true performance of All and singu-
lar The Above Promises Each Party doth Bind themselves to the
Other in the Penal Sum of Five Thousand two hundred Pounds current Money aforesaid IN WITNESS whereof they have hereunto set
their Hands and seals the day and year first above mentioned.
SEALED AND DELIVERED IN THE PRESENCE OF   Sam'l Wise)
                                            W'm Jackson)[Wit.]

Thomas Bingham   Ely Kershaw   Philip Pledger
George Hicks   Thomas Lide   Benj'm Rogers
Charles Bedingfield   Thomas Ellerbee   Claudius Pegues

    WHEREAS it may be Necessary to have some Alterations In the
Inside work of the Church it is agreed Between both Parties
that any alteration that shall be made hereafter shall not Break
the intent and meaning of the within Instrument of writing Provided the Alterations are agreeable to both parties.

Witness: Sam Wise   Thomas Bingham
         Wm Jackson   Ely Kershaw
         Jesse Edwards   Philip Pledger
                              Thomas Lide
                              Benj'n Rogers
                              Charles Bedingfield
                              Thomas Ellerbe
                              Claudius Pegues

SIR Please to Pay unto Ely Kershaw on Order One Hundred & Sixty
Pounds Currency of So. Carolina being the Ballance of the Sum
Provided for Parochiel Charges for the Parish of Saint Davids
the 16 April 1770   Claudius Pegues
   To   William Godfrey
Jacob Motte, Esq'r   Thomas Lide
Public Treasurer   Charles Bedingfield

SIR Please to Pay unto Rev'd Mr. James Foulis Twenty Pounds
Curency of South Carolina in Part of the Sum Provided for Paro-
chal Charges for the Parish of Saint Davids
 3 July 1770   Claudius Pegues
To   Samuel Wise
Jacob Motte, Esq'r   Ely Kershaw
Public Treasurer   Jesse Counsell
                                  John Pledger

Mr. Hogart   St. Davids Parish
     Sir   So Carolina 4 July 1770
There being a Clergyman wanted for this Parish we Have on the
Recommendation of Mrs. Betty Wise Agreed to wait for your
Acceptance of the Same on your Giving us an Answer in six Months
& your being here in Twelve Months from the Date Hereoff for fur-
ther Perticqulars we Refer to Mr. Wises Letter

At a meeting of the Freeholders for the parish of St. Davids at
the house of Mr. Wm. Lankfords the following Gentlemen were

10

unanimously Elected to serve as Church Officers for the Ensuing
Year, viz,

Jesse Counsell   Thomas Lide
Ely Kershaw   Thos. Ellerbee, Church Wardens
Chas. Bedingfield
Saml Wise   Vestrymen
Thomas Wade   George Hicks
Wm. Godfrey   Daniel Lundey
John Westfield   John Mitchell, Overseers of
                                   the Poor

William Davison Petission'd that his wife should be taken on the
Parish of St. Davids as an Object of pitty-
...Vestry Agreed to pay sixty pounds pr. Annum for the support
of Mary Davison wife of Wm. Davison who agrees to find... in All
Suffitient necessaries for that Sum...

St. Davids Parish to Sundries Dr. advanced by Chas. Bedingfield
To John Husbands for Bording a poor Woman   ... Ł 35.. 10
  ditto for hir funeral Expences   20
To Chas. Bedingfield for expences on receiving money
                  due sd. parish   5
To Norwood for Bording Elizabeth Losselwood till
                  Aug. 20th, 1771   50
To a Constable for summoning Norwood on Acct of
                  the parish ...   1..5
To Wm. Godfrey for getting sewing done for a poor
                  woman now dead ....   2..2.6
To Messrs. Ely Kershaw & Co their acct for
                  sundries for the Poor   8..12.6
To Mrs. Cooper for Bording a poor woman from
    Ester 1770 to Ester 1771   100
                               Ł 222-10--

Rec'd By the Church Wardens on acct of St. Davids parish
of Robert Weaver   Ł 80
of Henry Castles   40
                            Ł 120

October 1st, 1771

At a meeting of the Church officers at the house of Mr. Wm.
Lankford, Agreed, that Mr. William Lankford is to advertise for
the Vestrey Church Wardens & Overseers of the poor to meet at sd.
Lankfords on the first Tuesday in Jan'y Next by ten a Clock in
the fore noon and by there so doing will save their fine
Agreed that Walter McCalister be sumonid to appear to Mr. Wm.
Lankford's on the first Tuesday in Jan'y next & there give
security to the parish officers to keep the two mixed Blud Children in the parish, now in his care, & for proper Bringing them
up to Labour

At a meeting of the Vestry, Church Wardens & Overseers of the
Poor for the Parish of Saint David at the House of Mr. William
Lankford 14th January 1772

Present:
Thomas Wade   Thomas Lide
Charles Bedingfield   Thomas Ellerbee, Jun'r,
Wm. Godfrey   Church Wardens
Samuel Wise
John Westfield

11

Jesse Counsell   VestryMen   George Hicks
Ely Kershaw   Daniel Lundey, Overseers of
                                                the Poor

Mr. Joshua Edwards Appeard & informed the above Gentlemen that
James Scurlock a young lad had Liv'd with him above a year.
That his Father & Mother was both dead, he therefore disired the
Said Boy might be bound as an apprentice to him till he became
of Age, it was Agreed that the Said Edwards should appear on the
Third Tuesday in Feb'y next & bring with him the Said James
Scurlock, in Order to be bound Out to a Trade, as the Said
Church Officers shall then think Proper.
Agreed that John Husband be Summon'd, by the Clerk of this Ves-
try, to appear on the Third Tuesday on February next & to bring
with him Stephen Browns Three Children to be bound Out as the
Church Officers may think best & that Morgan Brown be Summon'd to
Appear at the Same time
Agreed that Samuel Hatfield be Summon'd to meet the Church Of-
ficers at the House of Wm. Lankford on the Third Tuesday in February next, and to bring with him Goodin a young Lad Lately in
his Employ, in Order that he may then be bound out to a Trade if
Approv'd off by the Church Officers.
Agreed that Mr. Thomas Wade, write to the Rev. Mr. Robinson, to
meet the Church Officers at Mr. Wm. Lankfords on the Third Tues-
day in February next, in Order to Perform divine Service, and if
he should then be Approv'd off by Said Church Officers, that they
Reccomend him home to take out Orders if this Place & their Proposals should be agreeable to him
Agree'd By the Church Wardens & Vestry that the Following Persons
be Appointed Commissioners for Building the Church in Saint
Davids Parish, Viz, Samuel Wise, Thomas Wade, Jesse Counsell,
John Kimbrough, James Kelly & Wm. Godfrey in the room of James
James, Robert Weaver Deceased & Thomas Crawford & James Thomson
leaving the Province & Alexander McIntosh & Thomas Ports refusing
to Act.

At a meeting of the Church Wardens & Vestry Men at the House of
Wm. Lankford 13th February 1772

Present:
Thomas Wade   Thomas Lide
Charles Bedingfield   &
John Westfield   Vestry Men   Thomas Ellerbee Junr, Church
Jesse Counsell   Wardens
Samuel Wise
Wm. Godfrey
      &
Ely Kershaw

Agreed that the Churchwardens Pay Walter McColister Twenty pounds
for maintaining & Burying John Dunpaten Late of this parish
Agreed that the Inhabitants of this Parish be taxed Two shillings
and six pence for every hundred acres of Land and Two shillings
and six pence for all negroes Slaves. Free negroes mulattoes
& Mustizoes for Defraying the Expence of maintaining the poor of
the sd. parish for the year one Thousand Seven Hundred & Seventy
One. The same to be Collected by Messrs. William Godfrey &
Charles Bedingfield & the Overplus if any should be to Be paid
into the hands of Thomas Lide and Thomas Elerbee, Jun'r Present
Church Wardens.
Agreed that James Scurlock be Bound out as an apprentice to
Joshua Edwards for the Term of Seven years.

12

Agreed that John Brown son of Stephen Brown Decesed be Bound
out to John Husbands to Learn the Shomaking Business Provided
he the sd. John Husbands can give sufficient Security to the
Church Wardens for Lerning him the sd. John Brown the sd. Trade
This day Charles Sparkes deli'd up to the Church Officers
Archabald Robinson son of Peter Robinson Late of this parish who
its agreed shall be Bound out to John Flanagan for the Term of
Eleven years.

Munday April the 20, 1772

At a meating of the Freeholders of the Parish of Saint Davids
At the House of Mr. Ely Kershaws the Following Gentlemen were
Unanimously Elected to Serve as Church Officers for the Ensuing
year Viz

James Kelley	Thomas Wade
Daniel Lunday	Wm. Henry Mills, Church Wardens
Jacob Johnson	
William Dewett	George Hicks
John Kimbrough	Male'h Murphey
John Jackson	Rob't Anderson, Overseers of
William White	the Poor
William Lankford, Clk.	

Agread the Rebecker Robertson be Bound to Paul Powers for Eight
years and that the sd. Powers Give her One years Schooling and
Two Cows and Calves at her Freedom & a New Sute of Good Cloaths.

12 April 1773

It is ordered that James Casey be paid Fifteen Pounds For Keeping a Poor Man.

It is Agr:d that Mr. William Henry Mills shal Draw an Order on
Joseph Gurley for the above Fifteen Pounds For James Casey. It
is Ordered that Robt Dooling be Paid Ten Pounds for Burying James
Role

THE PARISH OF SAINT DAVIDS DR to the UndrWritten Persons for
Maintaining the Poor there For the year 1772

To John Williams for a Poor Woman Seven Months and One Hundred
Pounds pr year Fifty Eight Pounds Twelve Shillings   to William
Davison For his Wife Sixty Pounds To Theophelis Norwood for a
Poor Woman Fifty Pounds   to John Williamson for Burying a Poor
Woman Ten Pounds

[Blank page]

At a meating of the Parishoners at the Parish Church of St.
Davids on Easter Monday being the 12 Day of April 1773 the
Undermentioned Gentlemen were Elected to Serve as Church Officers
for the Inseuing year

Col:o Charles Augustus Stewart	
Claud[s] Pegeus Esqr	
Capt Thos Lide	
Ely Kershaw	Vestrymen
Thomas Ellerbee	
Jesse Council	
William Dewett	

Phillip Pledger Esqr
Samuel Wise   Church Wardens

Alex:r Gordon
Maleciah Murphey   Overseers of the Poor
John Blakeney
William Lankford, Clk.

At a meeting of the Church Officers for the Parish of Saint
David at the Parish Church, on Monday 3d day of May 1773

Claudius Pegues, Esqr
Charles A. Steward, Esqr
Thomas Lide   Qualified to Serve as Vestry Men
Thomas Ellerbee &
Jesse Counsill

Philip Pledger
Samuel Wise   Qualified to Serve as Church Wardens

Alexander Gordon Overseer of the Poor

     Order'd that the Vestry Men & Church Wardens meet at the
Church on the first Monday in June, and that the Clerk Give
William Henry Mills Esqr Late Church ward in Notice thereof,
and likewise Request him to bring up the Papers & Accounts of
the Preceeding year The Clerk is Likewise to inform Mr.,Malachia
Murphey of Said Meeting & Request him to inform the Vestry of
the Situation of the Poor Woman at Mr. Benjamin James's & fur-
ther to Request Mr. Murphey to hyre Some Person to Remove the
Poor Woman at his House to the Parish from whence she came, the
Expence attending of which will be Refunded by the Vestry.

At a Meeting of the Church Officers for the Parish of Saint
David at the Parish Church on Munday 7th day June 1773

Present

Claudius Pegues Esqr
Chas. Augustus Steward Esqr.
William Dewitt   Vestry Men
Jesse Counsill &
Ely Kershaw

Philip Pledger, Church Warden

     Its Ordered that the Church Wardens bind for five years John
Morgan, to Serve as an Apprentice to Henry Counsill the Said
Counsill to Learn him the Blacksmiths Trade
ORDER'D that Hannah Howell be Bound as Apprentice to Abell Culp
'till she attains the Age of Eighteen years, or 'till She Marry's
ORDER'D that the Goods that Remains in the hands of John Flanna-
gan belonging to John Morgan, be Put into the hands of the Church
Wardens & they do Lay Out the Amount thereof as they think most
Convenient & advantagious to him
ORDER'D that the Church Officers meet the Second Munday in August

Philip Pledger Dr. to the Parish of Saint David for So Much Paid
him by John Downs by the hands of Col:o Steward this day   L 5

13 Sep 1773 John Morgan Bound to Henry Council Until he Arive
at the age of Twenty One to be Learnt the Blacksmiths Trade and
to be Learnt to Read write and Cast a Cast Accounts and to have

14

a good sute of Cloaths at his freedom

13 Sepr 1773 Bound Sarah Barker Aged about 13 to Mary Hollings-
worth Until She Arive at the Age of 18 and to have Six Months
Schooling and at her Freedom a Cow and a Calf a bible and a
Deacent Sute of Cloaths
Likewise Kesiah Barker about Six years Old bound to Mary Holins-
worth Until She arive at 18 and She is to Give her a years
Schooling and at her freedom one bible One Cow & Calf and One
Feather Bead

1 Augt   Hannah Howel bound to Abel Colp Until She arive to the
   1773   Age of 18 and to be Learnt to read & Write Supposed to
          be 12 or 13

13 Sepr 1773 Bound to Samuel Wise Mary Barker From the Age of 10
years While She Come 18 and Is to be Learnt to Read Write and
Cast Accounts and at her freedom to have a bible Cow and Calf a
Common prayer Book One Whole Deauty of Man & a Deacent sute of
Cloath

At a meeting of the Church Wardens & Vestry Men for the Parish of
Saint David at Mr. Burwell Boykins 20th Septemr 1773

It was agreed to by the Church wardens & Vestry to allow Doctor
Smith Ŀ 30 for mintaining & Curing Wm. Groves a Poor Man Likewise agreed to allow Neoma Heritage Sixty Pound P Anm.

At a meeting of the Parishoners at the Parish Church of Saint
David on Easter Monday the 4th day of April 1774 the undermentioned Persons was duly elected to Serve as Church Officers the
insuing year

Henry Counsill
John Andrew
Thomas Bingham   Vestry Men
John Heustiss
Burwell Boykin
Henry William Harrington
Aaron Daniel

Claudius Pegues, Esqr
Ely Kershaw   Church Wardens

John Kimbrough
Chas Evans Junr & Overseers of the Poor
Thomas Conner Senr.

John Flannagan this day Put into the hands of Phill Pledger Esqr
all the Effects that was left in his hands by Jane Morgan which
is to be disposed off for the use of John Morgan, for P. Pledger
gave John Flannagan a Receipt

The Parish of Saint David
1774   To Phil Pledger & Saml Wise Church Wardens Dr.
April   To Wm Davison for Boarding his wife   Ŀ   60
         To James Smith for Curing & Ment G. W. Groves   30
         To Neoma Heritage   60
         To Elisabeth Lislewood   50
         To James Shields for Ment & Burying Philip Hart 13. 11
         To Peter Roach for Attendance on do   27. 6. 6.
         To Alexander Gordon for Attendance on Eliz[a]
            Dunlap in her Sickness & Burying her   27. 9. 9

To Andrew Gibson for a Coffin & ca. for Philip
Hart   28.17 6
                                                 Ь   297. 4. 9

To Cash Paid Joshua Lucas for Keeping Thos Hinds 4
To Cash Paid Wm Davis for So much the Vestry
    allowed him as an addition to his Sallary   40
By Cash Received to John Downs P the hands of
    Chas. A. Steward Esqr   Ь   5
By Chas Bedingfield Esta. for a Ballance due
    the Parish when he was Church Warden   9. 9

At a Meeting of the Church Wardens & Vestry Men at the Parish
Church of Saint David on Monday 25th April 1774

Present

Henry Counsill
John Andrew
Thomas Bingham
Burwell Boykin
Aaron Daniel &
Thomas Ellerbee Junr., Vestry Men

Thomas Conner Senr
Charles Evans Junr, Overseers of the Poor

    The above Gentlemen met and Qualified to Act as Church
Officers for the Ensuing year
Agreed that the Clerk give Notice to Thomas Williams Geo Hicks &
William Ellerbee that they are Appointed to Assess the Parish to
Raise Three Hundred & Fifty Seven Pounds Thirteen Shillings and
One Farthing, to Reimburse the Church Wardens for Money advanced
by them the Preceeding year
Agreed that the Clerk Advertise for the Church Wardens So much
at the Parish Church on Saturday the 7th May near at Eleven
OClock

The Parish of Saint David
        To Phillip Pledger & Samuel Wise
    To so much allowed Charles Mason for Boarding
    David McCullough while under the Doctors hands Ь 37. 5.77 4

At a Meeting of the Church Officers at the Parish Church of
Saint David on Saturday the 7th May 1774

Present

Aaron Daniel
John Andrew
Henry Counsell   Vestry Men
Thomas Bingham &
Thomas Ellerbee Junr

Agreed that Thomas Lide be Appointed in Lieu of George Hicks To
assess the Parish for the Parish Tax for the Preceeding year
Thomas Lide Thomas Williams & William Ellerbee met Agreeable to
Appointment & Agreed that the Inhabitants Of this Parish be Taxd
three Shilling Current Money of South Carolina for every hundred
acres of Land & Three Shillings for all Negroes Slaves Free
Negroes Mulattoes Mestizoes for Defraying the Expence of Mentain-
ing the Poor of this Parish for the year one Thousand And Seven
Hundred & Seventh three the same to be Collected by Phillip

Pledger Esqr & Mr. Samuel Wise

South Carolina
Charraw District We being Appointed by the Church Wardens &
Vestry Men for the Parish of Saint David to assess the Said
Parish to Raise the Sum of Three Hundred & Fifty Seven Pounds
Thirteen Shillings & one Farthing to Reimburse the Churchwardens
for Money by them Advansed for the Relief Of the Poor of the
Said Parish during the Last year We do Therefore Agree that the
Inhabitants of the Parish aforesaid be Taxd Three Shillings for
Every Hundred Acres of Land & three Shillings on All Negroe
Slaves Free Negroes Mullattoes & Mestizoes the Same to be Collec-
ted & Recovered by Philip Pledger Esqr & Samuel Wise Late Church
Wardens

GIVEN UNDER Our hands
At Charraws 7 May 1774
Thomas Williams
Thomas Lide
Wm. Ellerbe

At a meating of The Vestry & Church Wardens of the parish of
Saint Davids on Monday the 13 Day of Febuary (sic) 1775

Present

Claudias Pegeus Esqr Church War^d
Thos Bingham
Henry Council
John Andrews
John Hewstes
Burwell Boyakin, Vestry Men

ORDERED

That the following Bonds to the Parish Be Entered

Ann Knight & James Sanders Dated 16 Feby 1773 Ł 3500
John Downs & Joshua Lucas Bond Dated the 20 May 1773 for the
Maintaining of there Bastard Children which Said Bonds are
Delivered in the hands of Claudias Pegues Esqr

Ordered

That Augustian Hargove be Put Under ed The Care of Doc^{tr} John
Ogle to be Cured of the Veneral Disease for Which Cure the Doctr
Is to have Ł 50-- Likewise that the Following Children be Bound
by the Parish Three Children Belonging to Wm. Groves 2 Boys &
one Girl The 2 boys to be Bound to John Hurd One Boy Named
Janes Weden[?] to be Bound to Philip Pledger Esqr 12 year of Age
One Girl Named Rebeckah Robertson to be Bound to John Heustis 9
year of Age
5 Children to be Bound Belonging to the widdow Morison

The Clark is to Write Indentures for the Above Children & to
advertise for the Vestry to meat At the House of Mr. Boyakins the
Last Monday in Febuary

13 February 1775

Mr. Arthur Clark
    Sir
          As the Church Wardens & Vestry are informed that Mr. John
Manderson gave you a Bond for the maintaining a Bastard Child
begotten with Dutch[?] Mary. And ther is some Charge which
the Parish is to pay for the nursing the said Woman.

Am by orders of the Vestry to desire you would remit the said
Bond to the Church Wardens in order to oblige Mr. Manderson to
defray the said Expence
Am   S^r your humble Servant

                              Claudius Pegues

The Parish of Saint David

                    To Claudius Pegues & Ely Kershaw D^r
To William Davison for Mintaining a Poor Woman   ₺   100
To Nioma Heritage   60
To Elizabeth Lislewood   50
To Peter Roach for attendance on Mrs. Dunlap   27..7.3
To Joshua Edwards for Mintaining Mrs. John
    Mandersons Bastard Child   20
To Charles Evans Junr for Boarding Rich   50
                                                  ₺ 307..7..3

South Carolina
Charraw District
        We the Vestry-Men for the Parish of Saint David do hereby
Agree that the Inhabitants of the Parish aforesaid be Taxed
Three Shillings for every hundred Acres of Land & three shillings
on all Negroe Slaves, Free Negroes, Mullattoes & Mestizoes the
Same to be Collected and Recoverd by Claudius Pegues & Ely Ker-
shaw, to defray the Sum of Three Hundred & Seven Pounds, Seven
Shillings, Three Pence by them advanced to the Poor of the Said
Parish during Last year
                          Given under our hand
                          at Chatham 24th day April 1775

                          Henry Councill
                          John Andrews
                          Thos Bingham
                          John Heustess
                          Aaron Daniel
                          Thos Ellerbe

[Two blank pages]

At a meating of the Freeholders and Inhabit^c of the Parish of
Saint Davids At the House of Mr. Phillip Singletons on Monday
the 24 Day of April 1775 The Under Written Gentlemen Was Elected
to Serve as Church officers for the Said year

H^y Wm Harrington, Esqr
William Pegues,   Church Wardens

Aaron Pearson
William Dewit
Joseph Pledger [stricken]
William Ellerbee
William Strother
John Donaldson [stricken]
John Westfield
John Jackson
Chas. Irby, Vestry Men

Daniel Sparkes
Robt Lowry
William Allen, Overseers of the Poor

At a meeting of the Church Wardens at Mr. Philip Singletons near
the Parish Church of St. David on Saturday the 12th Aug '75
Present

William Pegues
H Wm Harrington, Church Wardens

John Westfield
Charles Irby
Willm Dewit
William Strother, Vestry Men

The above Persons met & were qualified to Act as Church Officers.

It was agreed by the Church Wardens & the above four of the Vestry that Mary Judith be allowed three Pounds ten shillings per
month From the 12 July last for maintaining John Mandersons
Bastard Child, he it seems, having appeard before Arthur Hart
Esqr & Having g.... into a Recognizance for his appearances at
the Gen Sessions of the ... but has not yet given Security to the
Church Wardens it is [there]fore further agreed to postpone
writing to the said Jno Manderson till after next November Sessions when the matter may be finally settled. Ordered that the
Clerk do advertise for the Church Wardens and Vestry to meet at
the Parish Church on the third Monday in November next.

November 1775, As neither of the Church Wardens & none of the
             Vestry came this day all matters were left to
             stand over till Easter-money (sic)

[blank page]

    At a meeting of the Church Wardens & Vestry at Mr. Singletons
on Monday the eigt of April 1776
Present

Wm Pegues
H W Harrington, Church Wardens

Wm Dewit
Chas Irby
John Westfield, Vestry-Men

The Parish of St. Davids   Dr
            To Wm. Pegues & H W Harrington
  To Benjm James for maintaining Neoma Heritage   Ł   60..0.0
  To Joshua Edwards for ac of John Mandersons Bas-
     tard female Infant   11..10
  To ac for nursing& maintaining Mary Judith 3
     months   10..10
  To ac for Cloaths found the said Mary   5..10.
  To Wm Davison for maintaining his Wife   100..0.0
                                                    Ł 187.10.0

  To Doct^r Roach for curing Augustine Hargrove
                      of the Pox   80
                                                       267 10

Ordered that the Clark give notice to Thos Ellerbee Capt Lide &
Benjm Rogers to Assess the Parish to raise the sum of Two hundred
sixty seven Pounds ten shillings to Reimburse Wm Pegues and H W
Harrington the Church wardens for the last year for money advanced
by them to defray the expenses incured by the Poor of the said

19

Parish

Gave Wm Lankford an Order on Messrs Perroneau & Dart for Forty Pound Currency

At a meeting of the freeholders and Inhabitants of the Parish of St Davids at the House of Mr Philip Singleton on Moonday the 8th day of April 1776 the Under Written Gen^{lm} was Elected to serve as Church Officers for the ^e_s year.

       Col. George Pawley
       Claudius Pegeus, C. War.

Thos Elerby
Francis Gillispie
Capt John Blakeney
Thos Powe
Matthew Saunders
Capt Laml Benton
Buckley Kimbrough

Alexr Deubois)
Peter Roach) Oves^{rs}

William Lankford, Clk.

At a meeting of the Freeholders & Inhabitants of the Parish of St. David at the Parish Church on Monday the thirty first day of March 1777 the underwritten Gentlemen were Elected to serve as Church Officers for the said year

John Andrews)
Charles Irby) Church Wardens

John Kimbrough)
Thomas Lide   )
James Hicks   )
Thomas Powe   )
William Pegues)
Joseph Griffith)
Robert Lowry   ) Vestrymen

At a meeting of the Church Wardens and Vestry at the Parish Church on Saturday the 21st of June 1777

Present

John Andrews Church Warden

Thomas Lide   )
James Hicks   )
William Pegues) Vestrymen

The above Vestrymen met and were Qualified to act as Church Officers
It was agreed that the following Persons be appointed Overseers of the Poor
Benjamin Jackson)
John Pledger   )
John Jackson   ) Overseers of the Poor

Ordered that the Clerk do advertise for the Church Wardens, Vestrymen, & Overseers of the Poor to meet at the Parish Church on the first Tuesday in July and that in case of Non attendance they will be fin'd according to Act of Assembly

Agreed that a Letter be wrote to the Reverend Mr. Winchester to
Preach a Sermon on Saturday the 28th Instant for happy deliverance of this State from our cruel & oppressive Enemies on the
28th of June 1776

At a meeting of the Church Wardens and Vestrymen at the Parish
Church on Tuesday the first day of July One thousand seven hun-
dred and Seventy seven
Present

Charles Irby)
John Andrews)   Church Wardens

Thomas Lide   )
James Hicks   )
Joseph Griffith)
William Pegues) Vestrymen

Benjamin Jackson - Overseer of the Poor.

Order'd that the Clerk do write Letters to the following Persons
that were chosen Vestrymen & Overseers of the Poor to attenden
the first Tuesday in October at the Parish Church to Qualify

John Kimbrough)   John Pledger &) Overseers of
Thomas Powe   )   John Jackson)   the Poor
Robert Lowry) Vestrymen

At a meeting of the Church Wardens & Vestry at the Parish Church
on Monday the 20th of April 1778
Present

John Andrews)
Charles Irby) Church Wardens

Thomas Lide   )
James Hicks   )
William Pegues)
Thomas Powe   ) Vestrymen

Ordered That a letter be wrote by the Clerk to John Manderson
to appear at the next meeting of the Vestry and Church Wardens
to enter in Bond with sufficient Security for the maintenance of
his Bastard Child
Ordered That the Church Wardens bind Joseph Conner a free mulat-
toe as an apprentice to John Stephens till he arrives at the age
for (sic) Twenty one years.
Ordered That the Church Wardens do bind Elizabeth McDaniel as an
Apprentice to Mrs. Sarah Donaldson till arrives (sic) at the age
of eighteen years.
Gave Mr. Lankford an Order on the Public Treasurers for Eighty
Pounds for two years as Clark of the Vestry.
received of Col. Hicks ten Pounds which was recoverd before him
of James Blanton for fire hunting, for the use of the Poor.
Ordered That the above ten pounds be given to Sarah Rollins a
poor Woman

South Carolina)
Chiraw District) We the Vestry for the Parish aforesaid do
hereby agree that the Inhabitants of the said Parish be taxed
three shillings on all slaves free negroes, Mulattoes and musti-

zoes and three shillings on every hundred acres of Land the same
to be Collected and recovered by Chas Irby & William Pegues to
defray the sum of six hundred & ninety four Pounds seventeen &
sixpence for the poor of the Parish for four years past

                               Wm Pegues
                               Thos Powe
                               Thos Lide
                               James Hicks

Ordered That the Clerk do give notice to the following Gentlemen
to meet on the first tuesday in July at the Parish Church and
qualify as Church Officers for the Present year being duly elected

Benjn Hicks Junr   )
Wm Lide   ) Church Wardens
Benjn Hicks Senr   )
Clauds Pegues Junr)
Wm Thomas   )
[Fr]ancis Gillispie)
Thomas Ellerbee   )
Wm Ellerbee   )
John Speed   ) Vestrymen

Benjamin Rogers   )
Trustram Thomas   )
Wm Blassingame   ) Overseers of the Poor

The Twelth of Sepr 1778 It was Ordered by the Church Wardens of
the parish of Saint Davids that James Conner Should be bound to
John Hears to the age of Twenty One And Was bound and Now is one
year & Nine Months of Age

At a Meeting of the Freeholders & Inhabitants of the Parish of
Saint Davids at the Parish Church on Monday 27th March 1780 the
Underwritten Gentlemen was Elected as Church Officers for the
Ensuing Year

Wm Pegues   )
Benja Hicks Senr) Church Wardens

Claudius Pegues Junr)
Thos Powe   )
Charles Irby   )
John Westfield   )
John Andrews   )
John Wilson   )
Holden Wade   ) Vestry Men

John Husbands   )
Gutheridge Lyons)
Benja Jackson   ) Overseers of the Poor

Jesse Baggette, Clerk

At a Meeting of the Church Wardens & Vestry, at the Parish Church
on Tuesday 4th March 1780
Present

Wm Pegues   )
Benja Hicks Senr) Church Wardens

```
Charles Irby          )
Claudius Pegues Junr  )
John Westfield        )
Holden Wade           )    Vestry Men

John Wilson           )
Gutheridge Lyons      ) Overseers of the Poor
```

The Above Gentlemen Met & was Qualified to Act as Church Officers.

It's Ordered that the Church Wardens Bind John Feagans to Serve
as an Apprentice to James Shields, for the term of Ten years,
from the date above, to learn the Art of Leather Breeches &
Glove making.

Agree'd that the Church Wardens & Vestry Men Pay a Workman to
Repair the Church Doors Benja Hicks is appointed to employ a
Workman

Ordered that the Church Officers meet at the Parish Church on
Saturday the Sixth day of May, next.

At a meeting of the Freeholders & Inhabitants of the Parish of
Saint Davids at the Parish Church on Tuesday the 2d day of April
1782 The following Persons were duly Elected as Church Officers
for the ensuing year

```
Thos Ellerbee        )
William Strother     )  Church Wardens

Charles Irby         )
Claudius Pegues Junr )
John Westfield       )
John Wilson          )
Wm Lide              )
Wm Dewitt            )
Wm Pegues            )  Vestrymen
```

At a meeting of the Church Wardens & Vestry at the Parish Church
on Saturday the 13th of April 1782

```
Present        Wm Strother     Church Warden

               Charles Irby    )
               John Wilson     )
               Wm Lide         )
               Wm Pegues       )   Vestrymen
```

The above Gentlemen were Qualified to serve as Church Officers

John Combess a poor Boy nine years old was bound to Robert
Biggart by Wm Pegues one of the late Church Wardens to serve
till the age of Twenty one Years -- Indenture bearing date the
13th of March 1782

ORDER'D that
M. Hustiss & Wm Gordan & Robert Paslay) Overseers of the Poor

At a meeting of the Vestrymen at the Parish Church on Saturday
the fourth of May 1782

```
Present        John Westfield
               Willm Dewit
```

                    Charles Irby &
                    Wm Pegues

At a meeting of the Church Wardens and Vestrymen at the Parish
Church Saturday 3rd day of Augt 1782

Present

Wm Strother   ) Church Warden

Charles Irby)
Jno Willson   )
Wm Pegues   ) Vestrymen

Robt Pasley   )
Wm Gordan   ) Overseers of the poor

It's Order'd that Leep Stapleton is Bound apprentis to Guthridge
Lyons till he is twenty One years Old he being now thirteen Years
Old, Gutheridge Lyons is to give him the Said Boy two good home
Spun Suits of Clothing at the expiration of the time with a good
Horse bridle and Saddle the Horse to be worth Sixty Pounds Specie

Orderd that 3 Molatto Boys be bound to Wm Lankford till they
arrive at the age of 21 years Jim Hunt 18 years old Lewes Hunt
13 Years Old Saul Hunt 11 years old Jim Hunt to Serve out his
time without any freedom dues, each of the others to have each
a good Suit of home Spun Cloaths and each a Earling (sic) Colt
at the expiration of the time above mentioned

Orded'd that Aaron Kite a poor Boy be bound to Wm Lyons till
he be 21 Years Old he being now 15 Years Old, and at the Expiration of the time he the Said Kite is to receive from the Said
Lyons a good sufficient Suit of home Spun Cloths with a good
Horse bridle and Saddle worth Ƚ 50 Specie

Order'd that Isaac Ganey a poor boy be Bound to Thomas Lankford
till he is 21 years old at which age he is to receive a good
Horsebridle and Saddle and a good Sufficient Suit of Clothes
home Spun
NB the Said Ganey is 15 Years Old

Order'd that Randolph Johnson be Bound to Jno Willson till he
be 21 Years Old at the Expiration of which time he is to receive
one good Horse Bridle & Saddle with a good Suit of home Spun
Cloths the Boy

Orderd that Josiah Cumbess a poor Boy be bound to Joseph Booth
untill he being 21 Years Old at which time he is to have two
good Suits of home Spun Cloths with a Horse Bridle and Saddle
worth Ƚ 50 and one Year Schooling if Convenient NB Josiah
Cumbess is now 12 Years Old

Orderd that Joans Cumbest a poor Girl 5 year Old be Bound Francis
Robertson To the age of 18 years and the She is To have 1 years
Schooling and a Decant Sute of Cloathing at her freedom

Orderd that Edmund Kite A poor Boy 6½ years Old Likewise Girl
name Salle One 5 Years Old Be Bound to Ambras Singleton While
they are of Lawful Age the Boy is to have at his Freedom a Good
Horse and Saddle 2 Sutes of Cloaths and one years Scholing the
girl is to have 2 Sutes of Cloaths One Cow and Calf and One years
Schooling

Orderd that Mary Combest A poor Girl 6 years Old be Bound to
Thomas Lankford While She Comes to Lawful Age And is to Have 2
Cows & Calves at her Freedom and be Learned to reed and Deacently
Clothd When Free

At a meeting of the Freeholders & Inhabitants of the Parish of
St David, at the Parish Church on Easter Monday 1783 when the
following Persons were chosen for the ensuing year

Thos Powe   )
Clauds Pegues Junr)   Church Wardens

Charles Irby   )
John Andrews   )
Thomas Ellerbee   )
Benjn Hicks Junr   )
Robert Paslay   )
James Gillespie   )
Lam Benton   ) Vestrymen

At a meeting of the Freeholders & Inhabitants of the Parish of
Saint David at the Parish Church on Monday the 12th of April
1784 When the following Persons were chosen to serve as Church
Officers for the said Year

Benjamin Hicks Senr)
William Pegues   ) Church Wardens

Thomas Ellerbee   )
William Strother   )
John Westfield   )
Clauds Pegues Junr   )
John Wilson   )
Benjamin Hicks Junr   )
William Legate   ) Vestrymen

At the above time & Place the following Gentn were Qualified

Benjn Hicks Senr)
Wm Pegues   ) Church Wardens

Thomas Ellerbee   )
Wm Strother   )
John Westfield   )
John Wilson   ) Vestrymen

The following Persons were appointed Overseers of the Poor

      George Hicks
      John Heustess &
      Robert Paslay

At a meeting of the Church Wardens & Vestry men at the Parish
Church on Saturday the 16th of May 1784
Present

Benjn Hicks Senr   )
William Pegues   ) Church Wardens

Thomas Ellerbee   )
Clauds Pegues Junr)
Wm Strother   )
John Westfield   )

John Wilson   ) Vestrymen

George Hicks   )
Robert Paslay   ) Overseers of the Poor

Mr Clauds Pegues was this day Qualified

Orderd that Ł 11..10 Stg be allow'd for the maintenance of Thos
Also for one Year to Commence from the above date and that the
Church Wardens do employ Some person to provide for him

Order'd that Thomas Davis a poor man be allow'd Ł 5 starling for
his maintenance one year from the above date and that his sons
Thomas Davis and Frank[?] Davis be obliged to pay twenty one
Shillings stg. each into the hands of the Church Wardens for the
further Support of the Said Davis

Orderd that the Church Wardens do bind out John Owens (Alias
Williford) to Some handy Craft trade provided his father cannot
give Security to keep him off the Parish

Resolved that the Church Wardens & Vestrymen do meet the 2nd
Saturday in June next

At a meeting of the Church wardens and Vestrymen at the Parish
Church on Saturday the twelfth Day of June 1784
Present

Benjamin Hicks Senr)
William Pegues   ) Church Wardens

Thomas Ellerbee   )
Claudius Pegues   )
William Strother   )
John Westfield   )
John Willson   ) Vestry Men

Robert Parlsley   ) Overseer of the Poor
                        Carried over the same day

Ordered that the Church Wardens do bind out Johanna Combess a
female Child, about seven years old with the consent of the
mother to Robert Biggard, until she arrives to the age of
Eighteen years and that the Said Robert Biggard be obliged to
put her to some School untill she learns to read and write, and
at the expiration of the said time shall give her a suit of
Clothes

Ordered that the Church Wardens do bind out, Priscilla Inman, a
female Child, eight years old the sixteenth day of February last,
with the consent of the Grand Mother, to Richard George untill
she arrives to Age of Eighteen years and that the said Richard
George be obliged to put her to some School untill she learns to
read and write and at the expiration of the said time he the said
Richard George shall give her a Suit of Clothes.

Resolved that the Church Wardens & Vestry Men do meet and attend
at the Parish Church the Second Saterday in July next

At a meeting of the Church Wardens and Vestrymen at the Parish
Church on Saturday the fourth day of June 1785

Present

Benjn Hicks   )
Wm Pegues   ) Church Wardens

Thomas Ellerbee   )
Claudius Pegues   )
Benjn Hicks Junr   )
John Westfield   ) Vestrymen

Robert Paslay   Overseer of the Poor

The Parish of St David

To Benjn Hicks Senr & Wm Pegues   Dr

To Simon Lundy for maintaining Thos Allso   Ł 54. 6.8
To Thomas Davis   35
To Saml Shippen for ac   do Essex Bevellen[?]   30
To Rosanna McCoy a poor Woman   26
                                               145. 6.8

South Carolina
Cheraw District) We the Vestrymen for the Parish of Saint
David, do hereby agree that th Inhabitants of the Parish aforesaid be taxed one shilling old Currency on every hundred acres
of Land and one shilling like money on all Negroes, Slaves, Free
Negroes, & Mulattoes, Mestizoes, the same to be Collected and
recovered by Benjamin Hicks & Wm Pegues, to defray the sum of
One hundred and forty five pounds six shillings & Eight pence
like money by them advanced to the poor of the said Parish during
last year

                         Claudius Pegues)
                         John Westfield   )
                         Thos Ellerbe   )
                         Benjn Hicks   )
                         Robt Paslay   )Vestrymen

At a meeting of the Freeholders and Inhabitants of the Parish of
Saint Davids at the Parish Church the 25th June 1785 the under
written Gentlemen was Elected to serve as Church Officers for
the Ensuing year

Colo. Lam. Benton   )
Capt Calvin Spencer) Church Wardens

Thos Powe   )
Wm Ellerbe Senr   )
Jno Andrews   )
Holden Wade   )
Wm Pegues   )
   &   )
Morgan Brown   ) Vestry Men

Capt Spencer being Present took the Oath required, Also Wm
Ellerbe Senr Jno Andrews Jno Wilson Wm Pegues & Morgan Brown

Agreed that the Church Wardens & Vestry meet at the Parish Church
on Saturday 9th July 1785

At a meeting of the Vestry & Church Wardens at the Parish Church
on Saturday 9th July 1785

Present

Calvin Spencer   )   Church Warden

Wm Ellerbe Senr   )
Jno Andrews   )
Morgan Brown   )
Jno Wilson   )
Wm Pegues   )   Vestry Men

Holden Wade one of the Vestry attended & was duly quallified

Ordered that Trustram Thomas Moses Pearson Chas Dewitt & Wm
Strother be & they are hereby appointed Overseers of the Poor
for the Present Year

Ordered that Winney Combess be bound to Joseph Booth untill she
attains the age of Eighteen years, the Said Booth engages to
learn her to Read & Write & at the Expiration of her time the
Sd Booth engages to give her a good Suit of Cloths

Ordered that the Church Wardens & Vestry meet at the Parish
Church on the Second Saturday in Augt Next.

St David Church
Chatham S. C. Dec 25, 1819

The Revd Andrew Fowler missionary from the protestant Episcopal
Society in S. C. officiated in St Davids Church Chatham
    At Evening he baptized. Charlotte daughter of James A.
Harrington Esq He also officiated in Said Church the Sunday
following, after which he returned to Charleston.
    In January 1820, Mr Fowler again Visited Chatham and regu-
larly officiated in St Davids church every other Sunday when
the weather permitted in the capacity of Missionary from the
protestant Episcopal Society
    March 19th 1820 The Revd Mr Fowler baptized Mrs. Charlotte
Wilson wife of Jno Wilson Esqr of the Marlborough Dis in St
Davids Church
    April 2nd 1820 Mr Fowler administered the holy communion in
St Davids Church, it being Easter day and the first time the
Lords Supper was ever given in this church.
    Mr. John Wilson Mrs Charlotte Wilson and Mrs E. Toomer communed

St Davids Church Cheraw S. C.

At a meeting of the Episcopaliany of Cheraw and its vicinity
held at St Davids Church Feby 3 1823
Present   Thos Cotton
           Geo Andrews
           D. K. Dodge
           Jno S Punch
           Jno P Tamplit
           Benjn G[?] Rutland
           James A Harrington
           Joseph Pritchard
           Wilie Mebane
           Wm B Parker
           James A Anderson
           Erasmus Powe
           Edmd Laffon

James A. Harrington Esqr was called to the chair, and D. K.
Dodge appointed Sec^y to the meeting

The following Gent were duly elected to serve as Vestry men
& wardens for the ensuing year

James A Harrington)
Oliver H Kollock   )
Geo Andrews   )
D. K. Dodge   )
Joseph Pritchard   )   Vestry

Wilie Mebane   )
Jn P Tamplit   )   Wardens

After appointing D. K. Dodge Clerk It was resolved That the
Revd Mr. Wright the present officiating Clergyman together with
Joseph Pritchard Esq call on the Revd Mr Morgan presbyterian
clergyman the late occupant of the Pulpit to make such arrange-
ments as they may deem proper in regard to a mutual interchange
of Preaching
     Joseph Pritchard Esq was duly elected a Delegate to represent
this church in convention to be held in Charleston the ninth
Inst.
     On motion of Mr Harrington it was resolved that the vestry
& wardens of this church do of themselves & in behalf of the
Bishop of this Diocesse take possession of the Church of St
David in the Town of Cheraw and provided any other Sect or de-
nomination that Episcopalian may wish to preach therein when
not in their occupancy, application must be made to the Vestry
for the same
     No further business coming before this meeting it was
accordingly adjourned to Sunday 16th inst.

a true coppy
D. K. Dodge Sec^y

St Davids Church
1823

On Sunday the 15 Feby 1823 the Revd Thos Wright Missionary
from the united diocese of North & South Carolina officiated in
this church and administered the Holy Communion, there being
twelve communicants a collection was likewise made this day in
aid of the fund of the Society. Nine dolls 80/100 collected

D. K. Dodge, Sec^y

Sunday 2 March Service was performed by Mr Wright and baptised
Rebecca Ann Dodge daughter of D. K. Dodge
Monday 24 March the following pews were rented for one year
Payable Semi anually at the following prices

N° 1
    2
    3
    4   John Ellerbee   15 pd R. M.
    5
    6   by Charles Collins   at   10 50 pr ann
    7   " A Averill   "   20 00 pd
    8   by R. H. Rutland   "   11   pd
    9   " Ward Cowing   "   19
   10   " Geo Andrews   "   19
   11   " James Lyon & C. K. Dodge   20

29

```
12  "  Erasmus Powe      "      18
13  "  Jno Jinnings      "      23
14  "
15  "
16  "  Jno P Tamplet     "      21 pd
17  "  P Vannorden       "      11
18  "  J Pritchard       "      16
19  "  T Addison         "      11 pd
20  "  Geo Andrews       "      10 pd by O. H. Kollock
21  "  Wm Faulkner       "       9  50
22  "  Mr[?] Cotton      "      15  pd
23     Doct Ellerbee     "      15 pr ann
24     George T Hearsey         10 "    "
25
26
27
```

Sunday 6 May [April?] divine service was performed by Mr Wright and the Holy Communion administered, a collection was likewise made   8..60 collected

Friday May 9 1823 This church was visited by the Right Reverend Bishop Bowen Bishop of So Carolina and a Sermon delivered by him

The following persons were confirmed
    Mrs. Pritchard & two daughters Mary and Margarett Pritchard
    Mrs. Harrington Mrs. Kollock
    Mrs. Wilson Mrs. Mebane Mrs. Rutland James A Harrington

Sunday March 7th 1824 divine Service was performed by Mr. Wright and the Holy Communion administered

Good Friday 16th April 1824
Divine Service was performed by the Revd Mr Wright after which an Election was held for Vestry and Wardens to Serve for the ensueing Year and the following Gentlemen were Elected

```
        Present        Jno G Lance
                       James W Hathaway
                       James A Harrington
                       Erasmus Powe
                       John Ellerbee
                       Daniel K Dodge

George T. Hearsey    )
James A Harrington   )
Erasmus Powe         )
John P Tamplet       )
John G Lance         )
John Ellerbe         )   Vestrymen

O H Kollock      )
George Andrews   )  Wardens
```

Easter Sunday 18th April 1824 Divine Service was performed by the Revd Mr Wright and the Holy Communion was administered and a collection made of $9 12/100
                John P Tamplet Secretary

Good friday April 1st 1825 divine Service was to have been perford this day by the Revd Mr Hathaway but the boisterous State of the Weather prevented it
                Loper Secy

Easter Sunday April 3 1825
   Divine Service was perform'd by the Revd Mr Hathaway after
which an election was held for vestry & wardens to Serve for the
ensuing Year   the following Gentlemen were Elected

                Present   Jas A Harrington
                          Jno Ellerbe
                          L S Drake
                          David Martin
                          Geo Andrews
                          Jno B Billingsby
                          M Flemming
                          H G Loper

Geo T Hearsey   )
James A Harrington   )
Erasmus Powe   )
John Ellerbe   )
Richd Maynard   )
Jno G Lance   )
Henry G Loper   )   Vestrymen

Oliver H. Kollock)
Geo Andrews   )   Wardens

                        Henry G. Loper   Secretary
                        St. Davids Church
                        Cheraw S. Ca.

                     Morning
Second Sunday after Easter   April 17th 1825
   St Davids Church was this day visited by the Right Revd
Bishop Bowen Bishop of South Carolina and a Sermon deliver'd
by him   after Service Mrs Haws was Confirm'd   The holy communion
was also administer'd   the following persons were communicants
Mrs Richard Maynard   Mrs Jas A Harrington   Mrs O H Kollock
Mrs Jos H Towns   Mrs Hawes

                     Afternoon
   Divine Service was again perform'd by the Right Revd Bishop
Bowen
                     Loper Sec^y

At a meeting of the Vestry & Wardens of St Davids Church held
Tuesday morning 3d May 1825   Present

                James A Harrington, Chairn
                Richard Maynard
                Jno Ellerbe
                Geo Andrews
                B. H. Rutland
                H. G. Loper

The Vestry then went into an election for chairman (Vice ...J.
A Harrington Resignd) When Dr. Richd Maynard was duly elected

   A committee of three Gentlemen Viz Maynard Hearsey & Harrington were appointed as a Standing committe to act with full power
in all case in which the Interest of the Church is required

   The Vestry also Concur'd in the ordering of a Bell and
enclosure of the Church-yard
                     Loper Secty

                       31

At a Meeting of the Vestry & Wardens held on Wednesday 3d June
1826
    Present   Richard Maynard
                       James Harrington
                       Geo T Hearsey
                       Benj H Rutland
                       Geo Andrews

The Standing Committee reported that they had endeavord to pro-
cure estimates of the expences for enclosing the church yard
making double pannell doors & portico on the North side and for
erecting a Vestry room belfry & steeple & although they were not
able owing (to the indisposition of the person applied to) to
exhibit exact specifications yet they felt authorised in general
terms to assure the vestry that the Whole amount would not exceed
one Thousand Dolls.
    The Vestry then adjourned
                                  Loper   Secty

Sunday Morning June 12 1826
    This day were baptized during divine Service the infant Son
of Geo. T. Hearsey & Mary C. Hearsey by the Name of James Moffett
also the infant daughter of D. K. & Susan Dodge by the Name of
Indiana
                                  Loper   Secty

Sunday Morning June 27 1826
    This day was baptized the infant Son of O. H. & Sarah Kollock
by the Name of Cornelius

At a Meeting of the Vestry of St Davids Church held Jany 26 1826
Present
               G. T. Hearsey
               Richd Maynard
               James Harrington
               Ben Rutland
               H. G. Loper
               Jno G. Lance

On Motion Resolved that the Vestry offer to Mr. Hathaway four
hundred dollars for his Services during the present year And
five hundred Dolls provided they receive pecuniary aid from the
Episcopal Society in Charleston

On Motion of Coln Hearsey Resolved thatSuch repairs as have been
deem'd necessary to the Church be forthwith commenced and that a
loan be instituted for the purpose of defraying Such expences as
may be incur'd in Such repairs

Resolved that after Such repairs are completed So many pews be
disposed of at public auction as May be necessary to reimburse
the expences incurr'd

              The Vestry then adjournd

                        H. G. Loper   Secty

At a Meeting of the Vestry & Wardens of St Davids Church held
February 2, 1826
Present   Rich Maynard   P
             G. T. Hearsey
             Jas A Harrington
             Jno G. Lance

```
                Benjn Rutland
                O. H. Kollock
                G. Andrews
                H. G. Loper
```

On Motion of Jno. G. Lance order'd that a reconsideration be
taken of the resolution that was pass'd at the last Meeting- Viz
that certain repairs be put on the church and a loan be obtain'd
from the bank for the amount of costs and that the pews be sold
at public auction to defray the loan
Motion Made & Seconded that the repairs to the Church be made
for the Amount of the Estimate Render'd by Mr. Stennits

On Motion of Mr. Hearsey Resolved that the Committee do contract
for a loan until the first of January next from the Bank for the
amount of the Estimate

                The Vestry then adjourn'd
                        H. G. Loper   Secty

At an election held on Easter Sunday (1826) for Vestry and Wardens to Serve for one year the following Gentlemen were duly
elected
                Richard Maynard
                George T. Hearsey
                James A. Harrington
                John Ellerbe
                Benj. H. Rutland
                John G. Lance

                H. G. Loper, Pritchard, Billingsby
                [above in pencil]

At a Meeting of the Vestry & Wardens held April 7th 1826

     The Vestry then went into an election for Chairman of the
Same to Serve the ensuing Year which terminated in the election
of Dr. Richard Maynard.
     H. G. Loper was also elcted Secty for the Vestry for one
year.
     (previous to the election G. T. Hearsey was call'd to the
     chair. H. G. Loper Secty p'tem)

The Vestry then went into the consideration of Renting the pews
for One Year for the purpose of raising funds for the payment of
the Salary of the Pastor.

On Motion of Dr. Maynard Resolved that a part of the pews of the
Church be Sold at public auction On Saturday afternoon 15 Inst.
at 4 O Clock P. M. and a committee of Two consisting of Mr.
Hearsey & Maynard be appointed to Superintend the Selling of
Said pews
                The Vestry then adjourn'd
                        H. G. Loper   Secty

Saturday afternoon   April 15. 1826

     the following pews were Rented at public auction for One
Year payable Semi-annualy at the following prices

Pew No 1)
 "   "   2) Not rented
 "   "   3)

                            33
```
```

```
"   "   4)   Jno McDonald   $12.50
"   "   5)   Wm Chapman     $12.50
"   "   6)   Jos Pritchards $12.50
"   "   7)   R McQueen      $12
"   "   8)   B. H. Rutland  $11
"   "   9)   A P Lacoste    $14
"   "  10)   Ministers
"   "  11)   Jno G. Lance   $12
"   "  12)   O. H. Kollock  $20
"   "  13    J A Harrington $20
"   "  14)   G. T. Hearsey  $20
"   "  15)   R Maynard      $20
"   "  16)   Eras Powe      $20
"   "  17)   Jno Ellerbe    $15
"   "  18)   D. K. Dodge    $13
"   "  19)   Jos Lazarus    $10
"   "  20)   W H Robbins    $13
"   "  21)   Jno B Billingsby $11
"   "  22)   James Towns    $12.50
                          ─────────
                          $261.00
"   "  23)
"   "  24)
"   "  25)
"   "  26)   Not rented
```

Sunday Morning Sept 4 1825

Two children Son & Daughter of Franklin & Sarah Towns were this Morning Babtized by the Revd G. W. Hathaway as Elizabeth Kent & Henry Clark   Dr. John G. Lance Sponsor

The Infant daughter of the Revd G. W. Hathaway and Alice Hathaway was likewise babtized this morning by Mr H named Lavenia Alice Mr & Mrs Dr Maynard Sponsors
(NB This Should have been recorded Long since but the Memorandum was mislaid)

Sunday Morning October 22, 1826 the infant daughter of Mary & Benj G Turland was this morning Babtized by the Revd Geo. W. Hathaway as Flora Louisa   Mr & Mrs. Dr. Maynard Sponsor

Sunday Morning November 12th 1826
    This day the Reverend Mr Folker from Columbia was to have officiated and the Lords Supper was to have been ordain'd but unforseen circumstances prevented his reaching or coming at this time
                    H. G. Loper   Secty

On Sunday Morning 23 July 1826   The Reverend Mr Mason from Fayetteville perfor'd divine Service in the Church
                    H. G. Loper   Sec^y

[The stubs of several pages are found here]

No Records are lost by the leaves being cut out as it was done previous to this time

Sunday Morning   December 31, 1826
    This morning Prayers were Read by the Revd Mr Wright from No Ca and a Sermon preached by the Revd Mr Elliott from Charleston S C The Lords Supper was likewise administered this afternoon the Revd Mr Wright performd divine Service

Sunday Morning December 3d 1826
    This day the Revd Dr Gadsden from Charleston So Ca officiated
in our Church and the Lords Supper administer'd to the Members

[Blank page]

On Sunday the 20th May the holy communion was administered by
the Revd Mr. Elliott and a collection made the amount of which
was Three 7/100 Dollars $3 7/100)   1827

The Revd Mr. Elliot officiated for several years from this period
in St Davids Church It is regreted that the records of this
time are not transcribed in this book.
26 June 1832   J. A. Harrington

ADDENDUM:

    On page 14 after the entry"ORDER'D that Hannah Howell...."
should be the following:

ORDER'D That the Church Wardens bind out three Children Viz
Sarah, Mary & Kisiah Barker, to Such Persons as they may Judge
Proper

1   St. David's Church, Cheraw.
The General Assembly of the Province of South Carolina passed
an Act bearding date the 12th day of April in the year 1768 for
making a new parish out of part of the parishes of St. Mark's
Prince Frederick's & Prince George's "to go by the name of
the parish of Saint David." Fourteen gentlemen were by the said
Act appointed Commissioners of the said Parish, nine of whom,
viz. Claudius Pegues, Philip Pledger, Alexander Mackintosh,
George Hicks, Robert Alison,Thomas Lide, Charles Bedingfield,
James James & Benjamin Rogers, met at the house of Mr. C.
Bedingfield, on Monday Aug. 1st 1768. Three of these, viz.
Mackintosh, James & Alison, declined serving. An election
of Church officers was held, when eighteen votes were cast &
two Church Wardens & seven Vestrymen were chosen, who were
duly sworn in to their office on the next day, Augt. 2d. (For
additional particulars-see the Rev. Dr. Dalcho's History, p.
327)
      "The Revd. James Foulis officiated for some time in this
parish in 1770."
      On the 4th of July, 1770, the Vestry wrote a letter to the
Revd. Mr. Hogart, an English Clergyman & stated that "on the
Recommendation of Mrs. Betty Wise," they had "agreed to wait
for" his "acceptance" of the parish, he giving them "an answer
in six months," & "being here in (a) Twelve Month from the
Date Hereoff" &c. (See the Original Record.) Mr. H. did not
accept of the invitation; &"application was made in 1772 to the
Revd. Mr. Robinson to officiate & if approved of, the Vestry
(it was said) would recommend him for holy orders" Dr. Dalcho
thought that it was "probably that this gentleman was a minister of some other communion." May he not have been in Deacon's
orders? The original record of the Vestry (Jan. 14, 1772) is
in these words:"Agreed that Mr. Thomas Wade write to the Rev.
Mr. Robinson to meet the Church officers at Mr. Wm. Lankford's
on the third Tuesday in February next, in order to Perform
divine Service, & if he should then be approved off by said
Church Officers, that they then recommend him home to take out
orders, if this Place & their Proposals should be Agreeable to
him." (R. B. C.)

2 Memoranda June 21, 1777
At a meeting of the Church Wardens & Vestry at the Parish Church
on Saturday June 21st 1777, it was "Agreed that a Letter be
wrote to the Rev. Mr. Winchester to preach a Sermon on Saturday
the 28th instant for (the) happy deliverance of this State from
our cruel & oppressive Enemies on the 28th of June 1776." It
is not probably that this Mr. Winchester was a clergyman of the
Church of England. The Society for Propg. the Gospel has no
missionary of that name either in North or South Carolina or
Georgia, during the American Revolution. Their only Missionary
in S. C. was the Revd. Samuel Frederic Lucius, officiating
first (from the year 1770)to the Palatines at Coffee Town, in
Edgefield District, & after the Evacuation of Charleston,
attempting to go there again, but finding that impracticable,
staying in Charlestown until March, 1783, when he went to "the
Congaress, 142 miles from C---n" & found a number of his old
parishioners.
      There are no records extant of the Proceedings of the
Wardens & Vestrymen from Sat. July, 1785, until Christmas,
1819, when the Rev. Andrew Fowler, Missionary of the Prott.
Epl. Society in S. C. visited and officiated in "St. David's
Church, Chatham."
      See the account of Sir Peter Parker's attack on Sullivan's
Island & repulse on the 28th of June 1776, in Ramsay's History

of the United States, II, 105 & Marshall's Life of Washington,
II, 385. After writing the above I was informed by Genl.
Gillespie, that Mr. Winchester was a Baptist & afterward became
a Universalist. April 21, 1860. Robt. B. Croes.

3 Memoranda. May 9th, 1823

The Rt. Revd. Dr. Bowen, Bishop of the Diocese of South Carolina
first visited St. David's Cheraw, on Friday, May the 9th, 1823,
preached & confirmed nine persons, viz. Mrs. Pritchard, &
her two daughters, Mary & Margaret; Mrs. Harrington, Mrs.
Kollock, Mrs. Wilson, Mrs. McBanke, Mrs. Rutland & Mr. James
A. Harrington.

The Revd. R. B. Croes, of the Diocese of New York officiated
in St David's Church, as Minister pro-tem, nearly four months,
beginning on Sunday, Jan. 22, 1860.

4 Blank

5 Baptisms

1819 Decr 25th	by Rev. Andrew Fowler Miss P E S of So Ca Sponsors Charlotte N., daughter of Jas. A. & E. W. Harrington & Witnesses

1820
March   by Rev. A. F.
19th   Charlotte, wife of John wilson

1823
March   by Rev. Thos. Wright of No Ca
 2nd   Rebecca Ann, daughter of D. K. & Susan Dodge

1825
Sept   by Rev. Geo. W. Hathaway
 4th   Elizabeth Kent &) children of Franklin   Dr. John G. Lance
   Henry Clark   ) & Sarah Turner

 "   Lavinia Alice, daughter of Rev. Geo. W. and) Dr. & Mrs.
           Alice Hathaway   ) Maynard

1826
June   James Moffett, son of G. T. & Mary C. Hearsey
12th

 "   Indiana, daughter of D. K. & Susan Dodge

 26   Cornelius, son of Oliver H. & Sarah Kollock

October Flora Louisa, daughter of B. H. And Mary Rutland
  22   Dr. Maynard

1824   by Rev. Th. Wright of N. C.
June   John W., son of Jas. A. & E. W. Harrington

6   Baptisms
        By   ) Sponsors &
     Rev. Charles P. Elliott, Rector   ) Witnesses
  1827
  June
   10th   Randal Carter (cold.) servant of C. D. Wallace

37

24th	Henry W, son of Jas A. & E. W. Harrington) the Father
	born the 14th of February Mr. Jos Pritchard
	Mrs. Troy

24th   Henry W, son of Jas A. & E. W. Harrington) the Father
     born the 14th of February   Mr. Jos Pritchard
                    Mrs. Troy

"   Sarah A., daughter of Thos. E. &) Jas. A. Harrington
        Charlotte H. Powe   ) Mrs. H. Strong
     born the 5th May   ) Mrs. S. Kollock

August   Julia Agnes, daughter of Wm. &)
        Catherine Chapman   )   the Parents
        born the 15th June   )

Nov.   Elizabeth Hopkins born 12th July 1823)children of
11th   James Fayette   " 3rd Apl 1825) Joseph &
     John Marion   " 1st July 1827)Rebecca Townes
     [sponsors & witnesses:] the Parents & Mrs. C. K. Pritchard

1828
Jany   Virginia Hopkins Townes born Aug 10th 1826
11th   the Father Edmund Townes & Mrs. Jas. Townes

July   Thomas Chambers, son of John G. &) the Father
6th   Rosa Land born the 9th April) Lawrence Prince
                    Miss Auld &
                    Mrs. Harriet Chambers

27th   Alexander W. Ellerbe aged 12 years 3 mos. & 43 days
     Erasmus A. Powe   " 13 " 11 " & 6 "
     Mary Powe Ellerbe " 2 " 3 " & 2 "
     [sponsors & witnesses:] Erasmus Powe & Mrs. Esther Powe
     Mary Caroline Powe   ) Erasmus Powe
     Martha Ellerbe   Adults)
     John Ellerbe   ) Esther Powe &
     Erasmus Powe Ellerbe   ) Mrs. Kollock

     James Stingfield & Mary Ann
      children of Mr. & Mrs. Chas Collins the Parents

29th   Sarah E McCullough Adult Erasmus Powe &
                   Mrs. Ann Dewitt

"   John Dewitt son of Sarah E McCullough Erasmus Powe &
                   Sarah E. McCullough

"   Catherine servant   C. S. Maynard

"   Jeffry & Solomon servants of Mrs. E. K. Pritchard) Mrs.
     Francis Lin Scott free cold. child   )Pritchard

7 Baptisms   Sponsors &
    by Rev. Alexr W. Marshall, Rector   Witnesses

1829
Sept   John infant son of John & Martha Ellerbe (being ill
22nd   was baptised at the residence of Erasmus Powe)

October Caroline Harrington daughter of Thos E) Miss Mary Powe
11th   & Charlotte H. Powe)Margaret B. Prit-
                  chard & John Ellerbe

1830   Mrs E A Marshall
May   Kate servant of John Ellerbe Miss K Pritchard &
 23rd   John Ellerbe

June 8th   William Dewitt Clinton   son of Wm F &
               Caroline M Youngblood (aged six months)
               at Marlboro' Court House)

```
June       William Dewitt Clinton   son of Wm F &       ) Jacob S Alison
8th                    Caroline M Youngblood (aged six months ) Mrs McBurney
                       at Marlboro' Court House)             ) through Proxy
                                                             & Wm F Young-
                                                                      blood

July       Martha   daughter of Lemuel S & Ann Drake)
1st        (being ill was baptised at the house)      )

11th       Sarah Maria   daughter of Mr & Mrs Wingate )  the Mother[?]
                                                      )  Dr & Mrs Maynard &
                                                         Rev A W Marshall

October    Thomas Powe   son of Mr & Mrs Charles        the Parents &
3rd                      Collins                        Rev A W Marshall

1831
Jany       Richard Maynard   son of A W & E A   )   Dr & Mrs Maynard
2nd                      Marshall   aged 2 months and )        &
                             6 days               )   Rev J W Chanler

March      Edwin Gibbes   child of Maria Dr. Maynard's) Mrs E A Marshall
27th                                    servant       )
 "         James Boggs     "  "  Harriet Mrs.         ) Mrs C K Prit-
                            Pritchard's servant )           chard

July       Charles Thorp                      adult ) Dr Maynard
26th                                                ) John Elerbe

August                       daughters of Mr Jennings )  the Father &
     9th          at the Church in Wadesborough No Ca  )  Step Mother

                       infant daughter of Mrs. Hall )  Mr. Jennings &
                                                       Mrs E W Harrington

           John     servant of Mrs. H Strong       )  Mrs. H Strong

           Jane      "      Mrs. Troy              )  Mrs. Troy

           The three last named also baptised at Wadesborough
```

8   Baptisms

```
           by Rev A W Marshall   Rector            Sponsors &
1832                                               Witnesses
                Sarah Ann   child of Harriet Mrs Pritchard's)  Misses M & K
                                         servant        )  Pritchard

April      Dorothy Dewitt   wife of Josiah J. Evans ) Dr & Mrs Maynard
22         William Henry )
           Samuel Wilds  )      Children of          Mrs S E McCullough
           Edward Edwards)      D. D. & J. J.        Rev A W Marshall &
           Elizabeth Mary)         Evans             Mrs E A Marshall

           Margaret Julia Hawes           adult     the same witnesses

June       Desdemona   )  children of Mr & Mrs Wm   the Parents
3rd        Peter Dalton)          Pledger

8th        Elizabeth   wife of James R. Ervin
                       on her death bed
```

24th	John Witherspoon)	children	Mrs Esther Powe
	James Robert)	of	Mrs C H Powe
	Jane Witherspoon)	James R Ervin	Mrs E A Marshall
	Mary Caroline)		John Ellerbe
			Rev A W Marshall

July	Daniel Albert)	children of D K &	Mr & Mrs Billingsly
1st	Jane Fisk)	Susan Dodge	Mrs E A Marshall
			Rev A W Marshall

August	Frances)	children of	Rev A W Marshall &
19th	William Engel)	John & Mary	Mrs E A Marshall
	Virginia Caroline)	Stinemetz Dr & Mrs Maynard	
	John Billingsly)		) Mrs Pritchard &
			) John B Billingsly

Sept	Maria Hawes wife of John J Marshall	Mrs E W Harrington
16th		Dr Maynard

October	Thomas child of Maria Dr Maynard's	Dr Maynard
7th	servant	Mrs E A Marshall

May 8	Lucy William & Nicholas little	O H Kollock
	negroes of O H Kollock	

" "	Mike Spencer Henry John Alick Joshua)	J A Harrington
	Jesse Willis Edmund Tom George Scipio)	owner
" "	Mary Harriet & Rachel)	
	the above negroes Baptised in Marlboro'	

9 Baptisms   Sponsors &
    by Rev A W Marshall Rector   Witnesses

May 14th	aged 90 to 100 servt. of J. A. Harrington
	(2) little negroes of J. A. Harrington
	)John Ellerbe & Mrs.
Nov 4	Charity Beck & Wisdom servants of John)E A Marshall
	Ellerbe)Miss Pritchard & Kate
	Charlotte servant of Mrs. Esther Powe) Mrs Esther Powe &
	)Mrs E A Marshall
	)Rev A W Marshall for
	the above

11th	Sally Cantey wife of John N Williams)
	Elizabeth B Witherspoon adult)Mrs S E McCollough

Decr	John Dewitt adult) Dr Maynard &
30th	) Ann Dewitt

1833
Jany 26	Serena Inf daughter of S C & J N Williams) The Mother &
	at the Male Academy Society Hill) E B Witherspoon
	Sarah Helen daughter of J J & D D Evans) The Mother
	at the Male Academy Society Hill) Mrs McCollough
	) Rev A W Marshall

27	Ann Elvina wife of Lemuel S Drake) the husband &
	) Mrs E A Marshall

    2 little negroes of James A Harrington

Febry	Steven servant of James R Ervin) Dr Maynard's Tom
3rd	) Mrs Ellerbe's Kate

[Febry 3rd] Washington child of John Ellerbe's) Mrs E A Marshall
                                 Charity   ) Miss M B Pritchard

March   Elizabeth Evans   wife of C B Pegues   Mr & Mrs J B
  3   Rebecca A E Pegues   adult   Billingsly &
         Francis Gillespie)   children   Rev A W Marshall
         Nicholas Bedgegood)   of   Sponsors & Witnesses
         Christopher Claudius)   C B & E E   Rev. A W Marshall
         Charles Augustus   )   Pegues   Mrs E A Marshall
                                                   Witness

  24th   Harriet   servant of James R Ervin   Miss M B Pritchard &
   "   Caroline negro child belonging to   Mr Ellerbe's Kate
                   John Ellerbe   Sponsor & Witnesses

10 May   Charlotte Powe   ) children   Mr & Mrs Harrington
   5th   Elizabeth Evans   )   of   & Mrs C H Powe
          Josiah Edward Evans) C B & E E Pegues   Mrs D D Evans
                                                  Jas A Harrington

   "   Erasmus William   son of   Mrs McCollough
                   Thos E & C H Powe   Jas A Harrington

   "   Adeline Alice   daughter of   Mrs A E Drake &
                   John & Mary Stinemetz   Dr A Hopton

   "   Mark   servant of Jas A Harrington   Jas A Harrington

July   Henrietta Kelsal   infant daughter)   Mrs E A Marshall
 7th   of Wm H & H K Robbins   )   Miss M B Pritchard

14th   Hannah (inft)   servt of Mrs Pritchard Miss M B Pritchard

   "   Margaret child of Wisdom & Beck servants) Miss M B Pritchard
                   of John Ellerbe   ) Ellerbe's Kate

25th   Laura Amanda   )   Children   )Mrs C H Powe
)   )Miss M B Pritchard
)   )John Ellerbe
)   of   )Cranmore Wallace
   "   James Francis)   ) Mrs E A Marshall
)   Lemuel S &   ) John Ellerbe
)   ) Cranmore Wallace
   "   Charlotte Powe)   Ann E Drake   )Mrs C H Powe
)   )Miss M B Pritchard
)   )John Ellerbe

   "   Mary Anna   Infant daughter of   )Mrs C H Powe
                         O H & Sarah Kollock   )Mrs E A Marshall
)Rev A W Marshall

   "   Langdon Kilham   Infant son of   ) The Father
                         D K & Susan Dodge   ) Mrs C Wallace
) Mrs John Morrison

October   Henry Cranmore son of) at   ) John Dewitt
 6th   Wm H & Maria A Snipes) Society Hill) Mrs S E McCollough
) Miss Julia Hames

11 1833   Elizabeth Witherspoon   Infant daughter) the Mother
   October   of John N & Sally C. Williams)
     27th   at Society Hill   ) Mrs E Witherspoon

                              41

Novr 17	Elizabeth wife of John D. Witherspoon at Society Hill	) J D Witherspoon) & Miss) D D Evans	

1834
April 2 Torn an old Servant of Jas A Harrington) Mrs C H Powe

26 Oliver Kollock) R Maynard
) Cranmore Wallace

Sept 14th Harriet infant child of Tom & Maria
servants of Dr. R. Maynard) the parents

Polly & 2 children of Harriet) Miss M B Pritchard
servant of Col Jas. R. Ervin) Mr. Ellerbe's Kate

Nov 2 Wm H. Robbins) Mrs H. K. Robbins
) O H Kollock

" Dolly Evans infant child of
C B & E E Pegues) Mrs Billingsly Proxy
) for Mrs D D Evans
) Mrs Rebecca Pegues
) Rev A W Marshall

Juliet infant daughter of
Cranmore & Juliet Wallace) the Parents
) Mrs Collins

Henry Peyton) Children Mrs. C. Billingsly
Moses) of J B Billingsly
Theodore) James & Sarah Sanders &
Mary Catherine) Rev A W Marshall

1835
Feby 12 Sarah Olivia wife of James Gillespie)
at his residence in consequence of her illness)

April 5 Mary Ann wife of Abner Hopton Mrs. C Pritchard

Mary Anna daughter of
Abner & Mary Ann Hopton)Miss E Stinemetz
)Mrs E A Marshall
) Rev A W Marshall

12 April 5 Mary Ann Infant daughter of
Lemuel L & Ann E Drake)
) Mrs M A Hopton

May 8 Sam an old Servant of O.H. Kollock The owners

George & 2 negro children of O H
Kollock Do

" 31st James Harrington Infant son of
Thos E & C H Powe) Mrs H Strong
) Mrs O H Kollock

Aug 16 Harriet & Kelsal 2 little negroes of
John Ellerbe) Kate &
) Charity

Decr 6 Miss Martha Louisiana Rogers of
Marlborough District) Mrs Pearson
) Mrs E A Marshall
) Rev A W Marshall

" " John Infant son of Tom & Maria servants
of Dr. R Maynard) Miss S A Marshall
)

42

[Decr 6]   Mary Sarah Laura Charity Lewis   )
           Washington Cicero & Allen little   ) Mrs E W Harrington
           negroes of E W Harrington Baptised at her)
           residence   )

1836
March   Henrietta Kelsal   daughter of)   the Parents
27   Wm H & H K Robbins   )

" 28   Rose an old servant of Mrs E W Harrington)
           thought to be near her end   )

April 29th   Catherine   )
            at the residence of A Shepherd Wadesboro)

June   Samuel Gillespie   infant son of   ) Mrs S Gillespie
26   C B & F E Pegues   ) A W Ellerbe
) Rev A W Marshall

Decr   Daniel)   children of   the parents
25   Frank)   Frank & Charlotte servts   &
       Lorenzo)   of Mrs. EstherPowe   Mr Ellerbe's Kate

1837
Jany   George Smith   at his residence in   )
17   Marlborough District being ill)

March   David Gregg   Infant son of   ) Miss Julia Hawes
26   John J & Maria H Marshall   ) Rev A W Marshall

13   March   Catherine Bedgegood wife of   ) The Husband
    23   Alexander W Ellerbe   ) Mrs E E Pegues

    "   John J. Marshall   ) O H Kollock
) John Ellerbe

April   Maria Elizabeth   Infant daughter of   ) the mother &
30th   Charity servt of John Ellerbe   ) Kate

May   John Alexander   Infant son of   ) Mrs E E Pegues
7   Alex W & C B Ellerbe   ) C B Pegues
) John Ellerbe

" 28   Mary Susannah   Infant daughter   ) Mrs C Billingsly &
        of Rev A W & E A Marshall   ) Miss S A Marshall &
) T C Marshall by
) their proxies Rev A W
) & E A Marshall

Octo   John Gasper Spergein Infant son   ) Miss F Stinemetz
15   of Abner & Mary A Hopton   ) the father &
) John Lynch

" 22   Josephine Elizabeth   infant daughter) the Parents
       of Wm H & H K Robbins   )

Nov   Eliza Vanorden   Infant daughter of   ) the Parents
12th   John & Ann Morrison   Miss E Vanorden

"   Franklin R Parker   ward of Mr & Mrs)
                John Morrison   )

43

```
1838
March   Louisa   Infant daughter of              ) the Mother &
  25         K C & C B DuBose                     ) Mrs E Witherspoon

Aug     James Gillespie Sen                       ) John Ellerbe
                                                  ) John J Marshall

  "     Mary Olivia )      children               ) Mrs H Gillespie
  "     Samuel James)        of                   ) Mrs M H Marshall
  "     Oliver Hawes)    James Gillespie Sen      ) Miss Julia Hawes &
                                                  ) John J Marshall

  "     Benjamin  Infant son of                   ) the parents
              John J & Maria H Marshall           ) Miss Julia Hawes
                                                  ) Rev A W Marshall

  " 26  Thomas Erasmus  Infant son of             ) The Mother &
              Thos E & C H Powe                   ) Mrs C B Ellerbe

Sept    Rosanna   daughter of Charlotte  servt )  Kate &
16th                 of Mrs Esther Powe        )  Mark

Decr    Elizabeth &          2 little negroes of ) Wisdom
 13          A W Ellerbe                          ) the father their
        Baptised at A W E's residence            ) Sponsor

14  1839
March   Archibald Strickland     adult
13th

April   at the residence of Jas Gillespie    )
10th    a large number of his little negroes)

  " 7th  Eliza Evans  Infant daughter of          ) the parents
              A W & C B Ellerbe                    ) & Mrs E Pegues

  " 21   Maria Ann   wife of Wm H Snipes          ) John Dewitt
                                                  ) Ann Dewitt
        Harriet Olivia) children of           ) John Dewitt
        John Dewitt   ) Wm H & M A Snipes      ) Ann Dewitt
                                              ) Julia Hawes

June    Rosalie  Infant daughter of               ) the Mother
15th         K C & E B DuBose                      ) & C H Powe

Aug     Sam  an old servant of C B Pegues)
9th                 on his death bed )

  " 18   Henrietta Frances Emma Infant daughter)  the parents &
              of Abner & Mary A Hopton        )  Sarah Gillespie

Nov 7th  Phosey   servt of Jas Gillespie at his residence

Decr 15th  Jim    servant of                      ) John Ellerbe
                  Geo H Dunlap                    ) Charlotte &
                                                  ) Mark
1840
Feby 3rd  Julius Augustus   Infant son of Kit
              servt. of Rev A W Marshall

May 3d   Samuel Gillespie  Infant son of          ) the Parents
              Wm & Elizabeth Godfrey              )
```

44

[May] 27   Julia, Alexander, Maria, Abram Charlotte) O H Kollock
            Roger & Nero   little negroes of O H Kollock)

June 3rd   little negroesof E W Harrington

  " 7th   Caroline Ann Infant daughter of   ) R E Collins &
                    Rev A W & E A Marshall   ) M C Marshall
) per proxy E A M

  " 28th   James Gregg Infant son of   ) Rev A W Marshall
                    John J & Maria H Marshall   ) Julia Hawes per
) M H M proxy

Aug 28   Josephine Baker daughter of Elizabeth Baker   )
            on the hill near the Bridges. She died soon after her Baptism)

15 Sept 6   Harriet   daughter of Harriet servt)
                        of Mrs Pritchard   )
             Laurie   son of Maria servt   )
                        of Mrs Pritchard   ) M B Pritchard

Octo 25   Abram   an old servant of   ) Patience his Wife
                   Mrs E W Harrington   ) Mark & Jim

Decr 11th   Mary Inf daughter of Eve) servants of   )
            Solomon Inf daughter of Vina) Thos G Powe   ) C H Powe

  " 13th   Georgiana   Inf daughter of   ) the parents
                    J H & Mary Pettus   )

1841
            Eleanor Esther Infant daughter of   ) The Mother &
            Thos E & C H Powe   ) Sarah Kollock
) per E A Marshall
) proxy

            Augusta Infant daughter of   ) The Mother &
                K C & E B DuBose   ) E Witherspoon

Feby 26   Van Buren   Infant son of Charlotte)   Esther Powe
                    servant of Mrs Esther Powe)

March   Virgil   Infant son of Adam & Eliza)   E W Harrington
  10   servants of Mrs E W Harrington)

16 Baptisms by Rev J W Miles missionary of P E Society of S. C.

A. D.
1841
September   Emma Engle at 4 months, daughter of) The Mother &
   5th   Thomas & Frances Bryan   ) Dr & Mrs Hopton

   "   Abner William Herschell at 1 month,)
            son of Abner & Mary Hopton.   ) The Parents

1842   By Rev. J. W. Miles, Minister of the Parish
February   At Gen. James Gillespie's: nine negro children: viz)
   11th   Martha: Rufus: David: Flora: Elijah" Ann: Julia:)Parents
            Alice: (& of the Est. Gillespie) Julius.   )

   13th   Chandler infant son of W & H. Robbins   Parents

45

March
2nd   At Mr. Kollocks: two negro infants James & Caroline

13th   Alexander: infant son of A. & C. Gregg) Parents &
) Mr & Mrs. Kollock

16th   At Mrs. Harringtons: five negro children:)Parents
       viz. Clayton, Emmeline, Amy, Nelson, Horace.)

June   At Mrs. Harringtons: two negro infants:
8th   Cicero & Ovid.

July
10th   George: infant son of   &   Bowman   Parents

September   Sarah Ann and Martha Jane: children of Mr. &
   20th   Mrs. Lyles: baptised on a sick-bed

            At Mrs. Harringtons, two negro infants, Ovid & Eastman
            At Mr. Kollocks, a negro infant

            Received Sarah Ann & Martha Jane Lyles into the Congregation
                                                    the Mother

October   Harriet Elizabeth, infant daughter of)   Parents &
                                Dr. & Mrs. Powe) Mrs. Harrington

December   Dr. Thomas Ellerbe Powe   )Mr. Kollock
   25th   )Mr. Robbins &
)Mrs. Harrington
   1843
January   Isaac Young: at 7 Months; son of   ) Parents &
   15th   [J. J. & Sarah L.?] Westervelt   ) Mr. Kollock

March   John Richardson: infant son of   ) the Mother
   12th   Charlotte, servant of Mrs. Esther Powe) Miss M. Cobia &
)Jim (a cold. commut.)

April 12th At Mrs. Harrington's, two negro infants

May   Mr. William Godfrey   Miss M. Pritchard
14th
           Claudia Elizabeth, child of William)Miss M. Pritchard
           Godfrey   ) & Mr. Godfrey

6 July   Alexander Gregg   ) O H Kollock
           by C E Gadsden(?)   ) Mrs C W Gregg
_____
           By the Revd. Henry Elwell, Rector.
_____
1844
Feby 11th At the house of Dr. A. Hopton,) Mrs. Stinematz
           James, infant son of Dr. A. &)   &
           Mary Ann Hopton   ) the Parents.
_____
           See the next page for an omission of a baptism
           on Sunday, March 31st 1844
_____
Good Friday At St. David's Church, John   ) Mr. A. Gregg
April 5th   Stafford, son of Duncan & Mary) Rev. H. Elwell
               Stafford   ) Miss Julia Hawes
             Also, James Alexander Smart &) Mr. A. Gregg
             William David Smart, children of) Revd. H. Elwell
             James & Martha Smart   ) Miss Julia Hawes

46

17

Also, John Goodwin, son of James) Mr. A. Gregg
and Sarah Goodwin   ) Revd. H. Elwell
) Miss Julia Hawes

18 Good Friday Also, Mary Jane Gales, child of)
    April 5th   Catharine Gales   )
                 Also, Elizabeth Smart, Martha)
                 Smart, & Ann Eliza Smart, chil-) Mr. A. Gregg
                 dren of James & Martha Smart   ) Mrs. Elwell
                 Also, Martha Jane Goodwin, &   ) Miss Julia Hawes
                 Laura Ann Goodwin, children of)
                 James & Sarah Goodwin   )

    April 12th   Eleanor Harrington Gregg, infant) The Parents &
                 daughter of Alexander & Charlotte) Mrs. Dr. Powe
                 Gregg   ,)

                 Also, Sarah Jane Bennett & Emme-) Mr. A. Gregg
                 line Bennett, children of Eliza-) Miss Julia Hawes
                 beth Bennett   ) Mrs. Elwell

    Omitted on the) John Douglas, child of Jno. J.   ) Jas. Gillespie Esq.
    preceding page) Westervelt & Sarah L. Westervelt) Mr. Downing
    March 31st   )   ) Mrs. R. Collins
       1844   )

    Friday Mg.   Mrs. Mary Stinemetz, Widow of) Dr. Hopton
    April 26th   John Stinemetz   ) Mr. Billingsly
) Mrs. Billingsly

                  Also Mary Stinemetz, infant) Mrs. Stinemetz
                  daughter of Thomas A. & Fran-) Mrs. Billingsly
                  ces Bryan   ) Mr. Billingsly

    Sunday
    afternoon
    Octr. 6th   Mary Ann Stafford & Louisa   ) Mrs. Gregg
                  Stafford, children of Duncan) Miss Julia Hawes
                  & Mary Stafford   ) Mr. A. Gregg

                  also Alexander Stafford & Daniel) Revd. H. Elwell
                  Stafford, children of Duncan &) Mr. A. Gregg
                  Mary Stafford   ) Miss Julia Hawes

                  Also William Thomas Goodwin &) Revd. H. Elwell
                  Charles Louis Goodwin, child-) Mr. A. Gregg
                  ren of James & Sarah Goodwin) Miss Julia Hawes

                  Also Maria Marshall Goodwin,) Mrs. Gregg
                  child of James & Sarah Goodwin) Miss Julia Hawes
                                                 Mr. A. Gregg

19 1845
    Jany 5th   After Evening Service at Church,
                  Rebecca a colored infant child,
                  belonging to Miss Julia Hawes   Miss Julia Hawes

    Feby 16   After the secdon Lesson at Evening
                  Service, John Henry, infant son of The Parents
                  Thomas E. & Charlotte H. Powe   A. Gregg, Esq.

                  At the same time with the above, Corne- The Parents
                  lius Kollock, infant son of Mr. & Mrs.   Bowman

                                  47

	March 16th	After the Second Lesson at Morning Service John George, son of Mrs. Elizabeth Keelyn, aged about six years.	John E. Edwards Revd. Henry Elwell
	April 13th	After the Second Lesson at Morning Service, Jamieson & John Edwards, children of Mr. & Mrs. Edwards.	Miss Julia Hawes Revd. Henry Elwell
	April 21st	On Mr. Kollock's plantation two in-) fant negroes, Nelly & Eli, the pro-) perty of O. Kollock Esq.)	Mr. & Mrs. Kollock
	May 22d	On Mr. Kollock's plantation four in-) fant negroes, Peter, Henry, Robert &) Jane...the property of John & Henry) Harrington)	Mr. & Mrs. Kollock
			Witnesses
	July 10th	At the house of her Mother, Ellen, lying dangerously ill, eldest daughter of Mrs. Mary Stinemetz	The Mother Mrs. F. Bryan Mrs. Bowne
	Octr 5	Mrs. Elizabeth Keelyn, daughter of John E. Edwards	John E. Edwards
20	Octr 26th	After the second lesson in the Morning Esther Louisa, daughter of Mr. & Mrs. Westervelt	the Parents
		At the same time, Julia, daughter of Mr. & Mrs. Waddill	the Parents Mrs. Torner
	Octr 29th	At the house of Alexr Gregg, Oliver Kollock, infant son of Alexander and C W Gregg	the Parents Dr. Powe

By the Rev. Alexander Gregg, Rector

	1846 June 21	After the second Lesson at Morning Service, James Miles Goodwyn, infant son of James and Sarah Goodwin	The Mother Mrs. C. W. Gregg John E. Edwards
		After the second Lesson at Evening Service, Mary Francis, infant daughter of Hiram and Barbara Lundsford	The Mother Mrs. C. W. Gregg John E. Edwards
	June 28	After dismission of congregation in the afternoon, Mary Jane, infant daughter of Charlotte, the property of Mrs. Esther Powe	The Mother Dr. Powe Mrs. C. H. Powe
21	Novr 8th	After the dismission of the congregation in the afternoon Frank, servant of Mrs. Esther Powe cold.	Dr. Powe Charlotte, (a communicant)

[Novr] 25th   At the residence of Mrs. Esther Powe,
              twenty five negro children, viz: Cato,
              Sharple Sr., Matilda, Abram, Alice,
              Grace, Calhoun, Eliza, George, Notoria,
              Julia, Sambo, John, Robert, Mary, Char-
              lotte, Charles, Sim, Martha Ann, Andrew,
              Richmond, Tom, Sharper Jr., Martha and
              Francis Ann.

Decr 18th   At the house of James Maynard, Gabriel
              and James, children of James and Mary
              Maynard

1847
Jany 14th   After the second lesson in the morning
              service, William Hinds, Infant son of The Parents
              William H. and Sarah Tomlinson.

May 16th   After the second lesson in the morning,
              William Alexander, infant son of Dr.   The Parents
              Thomas E & Mrs. Charlotte W Powe.

              At the same time, Athalinda, infant   ) The Parents
              daughter of Alexander and Charlotte W.) Dr. & Mrs.
              Gregg.   ) Powe

22 June 14th At the plantation of O. H. Koluck in
              Marlboro District, before evening
              service for the negroes, Amelia, infant
              daughter of Samar, servant of O. H. Kollock

              At the same time and place, Olivia, Infant
              daughter of Eliza, & Mourning, Infant daugh-
              ter of Lucy, servants of Henry Harrington--
              Also, Carter, Infant son of Lavinia, servant
              of J W Harrington

    June 27th After the second lesson in the morning ser-
              vice, Henry Powe, Infant Son of Gideon W.
              and Sarah Duvall.   The Parents
                                           & Dr. S. E. Powe

    June 29th At the plantation of Dr. Thomas E. Powe,
              thirty one negro children: viz, William,
              Celia, Becky, Moses, Evans, Eliza, Drum,
              children of Hannah--Grace, Bob, Laura, Amy,
              Sappho, children of Hannah--Jack, Jim, Frank,
              George, Prince--children of Hagar--Tabb, Bogan,
              lyms(?), & Nelly, children of Rachael--Virginia,
              & Danid, children of Mary--Dallas, child of
              Chany--Hames & Fanny, children of Patience--
              Nelly & Daniel, children of Hannah--Washington,
              child of Viney--Mike, child of Louiza--& Abram,
              child of Jane, all the servants of Dr. Thos. C.
              Powe

23 July 25   Before morning service, Anna Charlotte,) the
              Infant daughter of James P and Laura) Parents
              Harrall   )

49

```
                    At same time and place, Edwin, infant) The Mother
                    son of Thomas A. and Frances Bryan   ) Wm Godfrey
                                                         ) Rev. A. Gregg

Decr 12th At St. Davids church, before morning) the Parents
          service, Sarah Jane, Infant daughter) Mrs. Turner
          of Edmond and Elizabeth Waddell      )

  "    "   At same time and place, Eliza Ann,  )
          Infant daughter of Duncan and Mary   ) The Mother
          Stafford.                            )

1848
Febry 1   At the residence of Dr. T. E. Powe, Judy,
          infant child of Jack and Mary(?), servants
          of Dr. Powe.

March 12th At St. Davids church, before morning)
           service, Ann Eliza, Infant daughter )the Parents
           of John J & Sarah Westervelt         )

  "    "   At the same time and place, Sarah    )
          Frances, Infant daughter of James and)the Mother
          Sarah Goodwyn                         )

  "    26th At St. Davids Church, before morning )the Mother
          service, Edmund Allen, Infant son of )Rev A Gregg
          Hiram & Barbara Lunsford             )
```

24

```
Aprl 2    At St Davids Church, before morning  ) Mother
          service, Sarah Frances, and Christian) Rev. A. Gregg
          Infant daughters of John and    Strick-
          lin.

Aug 6     At St Davids church, before morning) The Parents
          service, James Edgar, Infant son of) Dr. Powe
          James P and Laura A. Harrall        )

Decr 6    At the residence of O. H. Kollock, in)
          Marlboro, Mark, child of Jacob and  ) Mr & Mrs
          June--also Eve, child of Molly, all  )  Kollock
          servants of J. W. Harrington         )
          Also, Eleanora, child of Reuben and)
          Thamar, servants of O. K. Kollock  )

1849
March 12  At her residence in Cheraw, Elizabeth)J J Westervelt
          Davis Middleton (ill of a lingering  )Mrs M Godfrey
          sickness)

Aprl 29   At St Davids church, after second les-) Parents
          son in evening service, David Gregg,  ) Mr & Mrs
          Infant son of Alexr. & C. W. Gregg    )  Kollock

  "    "   Also, at same time and place, Franklin)
          Alexander, Infant son of Edward J. &  )The Parents
          Elizabeth Kent Waddell                )

  "    "   Also, at same time and place, Sarah  )
          Elizabeth, infant daughter of Gideon ) The Parents
          W. & Sarah Ann Duvall.               )
```

25 May 15 At the residence of Mrs. Esther Powe,)
             5 negro children viz-Carolina, child)
             of Charlotte, Charlotte, child of   ) Mrs. Powe
             Nelly--Cass, child of Vice, Wesley,) E A Powe
             child of Ann Sr.--Milly, child of   )
             Beck, all belonging to Mrs. Powe   )

    "   16   On Henry Harrington's plantation two Negro
             infants--Jimmy, child of   and M--(?)
             child of Cely

    Aug 13   At the house of the mother, Julius King,
             infant son of Sarah Stafford, in a dying
             state, at 19 months

    Sep 7   At the residence of J. D. Pickard, in Cheraw
             Ann Elizabeth (very sick) infant daughter of
             Warren & Marin Davis

    Oct 28   After the second lesson in the morning,) The Parents
             Charlotte Eliza, Daughter of Thomas B.) Wm Billingsly
             and Charlotte Pegues   )

    Decr 30th After the second lesson in the   ) P H Kollock
             morning, James Hewitt, aged about) J J Westervelt
             65 years.   )

    "   "   After evening services at church,) Mrs. C. W. Gregg
             Emma, child of Frank and Jane, the) the Parents
             servant of Alexr Gregg.   )

26 1850   At the residence of her brother)
    Jany 18th Sarah Stafford, aged about 35   ) Mrs. C. W. Gregg
             years & ill of consumption   )

    "   16th At the residence of Mrs. Esther)
             Powe, Margaret, infant daughter)
             of Beck, servant of Mrs. Powe &)
             George, servant of Dr. T E Powe)

    "   23   At the residence of O. H. Kollock,
             Rosamund, child of Lucy, servant of
             Mr. Kollock

    March 7 At the church, after second lesson)
             in the morning, John Marshall,   )Mrs Bryan
             infant son of Thomas A and Frances)Mrs Stinemetz
             Bryan.   )A Gregg

    June 14 At the church after second lesson) O H Kollock
             in the morning, James Goodwyn, aged) J J Westervelt
             about 45 years.   )

    "   22   At the residence of James Hewitt Sr) Rev. A. Gregg
             in Chesterfield district (He not) & The Father
             being able to take them to church))
             his daughter Hannah, aged 3 years &)
             infant son, Joseph   )

    "   30   At the church after second lesson in) the Parents
             the morning, John Harrington, Infant) W Godfrey
             son of J P & Laura A Harrall   )

51

27 [June 30] Also, Wm Irwin, Infant son of)
                John J & Sarah L Westervelt) the Parents

    Feby 28   At the church after second lesson)
              in the morning, Eleaner Harrington) The Parents
              Infant daughter of Henry & Caroline)Dr & Mrs Powe
              McIver   )

    Oct   At the church, after second lesson) the Parents
    20   in the morning, Robert Calhoun, In-) A Gregg
              fant son of James & Sarah Goodwyn)

    1851   At the church, after second lesson) the Husband
    March 2   in the morning, Mrs. Rebecca Irby) Mrs. C. W. Powe
              Harrington

    May 25   At the church, after second lesson) the Parents &
              in the evening, Mary Atha, Infant) Mr & Mrs Kollock
              daughter of Alexander & C W Gregg)

    Nov 9th   At his residence, Joshua Waters,   ) The wife
              confined by dangerous sickness   ) A Gregg

    1852
    Jany 4   In the church, after second lesson) the Parents
              in the evening, Elizabeth Irby, in-) Mrs. Dr. Powe
              fant daughter of H W & Rebecca Har-)
              rington.   )

    Feby 8   At the church, after morning service,) the Mother
              Mary Emma, infant daughter of M. G.) Mr. F. Bryan
              & Virginia Tarrh   )

    Apr 4   At the church after second lesson in) The Parents
              afternoon, Mary Drake, Infant daugh-) Mrs. A. Drake
              ter of J. P. and Laura A Warll(?)   )

28 April 4   At the church after second lesson in) Mrs. Drake
              afternoon, J. P. Harrall.   ) Mrs. Harlle
) Mr O H Kollock

    June 6   At the church, after dismissal of)
              congregation in afternoon, Reuben,) Rev. A. Gregg
              Infant son of Julia, my servant.   )

    July 18   At the Church, after second lesson   )
              in the morning, Martha Eliza, Infant)the Parents
              daughter of Gideon W & Sarah Ann Duvall)

    Septr 19 At the church, after the second lesson) The Parents
              in the morning, Mary Hanford, infant) Dr. T. E. Powe
              daughter of Henry and Caroline McIver)

    "   "   At same time and place, Edwin Alexander)the Parents
              Infant son of W and S Smith   )

    Octr 24   At the church, after second lesson in)
              the morning, Mary Ann Stafford, wife) Rev A. Gregg
              of Duncan Stafford   )

    Nr. 9th   At the residence of Mrs. Esther Powe) Parents
              Andrew, child of Charlotte, Jane, child) E. A. Powe
              of Ann, and Charlotte, child of Beck)

                              52

servants of Mrs. Powe   )

[Novr] 25   At the church after second lesson)
            in the morning Walter Norish, in-) the Parents
            fant son of William H & Julia   )
            Munson   )

1853
Jany 30   At the Church after the 2nd lesson) the Parents
            in the morning, Mary Lilian, Infant)
            daughter of T. E. B. & Charlotte Pegues

29   Jany 30   At the church, after 2nd lesson in)
                 the morning, Sarah Leak, infant   ) the Parents
                 daughter of J. J. & Sarah Westervelt)

     "   "   At same time & place, Wilson, infant) the Parents
                 son of Alexr & C. W. Gregg   ) O. H. Kollock

     "   31   At Gofer Hill, Mary Jane Jackson,) James Huntt[?]
                 adult in a dying state.   ) Rev. A. Gregg

     Feby 9th   At the Galton(?) residence, near) The Parents
                 Cheraw, William Asa, Infant son)
                 of John & Elizabeth Tucker   )

     March 27   At the church, after evening service)
                 Mary Jane, child of Anel & Jany(?)) Mrs. Powe
                 servants of Dr. T. E. Powe   )

     June 5   After evening service at church, Jo) Rev. A. Gregg
                 child of Leah, servant of Rev. A.   ) Mrs. C. W.
                 Gregg   )   Gregg

     October 13 At the church, after 2d lesson in)
                 morning, Charlotte Rosanna, Infant) The Parents
                 Daughter of Thomas E & C. H. Powe)

     "   "   At the same time & place, James)
                 Auld, infant son of H. W. & Rebe-) The Parents
                 cca J. Harrington   )

     "   27   At the residence of the Parents,)
                 Simeon, Infant Son of Hiram   ) The Mother
                 Lunsford, being sick   ) Mrs. Stafford

30   Octr 29   At the residence of the Parents,)
                 James Daniel, Infant Son of James) The Mother
                 and Betsy Clark, being sick   ) Mrs. Stafford

     Novr 21   At the church, after second lesson)
                 in afternoon, Ellen Shand, infant) The Parents
                 daughter of Cornelius and Mary Hen-)
                 rietta Kollock   )

     1854
     Jany 10   At the residence of the parents,)
                      infant daughter of Oliver &)
                 Sarah Stacy, badly burnt, & in a)
                 dangerous state   )

March 12 At the Church after evening service) Mr. O. H. Kollock
          Sam, my Servant   ) Mrs. Gregg
                                              Juri (Dunlap)

April 23 At the Church after second lesson) Mrs. C. W. Gregg
          in morning, Sarah, wife of James) O. H. Kollock
          Goodwyn   )

"   "   At same time and place, Elizabeth) Mrs. C. W. Gregg
          Ellen, child of Catharine Gale   ) The Mother

"   30   At the church after second lesson) The Husband
          in the morning, Sarah Rebecca, wife) Mrs. C. W. Gregg
          of G W Duvall   )

June 25   At the residence of M G Tarrh,   in)
          cheraw, Mary Alice, an infant negro)
          the property of R D Killen (sick))

31   July 2   At the church after the 2nd lesson in) the Parents
              the morning, Lemuel Drake, Infant Son) J J Westervelt
              of James P and Laura H Harrall   )

     Novr 19th At the church, after 2nd lesson in) The Parents
              the morning, Henry, Infant Son of) Dr. T. C. Powe
              Henry and Caroline H M'Iver   )

     1855
     Febry 11 At the church, after 2nd lesson in) O H Kollock
               the morning, John D. Middleton   ) J P Harrall

     March 18 At the church, after 2nd lesson in) J P Harrall
               the morning, David Goodwyn   ) Mrs. Stafford

     "   19   At same place and time, Sophia   ) Mrs. Stafford
               Goodwyn, his wife   ) Mrs. C. W. Gregg

     "   25   At the Church, after 2nd lesson in) The Mother
               the evening, Levica Ann, Hannah   ) Mrs. C. W. Gregg
               Elizabeth and Rebecca, children of) J P Harrall
               John and Massey Rushing   )

     Aprl 8   At church, after evneing service,) Dr. T. E. Powe
               Albert, child of Annette, servant) Mrs. C. H. Powe
               of Dr. T. E. Powe   )

     May 13   At church, after 2nd Lesson in after-) The Parents
               noon, Henry William, Infant son of) Dr. T. E. Powe
               Henry Willian & Rebecca Harrington   )

     "   15   At residence of Parents, near Cheraw,)
               Sarah Gilbert, infant daughter of John) The Parents
               & Elizabeth Tucker   )

32   May 20   At the church, after 2nd lesson in) James Hewitt
              morning, Phebe, wife of James Hewitt) Mrs. C. Gale

     "   "   At the church after afternoon service)
             William, child of Toney & Eliza, also) Dr. C. Kollock
             Maria, Sam & Logan, children of Sam &)
             Lucy, servants of Dr. C. Kollock   )

54

[May] 27	At the church before morning service) Mrs Mary Stine- Sarah Ann, wife of John Stafford) metz) John Stafford) Rev. A. Gregg

[May] 27   At the church before morning service) Mrs Mary Stine-
           Sarah Ann, wife of John Stafford   )   metz
) John Stafford
) Rev. A. Gregg

"   "   At same time & place, Louisa & Ann-) Dr. T. E. Powe
          ette, servants of Dr. T. E. Powe   )

Octr 28   At church, after 2nd lesson in after-) Mrs C W Gregg
          noon, Wilson, son of Alexr & C W Gregg) O H Kollock
) Dr. T. E. Powe

Nr. 11   At the church after afternnon services) Mrs C W Gregg
         Frank, child of Leah, servant of Rev.) Spencer,
         A. Gregg.   ) servant Dr.
) T F Powe

Decr 31   At the church, after 2nd Lesson, Henry) The Mother
         Jeremiah, and Leonora Kolcock, child-) Mrs J G Kollock
         ren of Jeremiah & Leonora Yates, of   ) O H Kollock
         Charleston, S. C.   ) Alex Gregg

1856
March 7   At the Church after 2nd lesson in af-)
         ternoon (5th Friday in Lent) Laura   ) The Parents
         Pauline, infant daughter of Jas P. &) Mrs. Ann
         Laura A Harrall   )   Drake

"   "   At same time & place, George Williams)
          infant son of John J. and Sarah West-) The Parents
          ervelt   )

33   June 13   At my own residence, Sue, infant son)
               of Julia, my servant in extremes.   )

"   29   At the church, after 2nd lesson in   )
         morning, Mary Wilson, infant daughter) The Parents
         of Cornelius & Henrietta Kollock   )

Sept 7   At the church, after 2nd Lesson in   )
         morning, Marine(?) Walker, infant son) The Parents
         of Gideon W. & Sarah Duvall   )

Sept 21   At the church, after 2nd Lesson in   ) Jacob Ganey
         morning, Harriet, wife of Jacob Ganey) Mrs. C.W Gregg

"   "   At same time & place, Laura & Lewis,) The Parents
          children of Jacob & Harriet Ganey   ) Mrs C W Gregg

Nov 2   At the church, after 2nd Lesson in   ) C Kollock
       morning, Francis Marini M'Iver   ) H W Harrington

"   30   At the church, after evening service) Miss J Prit-
         Ella Frances, infant child of Phil-)   chard
         lis servant of Miss J. Pritchard   ) Miss C Godfrey

"   "   At same time & Place, Rosetta, child)
          of Mose & Charlotte, servants of Rev) Mrs C W Gregg
          A Gregg.

Dec 14   At church, after evening service,   ) Mrs C W Gregg
         Sally, servant of Rev. A. Gregg   )

```
1857
Jany 11      At the church, after 2nd Lesson in ) The Mother
             morning, Thomas Powe, infant son of) Dr T E Powe
             Henry & C H M'Iver                )

34   Feby 15      After service in the afternoon, Nel-)
             son, Alonzo, Henrietta & Cato, chil-)Mrs C W Gregg
             dren of Laura & Cato, servants of   )
             Rev. A. Gregg                       )

     "  22       After service in the afternoon, Laura)
             & Nelson, children of Arthur, servant)Mrs C W Gregg
             of Jas. Powe & Zim(?), servant of Rev)
             A. Gregg                             )

     March 1     At Church, after 2d Lesson in Morning)The Parents
             Lucy, Elizabeth, infant daughter of  )Mrs S Turner
             Edmund T(?) & Elizabeth Kent Waddell )

     June 4      At the Church, Flornine Louise & Anna)The Mother
             Laval, children of William A. & Alice)Mrs Mary
             A Wilson                             )   Stinemetz
                                                  )Rev A Gregg

     March 18    After 2d Lesson, (4th Wednesday in  )The Parents
             Lent) Charlotte Powe, infant daugh-  )Mrs C H Powe
             ter of Henry W & Rebecca J. Harrington)

     June 13     At the Rail Road houses, Cesar, ser-)
             vant of Miss M T Miller (in a danger-) Mr. J. J.
             ous condition from injuried received)Westervelt
             on R. Road.)                         )

     July 19     At the church, after 2nd Lesson in  )
             morning, Charles Wilson, infant son ) The Parents
             of Cornelius & Henrietta Kollock.    )

     Decr 14     At her residence in this District,  )
             Mary Keid, an aged woman and very infirm)

1858
Jany 19      At his residence in this District, Eli )
             Wallace, in a dying state              )

35   Feby 28      At the church, after Evening services )Mrs C W
             Tamar, child of Julia, my servant     )   Gregg

     March 2     At the residence of the Parents, near)The Mother
             Cheraw, George Washington, child of  )Jas Goodwyn
             Samuel and Martha Jane Taylor        )Mrs. Goodwyn[?]

     May 2       At the residence of Mrs. Stinemetz, )The Mother
             the church undergoing repairs, Ida  )Mrs F Ryan
             Vendan(?), child of William & Alice )Claude Godfrey
             Wilson                              )Rev A Gregg

     July 25     At church, after 2d Lesson in morning)The Mother
             Cornelius Kollock, infant son of Alex)Dr C. Kollock
             & C W Gregg

     "  "        At same time & place, Alex Gregg, in-) The Parents
             fant son of J P & Laura A Harrall     )

                          56
```

Decr 5   At the Church, after 2nd Lesson, in)
          afternoon, Margaret Hawes, Infant   ) The parents
          daughter of Cornelius and M H Kollock)

1859
Feby 20   At the Church, after 2nd Lesson in)
          afternoon, Harriet Eleanor, Infant) the Parents
          daughter of Henry W and Rebecca J)
          Harrington   )

May 22   At the Church, after service in af-)
          ternoon, William, child of Cato &   ) Mrs C W Gregg
          Laura, servants of Rev. A. Gregg   )

" 29   At the Church, after 2d Lesson in the) Mrs F Bryan
          morning Harriet Mills Brock   ) Mrs W C Tarrh

36 June 12   At the Church, after 2nd Lesson in) The Mother
              the morning, Edward, infant son of) Dr. T. E. Powe
              Henry & C H M'Iver   )

Aug 21   At the church, after morning service)
          Allen, Horton, child of Julia, Mrs.)Miss J Robbin
          H. K. Robins(?) servant--also,   )Miss J C Prit-
          Charles Wesley, child of Phillis,   )   chard
          servant of Miss J C Pritchard   )

Sept 11   At the Church after 2nd Lesson in)
          morning, Keran Rebecca, infant   ) The Parents
          daughter of G. W. & S. R. Duvall   )

" 18   At the church, after morning service)
          Andrew Jackson, child of Amy, ser-) Miss G Robbins
          vant of Mrs. H. K. Robbins   )

" 25   At the Church, after 2nd Lesson in) The Parents
          morning, Nicholas Williams, infant) Miss J Robbins
          son of F. M. and H. K. M'Iver   )

Octr 30   At the Church, after 2d Lesson in   )
          Morning, Thomas Powe, infant son of) The Parents
          J. P. & Laura A. Harrall   )

1860
Sunday, Jan. 29th At St. Davids Church, Ditto, by the Rt.
Revd. Alexander Gregg, D. D. Bishop of the Diocese of Texas,
Eliza Williams, Wife of John W.Harrington) J. W. Harrington &
) Mrs Rebecca Harring-
                                                              ton
Edmund James Waddill   Witness, H. W. Harrington.
John Pickard Edwards   ditto, J. P. Harrall

Henrietta Cornelia, infant daughter of Dr. Cornelius &) Sponsors,
Mrs H. M. Kollock: Born on Wed. Dec.21, 1859   ) Parents.
                        Robert B. Croes, Minister pro. tem.
                                         of the parish.

Wed. night, May 16, I bapd. in private, Clarence William,
infant son of Mr. Ebenezer & Mrs. Margaret Wells. The
mother was sponsor. R. B. Croes.

37 Sunday   1861
    May 13th At the Church by the Rev. Mr. Kidney of Society
       Hill, Charlotte Harrington, infant daughter of Henry
       & E. K. McIver. The mother & Mrs. T. E. Powe were
       Sponsors.

    At the same time & place William Pegues, infant son of
    Henry & Rebecca Harrington. The parents were sponsors.

    On May 29th (Wednesday) the Bishop of the Diocese visited
    the Parish, & preached once. The Rev. Mr. Kidney preached
    the confirmation sermon & the Bishop confirmed the follow-
    ing persons Harriette Elizabeth Powe, Edmund James Waddell
    & John Pickard.
    [above entry marked through]

    Sunday
    Oct. 13 At the church, by the Rt. Rev. Bp. Gregg, of Texas,
             Aurelia Josephine, infant daughter of John F. &
    Sarah Westervelt. The parents and Miss J. E. Robbins-were
    sponsors.

    This church was open for services every sunday morning from
    the time that Bp. Gregg resigned in Oct. 1859 until Oct. 20,
    1861. The services were conducted by lay readers, Dr. T.
    E. Powe and Mr. H. W. Harringotn, excepting only a few
    months in the early part of the year 1860, when the Rev. R.
    Croes of N. Y. officiated in this church; and also excepting
    occasional services from clergymen of other parishes. The
    Rev. R. T. Brown of Fairfax C. H. Va having been called to
    this parish, assumed charge of it on Sunday Oct. 20/ 61.

    1862
    March 9th In Calvary Church Wadesboro N. C. by the Rev.
               R. T. Brown, Lucy Plummer, infant daughter of
               R. H. & M. Battle; sponsors the parents & Mrs.
               Ashe.

38 Baptisms by Rev. R. T. Brown

    1862
    April 6th   At the Church, after 2nd Lesson in Afternoon
                 service, Edmund James infant Son of E. J. & S.
                 Waddell Sponsors, Parents.

    May 8th   At the parents' residence Cheraw, Anna Elizabeth
                 Augusta infant daughter of E & M Wells. Spon-
                 sors Parents & Mrs. M. R. Brown.

    May 23d   At St. Davids Church after Second lesson in
                 afternoon service, Miss Jenny Brock.
                 Witnesses Mrs. V. Fawh & Mrs. E. Bryan

    June 1st   At St. Davids Church after 2nd lesson in after-
                 noon Service, Alexander Gregg, infant son of
                 Dr. Cornelius & Henrietta Kollock

    Septr 5th   At St. David's Church, after 2nd lesson in after-
                 noon service, Frances Gaillard, infant daughter
                 of Rev. J. M. & M. E. Greer, born June 19th
                 1862. Sponsors Mr. E. T. Gaillard, Misses Theo-
                 dora & Fannie Gaillard. (The parents of this child
    are refugees from Charleston during the war.)

October 17th   At St. David's Church, after the 2nd lesson
                 in morning service, Eliza Irby, infant daugh-
                 ter of John W. & Eliza W. Harrington: born
                 September 8th, 1862. Sponsors, Parents.

Decr. 28th   At St. David's Church, between morning & after-
                 noon services, Maria, infant child of Leopold &
                 Laura, servants of Mr. William Godfry. Sponsors
                 Mrs. & Miss Claudia Godfrey

39   March 30th   At St. David's Church, **afternoon**,   Parents &
                 after 2nd **Lesson**, Harriet Cardin,   Mrs K. Robbins
                 infant daughter of Lieut. Jas. H. &
                 Mrs. Josephine E. Powe born Jany 30tn
                 63

May 16th   At Mr. E. Wells, Cheraw, Florence Anne,   Parents &
                 aged 2 years & L month & Sarah Eliza- Mrs. E. Wells
                 beth aged 8 months children of $. E. & Miss E
                 Richd. W. & Sarah E. Raddy of Darling-   Raddy
                 ton District.

May 17th   Sunday after Ascension at St. David's Parents &
                 church, afternoon, after 2nd lesson,   Mr. E. F.
                 Nathaniel Chastaigner, aged 10 months, Walker
                 infant son of Mr. Jos. F. & Mrs. Emma
                 F. Walker, refugees from Charleston.

May 26th   At Westmoreland, near Cheraw, Henry
                 Herbert, aged 4 months, infant son Mrs. Jenkins
                 of Major Richd. & Mrs. Amarynthia   &
                 Jenkins & James Clarke, aged 8 months Mrs. Sea-
                 infant son of Dr. Jas. C. & Mrs. Ere-   brook
                 tina Seabrook, refugees from Wadmalaw
                 Island.

June 14th   At St. David's Church, before morning Her Husband
                 service, Jane, servant woman belonging Frank God-
                 to Mr. Jno K. McIver of Society Hill.   frey

July 15th   At St. David's Church, after 2nd lesson,
                 afternoon service, Henry William, infant Parents
                 son of James & Laura Harald aged   months

40   October 16th   At St. David's Church, Herbert Eben-
                 ezer, infant son of E. P. & Mrs. Maria Parents
                 Wells, aged 4 months.   & Miss E Raddy

Novr. 25th   At St. Davids Church, after Evening   Mrs. Eliza
                 Service, Cornelius Harrington, in- W. Harrington
                 fant son of Jeremiah & Leonora Eliza- Dr. C. Kol-
                 beth Yates, refugees from Mt. Plea-   lock &
                 sant near Charleston.   H. W. Harrington

Decr 4th   At Mrs. Ann Drake's residence Cheraw Parents,
                 Edward Thomas, aged 2 weeks, infant Miss Gaillard
                 son of Ed. T. & Mary Gaillard, & James & M. Brice
                 Francis aged 3 months, infant son of Parents, E.
                 Jas. F. & M. Drake   T. Gaillard, Mrs.
                                       Kendall & Mrs. Tomlin-
                                        son

1864 Jany 28th	At Westmoreland, Chesterfield District, near Cheraw, Julia Blanche, aged nine months, infant daughter of C. H. & Julia Blanche Leverett, refugees from Wadmelaw Island	Parents
March 9th	At St. David's Church, after 2nd Lesson afternoon service, Kinloch, aged 2 months, infant son of Thomas and Eliza Croft, refugees of Grace Church, Charleston.	Parents
May 8th	At St. David's Church, after 2d Lesson aftn. service, Annie Hicks, infant daughter of Cornelius & Henrietta Kollock, aged three months. Sarah Rebecca, infant daughter of H. W. & Rebecca Harrington, aged 3 months & Gertrude, infant daughter of E. T. & Elizabeth Waddell, aged 3 months.	Parents
41 May 9th	At the residence of the Parents near Cheraw, Henrietta Kelsall, infant daughter of Captn. Jas. H. & Josephine Powe, aged 2 months.	Parents & Mrs. K. Robbins
May 20th	At the residence of the Father in Cheraw, Emily Harmon, infant daughter of J. J. Westervelt, aged three months.	Father Annie W. Mrs. E. Westervelt
July 3d	At St. David's Church, after evening service Margaret Ann, Anna Jane, Mary Anne & Frances, children of Frank Godfrey & Jane, servants of Wm. Godfrey & J K McIver, Society Hill	Parents
" 31st	Harriett, child of the same	
August 2nd	At St. David's Ch., Margaret Elizabeth, infant daughter of Lt. S. G. & Harriett E. Godfrey, aged Five Weeks.	Mother Mrs. Margaret Godfrey & Dr. T. E. Powe
October 9th	At St. David's Ch. before evening service, Wesley infant of Flora & Dora, infant of Laura & Leopold, servants of Mr. Wm. Godfrey	Mrs. M. Godfrey & Miss E. E. Godfrey
Decr 4th	At St. David's Ch., after 2nd lesson Evening Service, William Allen Benton, adult, aet: at the same time & place Catherine, aet: 10 & Joseph Michal aet; 7, children of Chs. & Margaret Gayle	Wife & H W Harrington Mother & Grandmother
Decr 18th	At Grace Chapel near Cheraw, after 2nd lesson aftn. service, Frederick Perceval, infant son of C. H. & Julia Leverett, refugees from Wadmalaw, aged 4 months	Parents & Grandmother

1865
Jany 18th   At St. Davids Church, after 2nd   Grandparents
            lesson, aftn. service, Winthrop   Gꞁl. Williams
            Holmes, aged 7 years, son of Mr.   &
            Ketcham Augusta, Ga.   Miss Toney[?]

42   January 15th at Grace Chapel, near Cheraw, by Rev. W. O.
     Prentiss, Rector of St. Peter's Ch., Charleston, Julia Eva,
     infant daughter of Jas. La Roche & Wife, Madmalaw Island,
     aged 4 months. Sponsors Parents & Grandmother.

     April 9th After 2nd Lesson, Evening Service, St. David's,
     Cheraw, George William, infant son of Jos. F. & Emma Julia
     Walker (of Charleston) aged 4 months. Sponsors, Father &
     Mr. & Mrs. Walter.

     April 30th After 2nd Lesson, Evening Service, St. David's
          Church, Ardelia Williams, infant daughter of Saml. N.
     Brown & Nannie his wife, aged 4 months and 18 days.
     Sponsors Parents, GrandFather & Miss Tony, all of Charleston.

     May 7th At the parent's residence, Cheraw, after Evening
              Service, Sarah Ellen, aged 8 weeks, infant daughter
     of Major J. H. Screvan & Ellen W., his wife, refugees from
     Beaufort District. Godparents Dr. Dorr(?) & Mrs. Thos. &
     Miss Cornelia Screvan.

     May 24th On the Rail-Road cars, near Cheraw, Eugene, aged
              8 days, infant of   Smart &   his wife, refugees
     from Charleston.

     June 28th At the residence of Chancellor Dunkin, Cheraw,
              Sarah Harlston, aged 10 months, infant daughter of Mr.
          & Mrs. Alfred Dunkin, refugees from Waccamaw. Sponsors,
     Mother, Grandmother & C. H. Huger.

     July 2nd At St David's Ch., before morning service, Mrs.
          Elizabeth Davy Hearsey.
     Sponsors. Mrs. M. R. Brown, Mrs. Eliza Harrington & Mrs.
     Chs. DeSaussure.

43   July 2nd At St. David's Church, after 2nd Lesson, Evening
          Service, Mrs. Louisa Marion Prince, & at the same time &
     place, Catherine Gooch. At the same time & place, Lawrence
     William Thomas Ellerbie, infant son of Mrs. L. M. Prince &
     George William Thomas Ellerbie, infant son of Mrs. E. D.
     Hearsey. Sponsors & Witnesses, Wm. Godfrey, Chs. DeSaussure
     Mrs. DeSaussure & Mothers of children.

     August Two Infants on the Rail-Road cars, children of
             Refugees.

     Septr. 14th At the residence of Dr. C. Kollock, Cheraw,
             Mary Patterson, aged 5 weeks, infant daughter
             of Cornelius & Henrietta Kollock, Sponsors,
             Parents

     Octr 3d At the residence of Mrs. Ann Drake, Cheraw, Edwin,
             infant son of James and Laura Harrall, aged 1 month
             & 2 days, Sponsors, parents.

1866
April 1st   At the residence of its parents near Cheraw,
             Caroline Harriet, aged 10 months, infant daugh-
             ter of Henry and Caroline McIver.

See end of next page for an entry omitted in this place.

1866   By Rev. P. D. Hay
August 24   Fast (sic) of St. Bartholomew. At St. David's
            Church, Cheraw during morning service Charlotte
            Harrington infant daughter of Harriet and Gilles-
            pie Godfrey.
            Sponsors Dr. T. E. Powe, Caroline H. McIver and
            Claudia McLenn.

44   August 31st
             At the residence of her parents, Mary Salina, in-
      fant daughter of E. M. and Margaret Wells. The sacrament
      was performed in view of a surgical operation which she
      was to undergo and which it was apprehended would prove
      mortal.

      Nov: 25th
             At St. David's Chh., morning Service, Mary Pinckney,
      infant daughter of P. D. and M. P. Hay. Sponsors Hasilla
      Hay per prox. M. S. Pinckney, F. J. Hay, per prox.

      Nov. 25th
             At St. David's Chh., Evening Service, William Henry
      Robbins, infant son of J. H. and J. E. Powe. Sponsors,
      parents.

      1867   By Rgt. Rev. Alexr Gregg
      June 26th   At the residence of Mr. W. Godfrey, Elizabeth
                  Wilson, infant daughter of Dr. John K. & Mrs.
                  Claudia E. McLenn. Sponsors. The Parents and Mrs.
                  Margaret B. Godfrey.
                  At same time & place, William Francis, infant son
                  of Leopold & Laura Bates, (colored persons).
                  Sponsors, the Parents and Mr. W. Godfrey.

      1866 July ___th By Rt Revd. Thos F. Davis   In private
                  Sam, Sydney, Mary, Roger, and Ellen, children of
                  Rush & Charlotte Temple (cold.)
                  Sponsors, the parents and Dr. C. Kollock.

45   July 7th
                  At St. David's, morning service, John Wilson, son of
            J W & E W Harrington. Sponsors, parents and James H.
            Powe.

      1867   By Revd Jno W Motte, Minister of the Parish
      Aug. 26th At the residence of their parents, Thomas Wilson
                 & Claudia Helen (Twins), infant children of E. M. &
                 Margaret Wells. The Sacrament was performed in pri-
                 vate on account of the extreme illness of the child-
                 ren.

      Oct. 27th At St. David's Church, before Morning Prayer,
                 James Howard, infant son of C. Edward & Emma
                 E Jarrott. Sponsors parents & Mrs. F. Bryan
                 and Mrs. V. Fawk.

62

Nov. 24th At St. Davids Church, after the last Lesson at
           Evening Prayer, By the Rt. Revd. Alexander Gregg,
           Claudia Porcher, infant daughter of S. G. And H. E.
           Godfrey. Sponsors The Parents and Mrs. Claudia E.
           McLean.

1868
Feby 16th   At St. David's Church, after the last Lesson at
            Evening Prayer, Walter infant son of Jas P. and
            Laura Harrall. Sponsors the Parents and S. G.
            Godfrey.

April 25th Fest. St. Mark. At St. David's Church after the
            second Lesson at Morning Prayer, Charles Francis
            infant son of Mrs. Elisabeth Poston. Sponsors,
        the Mother, & Mrs. Catherine Cayle & Rev. John W.
        Motte
            At the same time & place, Henrietta Cornelia,
        infant daughter of Mrs. Mary Gayle. Sponsors the
        Mother & Mrs. Catherine Gayle & Rev. Jno W. Motte.

46   Oct 28th Fest. S. S. Simon & Jude. At St. David's Church,
         after the last lesson at Morning Prayer, Margaret Rebecca
        infant daughter of E. M. and Margaret Wells. Sponsors the
        father, Miss Elisabeth Reddy & Miss Rebecca Reddy.

        Oct 28th Fest. St. Simon & St. Jude. At St. David's Church,
        after the last Lesson at Morning Prayer, Martha LeNair in-
        fant daughter of Jas. F. & Ann E. Drake.
        Sponsors the parents & Miss Elizabeth Reddy.

        Oct. 28th Fest. St. Simon & St. Jude. At St. David's Church,
        after the last Lesson at Morning Prayer, Henry Thomlinson,
        son of Jas. F. & Ann E. Drake. Sponsors the parents & Mrs.
        Margaret Wells.

                    By Revd. Jno W. Motte, Rector.

Nov. 25th   In Private, Charlotte Eliza infant daughter of
            Betsy McAllister (cold.). Sponsors Mrs. F. M.
            Bryan & Rev. Jno W. Motte.

1869
April 25th At St. David's Church, after the last Lesson at
Morning Prayer, Thomas Powe infant son of S. G. and H. E.
Godfrey.
Sponsors the Parents & Dr. Thos E. Powe, maternal grand-
father.

May 9th At St. David's Church, after the last Lesson at
Morning Prayer, Pierce Butler Irby infant son of Jno W. &
Eliza W Harrington.
Sponsors the Parents & Jno H. Powe.

47   May 30th At St. David's Church, before Evening Prayer,
        Templeman Brown, infant son of Leopold and Laura Bates (cold.)
        Sponsors the parents & Mr. S. G. Godfrey.

        June 6th At St David's Church, after the Last Lesson at
        Morning Prayer, James McNair infant son of Jas. McN. &
        Bettie D. Alford.
        Sponsors the Mother, Mr. Wm. Godfrey & Dr. T. E. Powe.

Septr 9th In private Aaron Jackson (cold) aged 11 years,
son of Aaron & Jane Powe (The Sacrament was administered in
private on account of extreme illness)

Nov 16th In private, James Lockwood, infant son of Frank S.
and S. L. Gillespie. Sponsors the parents and Genl. James
Gillespie.

1870
Jany 3rd At the residence of his parents Florence, So Ca.
          Charles Edward infant son of C. Edward and Emma
          E. Jarrott. Sponsors Rev. L. F. Guerry, Revd.
          Jno W. Motte & Mrs. Mary S. Motte.

Jany 9th At. St. David's Church, after the last Lesson at
Morning Prayer, Mrs. Allan Eunice Cash. Witnesses Col. &
Mrs. Jno W. Harrington

Jany 9th At St. David's Church, after the last Lesson at
Morning Prayer, Alline Eunice, daughter of Col. E. B. C. &
A. E. Cash. Sponsors, the Mother, Revd. Jno W. Motte &
Mrs. Mary S. Motte.

48   Jany 9th At St. David's Church, after the last Lesson at
      Morning Prayer, Bessie Saunders, daughter of Col. E. B. C.
      & A. E. Cash.
      Sponsors the Mother, Col. Jno W. Harrington and Mrs. E. K.
      Harrington.

March 29th (24th day of Lent) At St. David's Church, after
the last Lesson at Evening Prayer, Charlotte Harrington,
infant daughter of Dr. Jas. H. & J. E. Powe
Sponsors, the father, Mrs. K. Robbins & Mrs. C. H. McIver.

March 29th. At a Missionary Station Samuel Gainey, infant
son of Samuel & Laura Goodwyn.
Sponsors the Grand parents Jacob & Harriet Gainey.

October 18th Fest. St. Luke. At St. David's Church, after
the last Lesson at Morning Prayer, Edward Morrell, infant
son of E. M. & Margaret Wells.
Sponsors The parents & Miss Elizabeth Reddy.

Novr 20th. At St. David's Church after the last Lesson at
Morning Prayer, Rosa Henrietta, infant daughter of Col. Jno
W. & Eliza W. Harrington.
Sponsors the parents & Miss Mary H. McIver.

Dec. 18th (4th Sunday in Advent) At St. David's Church, after
the last Lesson at Morning Prayer, William, infant son of
S. G. & H. E. Godfrey.
Sponsors the parents & Mr. Wm. Godfrey.

49   1871
      February 21st In private Elizabeth, relict of the late
      Crawford Ellerbe. This Sacrament was administered in pri-
      vate because of extreme illness from Consumption. Witnesses
      Mrs. Gideon Duvall and Miss Julia Hawes

March 12th (3rd S in Lent) At St. David's Church, after the
last Lesson at Morning Prayer, Emily Phillpot, daughter of
Mr. J. H. Gooch. Witnesses, Mrs. Low. M. Prince & Rev. Jno
W. Motte.

March 12th (3rd S in Lent) At St. David's Church after the
last Lesson at Morning Prayer, Margaret Florence, daughter
of Mr. J. H. Gooch. Witnesses Mrs. Low. M. Prince & Rev. Jno
W. Motte.

July 25th (Fest. St. James) At St. David's Church, after
the last Lesson at Morning Prayer, Mary Julia, infant daughter of Asa & Sarah J. Tuttle. Sponsors the mother, Mrs.
Mary Atkinson & Revd. Jno W. Motte.

July 25th (Fest. St. James) At St. David's Church, after
the last Lesson at Morning Prayer, Asa Solomon, infant son
of Asa & Sarah J. Tuttle. Sponsors the mother & Revd. Jno.
W. Motte.

August 1st In private Francis Samuel, infant son of F. 3.
and S. F. Gillespie.
Sponsors the parents, and Genl. James Gillespie.

August 9th At Grace Chapel, Chesterfield Co., Frances,
daughter of Mrs. Catharine Farmer of Charleston So Ca.
Sponsors Miss Julia Hawes & Mrs. Sarah R. Duvall.

August 20th At. St. David's Church, after the last Lesson
at Morning Prayer, Marcen Henry Howard infant son of Henry
F. & Sarah J. Duvall. Sponsors the parents & F. A. Waddill.

50 Septr 17th 15th Sunday after Trinity. At St. David's
Church, after the last Lesson at Morning Prayer, John Ward,
infant son of Revd. Jno W. and Mary Motte.
Sponsors Mrs. F. M. Bryan, Revd. P. D. Hay, J. Ward Motte.

Septr 21st Fest. St. Matthew. At St. David's Church, Mabel,
infant daughter of Alfred T. and Emma Peéle(?). Sponsors
The parents & Mrs. E. Donaldson

Septr 29th Fest. St. Michael and All Angels. At St. David's
Church, after the last Lesson at Morning Prayer, William,
son of Wm H. & Julia Monsun. Sponsors the parents.

Sept. 29th Fest. St. Michael and All Angels. At St. David's
Church, after the last Lesson at Morning Prayer, Annie,
infant daughter of W. H. & M. Monson. Sponsors the parents.

Septr 29th Fest. St. Michael and All Angels. At. St. David's
Church, after the last Lesson at Morning Prayer, Alice, infant daughter of W. H. & M. Monson. Sponsors, the parents.

Novr. 21st At Grace Chapel, after the last Lesson at Morn-
ing Prayer, Rachel, wife of John Atkinson.
Witnesses, Miss Julia Hawes, Mrs. G. W. Duvall, Revd. Jno W.
Motte.

Nov. 21st At Grace Chapel, after the Last Lesson at Morning
Prayer, Sarah, daughter of John & Rachel Atkinson.
Witnesses, Miss Julia Hawes, Mrs. G. W. Duvall, Revd. Jno W.
Motte

Nov 21st. At Grace Chapel, after the Last Lesson at Morning
Prayer, Catherine, daughter of John and Rachel Atkinson.
Witnesses Miss Julia Hawes, Mrs. G. W. Duvall, Revd. Jno W.
Motte.
At the same time & place, Rachel, daughter of John and Rachel

Atkinson Witnesses Miss Hawes, Mrs. Duvall & Rev. J W Motte

51   Nov 21st At Grace Chapel after the last Lesson at Morning
      Prayer Melissa daughter of John and Rachel Atkinson
      Sponsors Miss Julia Hwwes,Mrs. G. K. Duvall, Revd. Jno. W.
      Motte.

      Dec. 21st Fest. St. Thos. At St. David's Church, after
      the last Lesson at Morning Prayer William Henry Harrison,
      infant son of W. H. H. and Sarah J. Richards.
      Sponsors Revd Jno W. Motte & Mrs. Mary Stafford.

      Dec. 21st Fest. St. Thos At St. David's Church after the
      last Lesson at Morning Prayer Sarah Pattow daughter of W.
      H. H. and   Richards
      Sponsors Mrs. Mary Stafford & Revd. Jno W. Motte

      Dec. 21st Fest St. Thos At St. David's Church, after the
      last Lesson at Morning Prayer, Viola daughter of
      and Louisa McLaughlin.
      Sponsors Mrs. Mary Stafford & Revd. Jno W. Motte

      1872 April 25th Fest. St. Mark At St. David's Church, af-
           ter the last Lesson at Morning Prayer, Thomas Erasmus,
      infant son of Jas. H. and J. E. Powe Sponsors the parents.

      May 14th At Florence in private John Bryan infant son of
      C. Edward and Emma E. Smith
      Sponsors the Parents and Mrs. F. M. Bryan for Miss M. E.
      Tawh.

      June 23rd At St. David's Church after the last Lesson at
      Morning Prayer Talula Sherwood infant daughter of Jno W
      and Eliza W. Harrington.
      Sponsors the parents and Miss E. J. Harrington

52   Aug 7th In private Corrie Eila daughter of Capt. A. A.
      and   Pollock Sponsors Mrs. R. J. Pollock, Miss E. J.
      Harrington & Rev. Jno W. Motte

      Aug 7th In private Robert Alexander son of Capt. A. A. and
           Pollock,Sponsors, Mrs. R. J. Pollock, Miss E. J. Har-
      rington and Revd. Jno W. Motte.

      Aug 7th In private Nannie Seay daughter of Capt. A. A. and
           Pollock Sponsors the Mother, Miss E. J. Harrington
      and Revd. Jno W. Motte

      Aug 7th In private William Pegues son of Capt. A. A. and
      R. J. Pollock Sponsors the Mother, Miss E. J. Harrington
      and Revd. Jno W. Motte

      Augt 14th At Grace Chapel after the last Lesson at Morning
      Prayer, Frederick Alexander son of Mrs. Catherine Farmer of
      Charleston So Ca. Sponsors Miss Julia M. Hawes and Revd.
      Jno W Motte.

      Oct 20th At St. David's Church after the last Lesson at
      Morning Prayer Caroline McIver infant daughter of S. G. and
      H. E. Godfrey. Sponsors the father, Miss Mary H. McIver and
      Miss Meta Rogers.

Dec. 22nd   4th Sunday in Advent   At St. David's Church Howard, infant son of Leopold and Laura Bates (cold.) Sponsors The Mother, Mr. W. A. Benton & Revd. Jno. W. Motte.

1873

53   March 25th Fest. Annunc: At St. David's Church after the last Lesson at Morning Prayer, Thomas Francis, infant son of A. and M. J. Brown. Sponsors Mrs. C. Gayle & Revd. Jno W. Motte.

March 25th   Fest. Annunc: At. St. D. vid's Church after the last lesson at Morning Prayer, George Archibald, infant son of A. and M. J. Brown. Sponsors Mrs. C. Gayle & Revd. Jno W. Motte.

March 26th At St. David's Church, after the last Lesson at Morning Prayer, Caroline Harriet, infant daughter of John H. and Emily P. Powe. Sponsors, the parents and Mrs. S. E. Godfrey.

April 15th (Tues in Easter W.) At St. David's Church after the last Lesson at Morning Prayer, Allen Benton, infant son of E. M. and Margaret Wells. Sponsors the parents and W. Allen Benton.

April 15th (Tues in Easter W.) At St. David's Church after the last Lesson at Morning Prayer, Ida infant daughter of Alfred T. and Emma Peele. Sponsors, the parents, and Miss Annie K. Scoffin.

June 2nd (Monday in Whitsun week) In private Sidney Lockwood, infant daughter of F. S. and S. L. Gillespie. Sponsors, the parents.

June 18th At Grace Chapel, after the last Lesson at Morning Prayer, Sarah Leak, widow of Ervin Brunson. Witness Miss J. M. Hawes and Revd. Jno. W. Motte.

54   June 18th At Grace Chapel after the last Lesson at Morning Prayer, Reuben Raglan, infant son of E.and Sarah L. Brunson. Sponsors Miss J. M. Hawes and Revd. Jno W. Motte

June 18th at Grace Chapel after the last Lesson at Morning Prayer, Benjamin Franklin Ellerbe, infant son of E and Sarah L. Brunson Sponsors Miss J. M. Hawes and Rev. Jno W. Motte

July 2nd At Grace Chapel Wilkes Booth, infant son of Wm. and M. J. Barmar. Sponsors the Mother and Miss J. M. Hawes

Aug 18th In private, on account of extreme illness, Charles Wallis Ernest infant son of Jno D. and Sarah J. Pickard.

Sept. 28th At St. David's Church, after the last Lesson at Evening Prayer, Edmund Chapman infant son of Jas. F. and Ann E. Drake. Sponsors Miss Mary D. Harrall & Rev. Jno W. Motte

1874

Jany 1st Fest. Circumcision. At St. David's Church, after the last Lesson at Morning Prayer, Clara Edna Green, aged 14, daughter of Mary and Wm. Thos Graves. Sponsors Mrs. Jacob Gainey, Miss R. A. Reddy & Revd. Jno W. Motte

Jany 1st Fest. Circumcision. At St. David's Church, after
the last Lesson at Morning Prayer, Nancy Jane, aged 12,
daughter of Mary and Wm. Thos Graves. Sponsors Mrs. Jacob
Gainey, Miss R. A. Reddy, & Revd. Jno W. Motte.

55 Jany 4th At St. David's Church, after the last Lesson at
Evening Prayer, William Henry, infant son of Col. Jno W. and
Eliza W. Harrington. Sponsors the parents and Dr. Jas. H.
Powe.

Jany 5th At Dr. C. Kollock's residence, Robert infant son
of Aleck and Charlotte Tempel (cold.) Sponsors the parents

March 19th (5th Thurs in Lent) At St. David's Church, after
the last Lesson at Evening Prayer, Claudia Elisabeth, infant
daughter of Dr. Jas H. and J. E. Powe. Sponsors the father,
Mrs. Wm. Godfrey & Mrs. H. K. Robbins.

March 29th (Palm Sunday) At St. David's Church, after the
last Lesson at Morning Prayer, Elisabeth Waddill, infant
daughter of Henry P. and S. J. Duvall. Sponsors the parents
& Miss Martha E. Duvall

March 29th (Palm Sunday) At St. David's Church, after the
last Lesson at Morning Prayer, Carrie Mortimer, infant daughter of Wm. L. and Viola E. Reid. Sponsors the parents &
Mrs. S. J. Duvall

April 2nd (Maunday Thursday) At St. David's Church, after
the last Lesson at Morning Prayer, Arthur Fredric, infant
son of Wm. H. and Mary Munson. Sponsors the parents.

May 19th In private Claudia Elisabeth infant daughter of
Leopold (cold.) and Laura Bates (cold.)

56 June 21st At St. David's Church, before Morning Prayer,
Franklin Turner. Witness W. A. Benton.

July 12th In Private Mary Frances infant daughter of Betsy
McAllister (cold.)

Aug. 22nd In Private, Harriet Eleanor, infant daughter of
S. G. and H. E. Godfrey.

Oct. 6th In Private Emma, infant daughter of Alfred T. and
Emma T. Peele. Sponsors, the father, Mrs. Elisabeth Donal-
son & Mrs. Mary Motte.

Dec 7th In Private Emily Florence, infant daughter of Emily
P. and Jno H. Powe.

1875
March 25th Fest Annunc. At St. David's Church, after the
second Lesson at Morning Prayer, Henry Laurence Britton,
infant son of E. M. and Margaret Wells. Sponsors the parents

May 19th At Florence, Helen Alston infant daughter of C.
Edward and Anna E. Jarrot. Sponsors the father, Mrs. F. M.
Bryan, Mrs. Jno W. Motte

July 13th In Private Charles Irby of Marlboro' Co: Witness
C. Kollock, M. D.

Oct 17th   At St. David's Church after the Second Lesson at
Morning Prayer   Claudia Elisabeth, infant daughter of S.
G. and J. F. E. Godfrey.
Sponsors the parents and Mrs. Margaret Godfrey.

57   Novemr 3rd   In Private Robert infant son of Rev Jno W. and
Mary Motte aged 7½ hrs

1876
Jany 1st   At St David's Church after second Lesson at Morn-
ing Prayer   Emily Louisa infant daughter of Emily F. and
John H. Powe.   Sponsors the parents and Mrs. Mary H. Hardin

Jany 31st   In Private   Ellen Little daughter of Benj. and
Mary J. Tyson   aged 6 weeks.   Sponsors the Mother, John
Beaty & Ann E Beaty.

Feby 25th   In Private Margaret Agnes, daughter of Wm. E. and
G. Lillian Cook aged 4 weeks.   Sponsors Mrs. Margaret R.
Gaskins & Mrs. Mary Barton

March 17th   At St. David's Church, after second Lesson at
Morning Prayer, Virginia Shatton infant daughter of Capt.
A. A. and Rebecca J. Pollock.   aged 2 years 6 mos.
Sponsor the mother

April 8th   At St. David's Church after the second Lesson at
Evening Prayer Henry Herbert infant son of Wm. H. and Mary
Monson   aged 4 months   Sponsors   the parents

May 10th   At Home   Hary Lothrop infant son of Dr. Jno H.
and Josephine E Powe   aged 6 weeks   Sponsors the parents
and Mrs. H. K. Robbins

July 6th   At Home William Lockwood son of F. L. And S. L.
Gillespie   Sponsors the parents   aged 10 months

58   July 16th   At St. David's Church after the second lesson at
Morning Prayer   Edmund Walker son of Sarah J. and Henry P
Duvall   aged 2 months.   Sponsors Miss Lucy E Waddill, E. J.
Waddill G. W. Duvall

July 25th   At St David's Church, after the second Lesson at
Morning Prayer, Mary Lilian, daughter of E. M. and Margaret
Wells   age 3 months.   Sponsors the parents and Miss Mary L.
Reddy

Dec 3rd   At St. David's Church after the last Lesson at
Evening Prayer Dora Priscilla   aged 12 years   daughter of
A. Catherine and T. Franklin Sherrill   Sponsors Mrs. Pri-
scilla Ogburn, S. G. Godfrey

Dec 3rd At St. David's Church after the last Lesson at
Evening Prayer, Martha Custis   aged 10 years   daughter of
A. Catherine and T. Franklin Sherrill   Sponsors Mrs. Pri-
scilla Ogburn, S. G. Godfrey

Dec 3rd   At St. David's Church, after the last Lesson at
Evening Prayer, Mary Ann Epps aged 8 years daughter of A.
Catherine and T. Franklin Sherrill   Sponsors   Mrs. Priscilla
Ogburn, S. G. Godfrey

1877 March 4th At St. David's Church, after the second
Lesson at Morning Prayer Eleanor McIver, aged 4 mos.
daughter of Jas. D. and Mary H. Hardin
Sponsors The parents & Mrs. Caroline H. McIver

July 22nd At Christ Church, Mars Bluff, at Evening Prayer,
George McClenaghan born Jany 4th 1870, son of Jno W and M.
A. Wilson. Sponsors Mrs. M. A. Wilson, W. J. Maxwell, Rev.
Jno W. Motte.

59   Nov 21st At Grace Chapel John Atkinson, aged 63 years.
Witnesses Miss Julia W. Haws, Mrs. Rachel Atkinson

Nov 21st At Grace Chapel, John aged 3 years, son of
Charlotte & Jno F. Edwards. Sponsors Miss J. M. Haws, Mrs.
Rachel Atkinson.

Dec 3rd At Home in Marlboro Co., Waite Emmeline aged 8
yrs daughter of David and Elizabeth Richardson

Dec 3rd At Home in Marlboro Co., Loucy Caroline aged 6
yrs daughter of David and Elizabeth Richardson

Dec 3rd At Home in Marlboro Co., William Parker aged 3
yrs son of David and Elizabeth Richardson

Dec 3rd At Home in Marlboro Co.
 Julia Motte)
 Ellen Buist) aged 4 months
 Maria Thomas)
children of David and Elizabeth Richardson

Dec 16th In St. David's Church after the second Lesson at
Morning Prayer Marian Gillespie born Nov. 1st 1877 daughter
of S G. and Harriet E. Godfrey
Sponsors the parents & Miss S. B. DeSaussure

Dec 16th In St. David's Church after the last Lesson at
Evening Prayer, Francis Marion West Born Sept. 5th 1851
Witness, F. R. Waddill, M. D.

60   Dec 21st Fest. St. Thos. In St. David's Church after the
second Lesson at Morning Prayer Lemuel LeNair son of Jas.
F. and Ann E. Drake Born Aug. 4th 1875. Sponsors the
parents & Rev. Jno W. Motte

1878 Feb 17th In St. David's Church after the second Lesson at Morning Prayer Charlotte Wilson Born Nov 27th 1877
daughter of Emily P and John H Powe. Sponsors the parents
& Mrs. C. H. McIver

March 15th In St. David's Church after the second Lesson
at Morning Prayer, Lewis, born July 15th 1876 son of John
and S. Frances Eddings. Sponsor the Mother.

April 12th In St. David's Church at Morning Prayer Mary
Alline Born April 10th 1878 daughter Polston Sponsor
Mrs. Catherine Gayle

April 12th In St. David's Church at Morning Prayer William
Madison Born   son of Sarah D. Tuttle Sponsor Mrs.
Catherine Gayle

April 12th   In St. David's Church at Morning Prayer James
Eagan   Born   son of Sarah J. Tuttle, Sponsor Mrs. Catherine Gayle

June 16th   Trinity Sunday in St. David's Church at Morning
Prayer   Henry Powe born April 29th 1878 son of Henry P.
and Sarah J. Duvall.   Sponsors Dr. C. Kollock, W. A. Benton,
Mrs. W. A. Benton

61   Dec 15th   In St. David's Church after the last Lesson at
Morning Prayer   Mary Pauline born Sept. 15th 1878 daughter
of Mary D. and Danl. H. Reid.   Sponsors the parents & S.
Pauline Harrall

Dec. 27th   In St. David's Church after the second Lesson at
Morning Prayer   William Homer born   son of Wm. H. & Mary
Monson   Sponsors, the parents.

1879 Feby 9th   In St. David's Church after the second Lesson
at Morning Prayer   Meta Inglis born Nov 23rd 1878 daughter
of Jas D. and Mary H. Hardin   Sponsors, the parents.

Feby 9th   In St. David's Church, after the second Lesson at
Morning Prayer   Mabel born Nov 6th 1878 daughter of Thos P
and Susan R. McIver   Sponsors, the parents and Mrs. Sarah
A. Duvall

March 2nd   In St. David's Church after the second Lesson at
Morning Prayer   Edmund Waddill, born Dec. 27th 1878 son of
Henry W. and Lucy E. Harrington.   Sponsors the father and
Mrs. Sarah Nisbet

March 21st at Home in Marlborough Co. Randolph Pegues born
Nov 2nd 1877 son of Frank S. and S. L. Gillespie   Sponsors
the parents

April 20th in St. David's Church, after the second Lesson
at Morning Prayer   Margaret McLean born Nov. 29th 1878 daughter of Wm. L. and Viola C. Reid.   Sponsors the parents &
Mrs. Mary Motte

62   June 3rd   In Private   Henry Alexander born July 26th/79
son of Elizabeth Polston

Sept 14th In St. David's Church after the second Lesson at
Morning Prayer   Eleanor Josephine born Aug. 1st 1879 daugh-
ter of S. G. and Harriet E. Godfrey.   Sponsors the parents
& Mrs. Caroline H. McIver

1880 Feby 27th   In St. David's Church after the second Lesson at Morning Prayer   Gussie born Sept. 26th 1879 son of
John and S. Frances Goodwin   Sponsor   the Mother

April 4th   In St. David's Church after the second Lesson at
Morning Prayer John Henry Born Feby 17th 1880 son of John
H. and Emily P. Powe   Sponsors the parents & Dr. Jas. H.
Powe

June 29th   In St. David's Church   Annie Laurie McLean Born
April 10th 1878 daughter of E. M. And Margaret Wells   Sponsors the parents and Miss Rebecca A. Reddy.

June 29th in St. David's Church Joseph Blaine Born Jany
20th 1880 son of E. M. and Margaret Wells. Sponsors the
father, Miss E. J. Reddy & H. E. Wells

Aug 15th In St. David's Church Lucy Nisbet Born June 22d
1880 daughter of Henry W. and Lucy E. Harrington. Sponsors
the parents & Mrs. Mary Motte

63   Sept 29th in St. David's Church after the second Lesson at
Morning Prayer Gideon Walker Born Oct. 9th 1878 son of
Marun W. and Margaret D. Duvall. Sponsors the parents.

Sept 29th In St. David's Church, after the second Lesson
at Morning Prayer Howard Born Feby 28th 1880 son of
Marun W. and Margaret D.Duvall Sponsors the parents

Dec 5th In St. David's Church after the second Lesson at
Morning Prayer Fannie Benton Born Sept 17th 1880 daughter
of Henry P. and Sarah J. Duvall. Sponsors Mrs. Susan R.
McIver, Mrs. Fannie Benton & M. W. Duvall.

Dec. 22nd At. Home by Rt. Rev. Alex Gregg, D. D. Alexander
Gregg   Born Dec. 20th 1880 son of Ellen S. and D. F. A.
Waddill Witnesses Mrs. M. H. and Dr. C. Kollock and on
1881 April 17th Easter Day was received into the Church by
the Rector the parents being Sponsors

1880 Dec. 26th In St. David's Ch: after the second Lesson
at Morning Prayer Samuel Gillespie Born Nov 20th 1880 son
of Harriet E. and S. G. Godfrey
Sponsors Mrs. E. M. Godfrey, W. R. Godfrey and Jas. H. Powe,
M. D.

1881 Jany 16th In St. David's Ch: after the second Lesson
at Morn. Prayer Henry Harrington Born Oct. 11th 1880 son
of Lemuel D. and Charlotte P. Harrall. Sponsors the parents and Jas. P. Harrall

64   March 30th In Private. William Anderson Born February
28th 1876 son of Louis and Henrietta Gainey. Sponsors the
Mother & Grandmother Mrs. Harriet Gainey.

March 30th In Private Laura Jane Born June 28th 1879
daughter of Louis and Henrietta Gainey. Sponsors the Mother
& Grandmother Mrs. Harriet Gainey

May 15th In St. David's after the second Lesson at Morning
Prayer Laura Born Feby 20th 1881 daughter of Danl. H. and
Mary D. Reid Sponsors the Parents

June 7th In St. David's after the second Lesson at Morning
Prayer Louis Alexander aged 9 years son of Louis and
Henrietta Gainey. Sponsor the Grandmother Mrs. Harriet
Gainey.

June 7th in St. David's after the second Lesson at Morning
Prayer James Thomas aged 8 years son of Louis and Henrietta Gainey. Sponsor the Grandmother Mrs. Harriet Gainey.

June 19th In St. David's after the last Lesson at Evening
Prayer Laura Louise Born March 16th 1881 daughter of
J. Edgar and Laura L. Harrall Sponsors the Parents

June 22nd At Home   Edward Roscoe Born June 13th 1880
son of William H. and Mary Monson

65   Sept 10th In Private   Duvall Born Sept 10th 1881   son
      of Thos P. and Susan R. McIver

      Dec 2nd In Private   Clarence Kinmay   Born April 3rd 1880
      son of Frank S. and S. L. Gillespie

      1882 Feby 13th In Private (sickness) John Huntley Born
      January 8th 1882 son of E. W. and Margaret Wells

      April 23rd in St. David's after the second Lesson at Morn.
      Prayer Ernest Born Feby 5th 1882 son of Marun W. and
      Margaret D. Duvall. Sponsors the father, Mrs. Susan W.
      McIver, & H. R. Duvall

      May 28th In St. Davids, after the second Lesson at Morn.
      Prayer Cornelius Kollock born April 17th 1882 son of Ellen
      L. and Frank A. Waddill, M. D. Sponsors Dr. C. Kollock and
      Mrs. M. H. Kollock

      Aug 10th In Private Jessie Graham Born April 8th 1882
      daughter of Saml M. C. and Mary E. Moore

      Aug 13th In St. David's Church after the last Lesson and
      Eve. Prayer Agnes Evans Born Feby 28th 1880 daughter of
      Dr. Jno K. and Agnes B. McLean. Sponsors the Parents &
      Mrs. W. R. Godfrey

66   Aug 15th At Home Gustavus Adolphus Born Sept. 9th 1870
      son of Franklin & Catherine R. Sherrill Sponsors The Mother
      & Mrs. Priscilla Ogburn

      Aug. 15th At Home Daniel William Born Sept. 22nd 1872
      son of T. Franklin & Catherine A. Sherrill. Sponsors the
      Mother & Mrs. Priscilla Ogburn

      Aug. 15th At Home Adrianna Harriet Born Sept. 21st 1874
      daughter of T. Franklin & Catherine A. Sherrill. Sponsors
      the Mother & Miss Dora P. Sherrill.

      Aug. 15th At Home Anna Alberta Born Dec. 30th 1880 daugh-
      ter of T. Franklin & Catherine A. Sherrill Sponsors The
      Mother & Miss Dora P. Sherrill

      Aug. 15th At Home Catherine Eliza Born March 31st 1879
      daughter of T. Franklin & Catherine A.Sherrill. Sponsors
      the Mother & Miss Dora P. Sherrill

      Aug. 15th in Private Charles Clingman Born Feb 1880
      son of John J. & Emma Liles Sponsor the Mother

      Aug 15th. in Private Arthur Vanderbilt aged 10 mos. son
      of John J. & Emma Liles Sponsor the Mother

67   Oct 6th In Private Francis Motte   Born Jany 15th 1879
      son of James F. and Ann E Drake

      Oct. 15th In St. David's Church, after the second Lesson
      at Morn. Prayer Edward Hanford Born Aug. 4th 1882 son of
      Thomas P. and Susan R. McIver. Sponsor the parents &
      Edwards McIver, Esqr.

Oct 22nd In St. David's Church, after the second Lesson at
Morn. Prayer Florence Marion Born July 30th 1882 daughter
of John W. and Emily P. Powe. Sponsors the Parents & Miss
Margaret E. Godfrey.

Novr 26th In St. David's Church after the second Lesson at
Morn. Prayer, Thomas Franklin Sherrill   Born Nov. 17th
1831. Witness Mr. S. G. Godfrey

1883 April 8th In St. David's after the second Lesson at
Morn. Prayer Edith Born Novr. 5th 1882 daughter of Henry
P. and Sarah J. Duvall. Sponsors the parents and Miss
Elizabeth W. Duvall

April 29th In St. David's after the second Lesson at Morn.
Prayer   Ruth Born Feby 16th 1883 daughter of Henry W.
and Lucy C. Harrington. Sponsors the parents and Mrs.
Rebecca J. Pollock.

July 10th At Home   Alexander Pollock Born April 3rd 1883
son of Lemuel D. and Charlotte P. Harrall. Sponsors the
father and Mrs. Rebecca A. Pollock.

68   Sept 16th In St. David's after second Lesson at Eve. Prayer
Julian Cecil   Born June 14th 1875 Son of James and Lizzie
C. Coker. Sponsors Mrs. W. R. Godfrey, D. F. R. Waddill,
R. H. Pegues.

Nov. 1st In St. David's after second Lesson at Morn. Prayer
John Harrington   Born Sept. 7th 1883 son of S. G. and H.
E. Godfrey. Sponsors Mrs. W. A. Benton, W. A. Benton & Jno
H. Powe.

1884
May 11th In Bennettsville at Home Thomas Loraine Born
Aug 31st 1882 son of Sarah E. and Thomas M. Webster

July 27th In St. David's after second Lesson at Morning
Prayer William Evans Born March 12th 1884 son of Marun W.
and Margaret D. Duvall. Sponsors the parents and Miss
Sarah E. Duvall

Sept 7th At Home Mildred O'Roddy Born Aug 30th 1883
daughter of E. M. and Margaret Wells. Sponsors the parents
and Miss Rebecca A. Reddy

1885
Jany 25th In St. David's after the last Lesson at Morning
Prayer James Edward Born Dec. 11th 1884 son of John H. and
Emma P. Powe. Sponsors the parents and Dr. James H. Powe

April 2nd In St. David's after the last Lesson at Morn.
Prayer, Marian Emmons Born Oct. 10th 1882 daughter of Wm
H. and Mary Monson. Sponsor the Mother

69   June 24th At Home John Henry son of Charles H. and
Carrie McAllister (cold.)

Aug 2nd In St. David's after the last lesson at Eve. Prayer
Henrietta Born July 19th 1881 daughter of Louis and Henrietta Gainey. Sponsor Mrs. Harriet Gainey the Grandmother

Sept 7th At Home Lydia Maud Born May 19th 1885 daughter
of Louis and Henrietta Gainey

Nov 1st In St. David's at Evening Prayer Gordon Leslie
Born Jany 2nd 1885 son of Charlton & Fannie M. Shatney(?)
of Rochester N. Y. Sponsors the father, Jno F. McNair, Mrs.
Winnie S. McNair.

Nov. 25th In St. David's at Morn. Prayer Annie Laurie Born
Aug 12th 1885 daughter of Lemuel D. and Charlotte P. Harrall
Sponsors the parents and Mrs. Mary D. Reid.

1886 Feby 7th In St. David's at Eve. Prayer Thomas William Born Oct. 12th 1885 son of Richard H. and Sarah E.
Pegues. Sponsors the Parents

March 21st In St. David's at Morn. Prayer Helen Born Nov.
19th 1885 daughter of Thomas P. and Susan R. McIver.
Sponsors the Parents

70   April 19th Monday in Holy Week
    In St. David's at Morning Prayer Harriet Emily Born
Feby 27th 1886 daughter of S. Gillespie & Harriet E. God-
frey. Sponsors the father, Mrs. Josephine E. Powe and
Mrs. Emily P. Powe.

June 20th Trinity Sunday In St. David's Church at Morning
Prayer Margaret Evans Born March 14th 1886 daughter of
Marun W. and Margaret D. Duvall. Sponsors the parents

August 15th 8th S. after Trinity. In St. David's Church
at Morning Prayer Hannah Lide Born June 12th 1886 daughter of Mary D. and Wm. C. Wilson of Society Hill, S. C.
Sponsors: Mrs. Elisabeth M. Godfrey, Miss Elisabeth W.
McLeah, W. R. Godfrey

August 19th At Home Jennie Marshall Born April 7th 1880
daughter of John H. & Mary Ella Harrall Sponsors the
Father, Mrs. Laura A. Harrall.

August 19th At Home Alice Elisabeth Born Nov. 1st 1881
daughter of John H. & Mary Ella Harrall Sponsors the Father,
Mrs. Mary D. Reid.

71   August 19th At Home James Ernest Born July 23d 1883,
son of John H. & Mary Ella Harrall Sponsors James P. Harrall, Lemuel D. Harrall

August 19th At Home Mary Ella Born March 22nd 1885 daughter of John H. and Mary Ella Harrall. Sponsors the Father,
Miss L. Pauline Harrall.

Novr 21st In St. David's Church at Morning Prayer William
Gregg Born Aug 7th 1886 son of Dr. Charles W. and Gertrude
E. Kollock. Sponsors Caspar A Chisolm, F. A. Waddill, M. D.,
Miss Annie H. Kollock

Dec. 24th In Private Gertrude Born Nov. 13th 1886 daughter of Henry W. and Lucy E. Harrington

1887 Jany 16th In St. David's Ch. at Morning Prayer, Roland
Davis Born Nov. 18th 1886 son of John H. and Emily F. Powe
Sponsors the Parents & S. E. Godfrey

April 10th Easter Day In St. Davids Ch. at Morning Prayer
Stuart Strother Born March 1st 1887 son of Minnie Charle-
ton and John T. McNair. Sponsors George S. C. Strother,
Toronto Canada, Frank W. Strother, Toronto, Canada, Mrs.
Jessie E. McNair.

72   1888
March 10th In private Mary Crawford daughter of Elisabeth
and Crawford Ellerbe. Witness Mrs. Sarah A. Duvall

April 15 In St. David's at Morning Prayer, Annie Kollock
Born July 2, 1888 daughter of Henry W. and Lucy E. Harring-
ton. Sponsr. the Mother, Miss Sarah D. Duvall, Dr. F. A.
Waddill.

Aug 19th In St. David's at Evening Prayer Elisabeth Turner
Born July 12th 1888 son of Ellen S. & Frank A. Waddill, M.
D. Sponsors Mrs. F. M. Benton, Mrs. Lucy E. Harrington,
Edmund James Waddill.

1889
July 11th In St. David's at EveningPrayer Annie Eliza
Born April 12th 1889 daughter of Margaret D. and Marun W.
Duvall. Sponss. The Parents and Miss Martha Duvall By
the Rev. Chas. C. Quin, Rector of Calvary Church, Wadesboro,
N. C.

Dec 12th In St. David's at Evening Prayer by the Rev. Chas.
C. Quin of Wadesboro, N. C. Katherine Elizabeth Born
Sept. 3rd 1889, Daughter of John H. & Emily P Powe.
Sponss. The parents and Mrs. Elizabeth McLeod.

73   Dec 2nd In St. David's by the Rev. C. C. Quin, William
Motte Born July 9th 1889 Son of Walter N. & Henrietta C.
Munson. Sponsr. The parents & Mrs. J. M. Brown

Dec 2nd In St. Davids by Rev. Chas. C. Quin, Mary Ann Born
Oct. 1st 1876 Daughter of Irving A. & Amanda Hewitt Sponsr.
Mrs. M. R. Godfrey & Mrs. S. G. Godfrey.
        Also at same time and place
Benjamin Harllee Born Oct. 3rd 1878 Son of Irving A. and
Amanda Hewitt Sponsr. Mrs. S. G. Godfrey and Mrs. W. R.
Godfrey
Lilly May Born July 25th 1881 Daughter of Irving A. and
Amanda Hewitt Sponsrs. Mrs. S. G. Godfrey and Mrs. W. R.
Godfrey
Alexanda Hilliard Born Nov. 24th 1884 Daughter of Irving
A. and Amanda Hewitt Sponsrs. Mrs. S. G. Godfrey and Mrs.
W. R. Godfrey.

1890
March 4th in St. David's at Eve. Prayer By Rev. J. W. Motte
Rector, St. Andrew's, Darien, Ga. Ellen Kollock Born
Aug. 6th 1889 Daughter of Henry P. and Sarah W. Duvall
Sponsors Miss Ellen S. Waddill, Rev. Jno W. Motte

[pencil note:] Following entries by Rev. A. A[?] McDonnough

March 13th In St. David's, Henry Walker Born Sept. 14th
1889 son of Thomas P. and Susie R. McIver. Sponsors: Father
and Mother

76

74   Dec. 28th In St. David's Albert Cleveland Born Aug. 3rd
1884 Son of John T.and Mary A. Glover Sponsors Dr. J. H.
Powe, John T. Glover and Miss J. C. Pritchard

Dec. 28th Same time and place Josie Hamer Born Dec. 2nd
1887 daughter of John T. and Mary A.Glover Sponsors, Mother, Miss J. C. Pritchard and Dr. J. H. Powe, Mrs. Robt.
Godfrey.

1891
April 25th In private on account of extreme illness, Paul,
born April 1st 1891, son of James M. and Dora P. Thompson

May 31st In St. David's Douglas Breckenridge Born April
25th 1891 son of John T. and Mary C. McNair Sponsors The
father; Rev. A. A. McDonough, and Mrs. Agnes McLean

1892
April 3rd In St. David's Mary Emma Born Oct. 14th 1891
daughter of Walter N. and Henrietta C. Monson. Sponsors
Parents & Miss Rebecca Reddy.

April 17th In St. David's Cornelia Kollock born Aug. 16th
1891, daughter of John T. and Mary A. Glover Sponsors:
Mother; Mr. S. G. Godfrey, and Mrs. Elizabeth M. Godfrey

75   1893
July 23d In St. Davids at Evening Service Ichabod Futrell
aged 58 years; Sponsors Mr. and Mrs.W. R. Godfrey

Oct. 15th In St. David's: at Morning Service, Charlotte
Harrington Born July 22nd 1893 daughter of Mr. and Mrs. L.
D. Harrell; Sponsors The parents and Mrs. A. A. Pollock
and Miss L. Pauline Harrell.

Oct. 29th In St. David's: At Evening Service, Thomas Franklin Born Dec. 19th 1879: At same time and place, John Henry
Born Dec. 24th 1883; both sons of Mrs. Ichabod Futrell by a
previous marriage--Sponsors The Mother Mrs. Mary Jane
Futrell, and her husband Mr. Ichabod Futrell, step-father of
the boys; and Mrs. Elizabeth M. Godfrey and Rev. A. A. Mc-
Donough.

Dec. 24th In St. David's at Evening Service, William Thomas
Born Sept. 2nd 1893, son of Mr. and Mrs. William Thomas
Thrower. Sponsors William Godfrey, Samuel Gillespie God-
frey and Caroline McIver Godfrey.

76   1894
April 22nd In St. David's At Evening service, Julia Norrish
Born Sept 15th 1893 daughter of Walter N. and Henrietta
Cornelia Monson. Sponsors: Parents and Miss M. Lilian Wells

May 6th In St. David's Church at Evening Service, Cornelia
Eugenia Norton (Norton surname) about 4½ years old: Adopted
daughter of Mr. and Mrs. Ichabod Futrell; Sponsors Mr. Ichabod Futrell, Mrs. W. R. Godfrey, and Mrs. A. B. McLean.

1895
May 5th In St. David's Church; at Morning Service, James
Robert Born Dec. 16th 1894 son of W. Thomas and Margaret E.
Thrower Sponsors Mr. and Mrs. S. G. Godfrey and Edward Mc-
Iver as proxy for William Godfrey

77   Name   James Presley Harrall
        Birth   Nov 24th 1895
        Baptism March 26th 1796 at St. Davids Church
        sponsors Thomas Harrall & Parents
        Parents Mr. L. D. Harrall Mrs. L. H. Harrall
        Minister   Thomas P. Baker

        Name   Shady Stanton born 26th
        Birth   of May 1885
        Baptism April 14 1896
        Sponsors Lillian Wells
        Parents
        Minister Thomas P. Baker

        Name   Bessie McCall
        Birth   18th of May 1884
        Baptism April 14 1896
        Sponsors
        Parents
        Minister   Thomas P. Baker

        Name   Martha Arnold Baker
        Birth   September 2 1896
        Baptism November 1st 1896
        Sponsors Dr. & Mrs. F. A. Waddill & Miss L. Wells
        Parents Thomas P. and Mattie S. Baker
        Minister   Thomas P. Baker

78   While in Charleston, Feby 17- 97 I baptised, Resi-
        Feby   dence Smith Street, Alexander Dillingham, born Jany
        17   21 1897 son of James and Annie Kollock Dillingham
        1897   Thomas P. Baker, Rector St. David's

        Sponsors (Dr. Cornelius Kollock; Ellen S. Waddill
                 (Dr. Chas. W. Kollock

        28 Decr 1897 The Innocents Day I baptised the following
                      Children:
                      Gillespie Godfrey Thrower
                      born Aug. 26th 1897
                   son of Capt. Thomas & Maggie Godfrey Thrower
              Sponsors:

        28 Dec 1897 John Watts   born Feby 1st 1892
                     son of R. C. Watts
              Sponsors: Parents & Nell Harden

        28th Decr 1897 Elizabeth Cannon Watts
                        born Aug. 13th 1887
                        daughter of R. C. Watts
              Sponsors Parents
                 Baptism in St. Davids Church
                                Thomas P. Baker, Rector

79   Name   Alexander Anderson Pollock
        birth   May 1831
        Baptism June 19th 1898
        place   at residence in Cheraw (_?_ ill)
        Sponsors His wife & T. P. Baker
        Minister   Thomas P. Baker

```
Name        Mary Elizabeth Baker
birth       born May 20 1898
Time &      Aug 7th 98, St. Davids church
place       after second Lesson Evening Prayer
Sponsors    Agnes McLean & E. Walker Duvall
Minister       Thomas P. Baker

Name        Carrie Hicks
   "        Hicks      were baptised
in St. Davids church during summer of 1898 by Thos P. Baker,
rector  Sponsors: Miss Lillian Wells, T. P. Baker
```

80   In St. Davids Walter Herbert infant son of Walter N. &
Henrietta Monson   by Thos P Baker

```
April 30 1899  St. Davids   Clarence Clifton infant son of
C. C. Medlen & Gertrude Perkins Medlen  Born Jany 19 1898
     Sponsors   Mrs. W. R. Godfrey
     Minister   Thomas P. Baker
```

May 7 1899 in St. David's Church   Gertrude Waddill infant
daughter of Rev. J. S. Hartzell & Gertrude Waddill Hartzell
Born Octo. 24th 1898 at Mt. Pleasant, S. C.
```
Sponsors     Mrs. H. P. Duvall
   "          H. G. Osteen
             Mr. E. Walter Duvall
Minister  Rev. J. S. Hartzell
```

81   June 21, 1899 at St. David's Nannie Seay (Pegues) infant
daughter of Waddill Pegues and Nannie Pollock Pegues   Born
January 13 1899 Baptised June 21 -99 by Thomas P. Baker
Rector St. Davids
```
     Sponsors    Miss Irene Wannamaker
                 Mrs. Rebecca Pollock
                 Mr. L. D. Harrall
```

July 12 1899 at Church Edwin Powe Guy son of James Lindsay
Guy and Emily Powe Guy Born January 23 1899
```
Sponsors     John H Powe
             OBerry Powe
             Mrs. John Powe
                      Thos P. Baker, minister
```

82   At St. Davids Church on the morning of Sept. 8 1899 William
Hicks son of Maggie G. and W. T. Thrower born Aug 5th 1899
```
Sponsors:  Mr. John H. Powe
           Wm. Godfrey
           Miss M. G. Godfrey
                    Thomas P. Baker, minister
```

At his home on Church St. in Cheraw December 4th 1899
John Fletcher Grant Age about 54 years Witnesses Thos
P Baker, Mrs. W. R. Godfrey and Miss Hewitt.
Minister   Thomas P. Baker

83   At St. Davids Church, Evening Prayer, June 3, 1900
Carrie McIver daughter of William and Cora Page Godfrey
born April 19th 1900   Sponsors: The parents and Eleanor
& Hattie Godfrey   Thomas P. Baker, minister

A. D.   1901
Mary Elizabeth daughter of Mr. D. M. and Mrs. M. A. Stubbs
baptised 19th Mch 1901 in St. Davids church by the rector

The baptized was born Nov. 19th 1900. The sponsors were
Mr. W. A. Benton, Mrs. F. A. Waddill and Mrs. M. A. Stubbs
C. W. Boyd, rector

1901 A. D. Thomas Baker Monson
On the 19th May 1901 I baptized Thomas Baker son of W. N.
and H. C. Monson at St. Davids Church at Morning Prayer.
The baptized was born Jan 5th 1901. The Godfathers were
the father Mr. W. N. Monson and Mr. Lemuel Harrall and the
godmother Miss Emma Monson.   C. W. Boyd, Rector.

84   Eddings
On the 7th June 1901 at their home in Cheraw I baptized
James David Walker born Sept 8th 1894 and Wm Brooks born
Jan 29 1899 children of Mr. W. M. and Mrs. Hattie K. Eddings
C. W. Boyd, Rector

      On the 1st day of September 1901 at St. Davids Church
in Cheraw I baptized Margaret Wells daughter of Eugene
Charles McGregory and Daisy Wells McGregor   born
Rebecca Covington, Helen Green and Ebenezer Wells being god
mothers and godfather respectively.   C. W. Boyd, Rector

                    Thrower
On March 11th 1902 in St. Davids Church I baptized Harriet
Powe daughter of Mr. W. F. and Mrs. Margaret Elizabeth
Thrower born Oct. 2nd 1901.
Godmother Mrs. H. E. Godfrey and Miss M. E. Duvall
Godfather Edward McIver, Esq.   C. W. Boyd, rector

85   On the 16th June 1902 at St. Davids church I baptized Emma
Mordecai daughter of Mr. Bledsoe of Raleigh N. C.   She
was born Aug 1885. Witnesses Mr. & Mrs. R. W. Godfrey
                        Mrs. Agnes McLean

      Pregues
      On 16th June 1902 I baptized Rebecca Pollock daughter
of Mr. E. W. and Mrs. N. S. Pegues at the home of Mrs.
Pollock in Cheraw Born 5th Oct 1901   C. W. Boyd

      Godfrey
      On the 23d July 1902 I baptized Nancy Page daughter of
Mr. William and Mrs. Cora Godfrey at St. Davids Church
Nancy Page was born 12th June 1902.   C. W. Boyd

      Eddings
On the 26th Nov 1902 at their home in Cheraw I baptized
Daisy Etoil born Aug 29th 1902 daughter of Mr. W. M. and
Mrs. H. K. Eddings   C. W. Boyd, rector

86   On the 25th Feb 1903 at St. Davids church I baptized Francis Wilson son of Arthur and Charlotte W. Kittrell born
2nd July 1902.   C. W. Boyd, Rector
Sponsors John H. Powe
         J. Henry Powe
         Charlotte W. Kittrell

On the 9th Mch. 1903 at her home three miles from Cheraw
I baptized Blanche Alene wife of G. W. Martin
Witnesses G. W. Martin
           M. G. Boyd   C. W. Boyd, rector

On the 18th of October 1903 at St. Davids church I baptized
Harriet Powe daughter of William and Cora H. Godfrey born
the 4th Sept 1903   C. W. Boyd, rector
Sponsors Wm. Godfrey
        Mrs. H. E. Godfrey
        " M. E. Thrower
    Miss H. E. Godfrey

87   On the 6th of March 1904 at St. Davids Church I baptized
Marion Godfrey daughter of The Rev. C. W. and Marion G.
Boyd   born on 4th Jan. 1904.
Godfather   Godmothers
Wm. Godfrey   Mrs. M. A. Boy
                  " Ellen Waddill
           Miss Claude Godfrey

On the 1st May 1904 at St. Davids Church I baptized George
Wythe son of G. W. Martin and Blanche A. Martin
                      C. W. Boyd

On the 21st July 1904 at the home of her parents I baptized
Frances Pemberton daughter of Thos. Powe and Carrie Pemberton Harrall.   C. W. Boyd

At St. Davids church Nov 6th 1904 I baptized Sarah Leon
Thomas aged about 14 years   C. W. Boyd

88   At St. Davids church on the 26th Dec 1904 I bpatized John
Harrington son of W. T. and M. E. Thrower born the 27th
Sept 1904   C. W. Boyd

At their home Feb. 16th 1904 I baptized
(1) Peter T. Cassidy
(2) Allie W. Cassidy aged 14 and 16 years respectively
                     C. W. Boyd

At St. Davids church on the 30th April 1905 I baptized Marion
Gravely daughter of G. W. and Blanche A. Martin, born 22nd
Oct 1904   Sponsors Miss Lulu Harrington and the parents
                     C. W. Boyd

On the 8th June 1905 I baptized at St. Davids church, Caroline Fernandez daughter of myself and wife Marion G. Boyd
born 30th Mch. 1905 Sponsors S. G. Godfrey, Mrs. C. B.
Robinson, Miss Etta Powe and Miss Eleanor Godfrey
                     C. W. Boyd

On the 1st day of October 1905 I received into the church
Rebecca Pollock daughter of Mr. and Mrs. E. W. Pegues
having baptized her privately 16th June 1902
                     C. W. Boyd

89   On Oct 1st 1905 I baptized at St. Davids Church, Virginia
Lee born May 2nd 1905, daughter of Mr. and Mrs. E. W. Pegues
Sponsors:

Oct. 1st 1905 I baptized at St. Davids Church Margaret
Dewitt born June 19th 1894, daughter of Mr. and Mrs. W. D.
Evans
Sponsors: Mrs. W. R. Godfrey
         " E. W. Pegues

Nov. 14th 1906, in Cheraw, I baptized Harriet Powe, daughter of Mr. and Mrs. J. M. Jackson of Bennettsville, S. C.
Born Aug. 26, 1906
Godfather: Mr. J. M. Jackson
Godmothers: Mrs. J. M. Jackson
            Mrs. Harriet Lunch

Cheraw S. C. 19 March 1905 at residence of parents baptized by Revd. J. S. Hartzell
Wade Son of Edmond James and Loretta Waddill born Jany 4 1905
Godparents The parents and Mrs. Gertrude W. Hartzell
        Recorded by W. E. Godfrey (warden)

90   On the 24th Mch. 1907 at St. Davids Church I baptized Charles William son of Rev. C. W. and Mrs. M. G. Boyd born Dec. 21st 1906
                                    C. W. Boyd, rector

On the 6th day of Oct. 1907, at St. Davids church I baptized John Mitchell son of Mr. John Mitchell and Mrs. Witsell born June 13th 1907   C. W. Boyd, rector

On the 3d day of Nov. 1907 at the home of his parents in Cheraw, I baptized William Ancrum, son of Mr. and Mrs. W. A. Boykin   C. W. Boyd, rector

On the 29th day of Dec. 1907 at the home of his parents I baptized William McLean son of Mr. William and Mrs. Agnes Hickson
Sponsors: Evans Willson
          Elizabeth McLean
          E. Walker Duvall
          Eleanor Duvall   C. W. Boyd, rector

On the 14th day of April 1908, at St. Davids Church I baptized Howard Eliot son of H. P. Duvall Jr. and Mrs. Irene Duvall   C. W. Boyd, rector

91   On the 14th day of April 1908 at St. Davids Church I baptized Mildred Claudia daughter of Mr. Ernest and Mrs. Mildred Duvall   C. W. Boyd, rector
        Born Jan 28, 1908

On the 30th of August 1908 at St. David's Church Margaret High daughter of Wm. and Cora High Godfrey (born March 17, 1908) was baptized by Rev. C. W. Boyd, late rector of the Church. Sponsors Mrs. Margaret Thrower, Alfred G. and Mrs. Margaret Page.   Recorded by A. S. Thomas,
                                                Rector

On the 12th day of October 1908 at the home of her grand father D. W. Evans I baptized Mary Evans daughter of Henry Jordan and Nell Thurmond (born Aug 18, 1908) Sponsors: Alexina Evans, Lucy Clark, Sam Evans, Claud Kiser
                                    A. S. Thomas, rector

On the 6th day of January 1909 at St. David's Church, I baptized Ralph Gandy (born Sep. 20, 1908) son of G. W. and Blanch E. Martin. Sponsors: G. W. Martin, L. H. Powe, Mrs. C. F. Pendleton.   A. S. Thomas, Rector

On the 8th day of January 1909 at St. David's Church I baptized Marion Humes (born April 30, 1908) daughter of Phil & Marian Humes Turner. Sponsors: Mr & Mrs. E. W. Duvall, Susie Turner, Mr. & Mrs. Ralph Calder Turner.
A. S. Thomas, Rector

On the 15th day of December at St. Davids Church, I baptized Mary Cyrene (born Sept. 5, 1908) daughter of G. Walker and Mary Duvall. Sponsors: J. H. Emack, Miss Bell McConnell, Miss Eliza Duvall
A. S. Thomas, Rector

92 On the 15th day of April 1909 at St. Davids Church I baptized John Lewis (born Sep. 4, 1908) son of John Andrew and Laura Gainey Hill. Sponsors: L. H. Power, Mrs. W. A. Godfrey.
A. S. Thomas, Rector

On the 19th day of May 1909 at St. David's Church I baptized Thomas Powe son of Thomas P. and Carrie Pemberton Harrall born Sep. 21, 1908. Sponsors A. S. Thomas & Parents
A. S. Thomas, Rector

On the 20th day of June 1909 at St. David's church I baptized Eleanor Humes (born Apr. 3, 1909) daughter of E. Walker and Eleanor Humes Duvall. Sponsors: H. P. Duvall, Lulu Harrington, Marion Turner.
A. S. Thomas, Rector

On the 6th day of June 1909 at Ruby, S. C. I baptized David McGregor (born Aug. 31, 1908) son of H. H. and Kate Harrall. Sponsor: Annie Laurie Harrall.
A. S. Thomas, Rector.

On the 17th of June 1909 at their home in Marlboro Co., I baptized Frank Wilds (born Dec. 14, 1908) son of Frank Wilds and Kate Pegues. Sponsors: Olin Pegues, H. R. Witsell, Mrs. A. S. Nowel, Pattie Coachman. A. S. Thomas, Rector

On the 11th of October 1909 at the house of Mrs. McLean, I baptized Benjamin Reeves, son of William and Agnes Hickson (born July 2, 1909) Sponsor: Mr. & Mrs. W. R. Duvall.
A. S. Thomas, Rector

On the 3rd day of November at St. David's Church I baptized Mareen Walker (born July 14, 1909) son of Ernest and Mildred Duvall. Sponsors: G. Walker Duvall, Mary Duvall.
A. S. Thomas, Rector

93 On the 17th day of November 1909 at residence of grandmother Mrs. H. E. Godfrey Gillespie Godfrey (born Oct. 18, 1909) son of Rev. C. W. and Marian G. Boyd was baptized by his father Rev. C. W. Boyd Sponsors C. R. Robertson, William Gillespie and Hattie Godfrey.
Recorded by A. S. Thomas, Rector

On the 28th day of April 1910 at St. David's Church, I baptized Henry Carrison (born Jan. 30, 1910) son of Albert Sidney and Emily Jordan Thomas. Sponsors: Rev. Harold Thomas, H. G. Carrison, Jr., Margaret C. Miller, Eleanor Walter Thomas
A. S. Thomas, Rector

On September 21, 1910, at St. Davis Ch., I baptized Gideon Walker (born June 5, 1910) son of Gideon Walker and Mary Duvall. Sponsors: Ernest H. and Mildred Duvall.
A. S. Thomas, Rector

On October 30, 1910, at St. David's Church I baptized
Theodore Wannamaker (born July 26, 1910) son of H. P. Jr.
and Irene Duvall. Sponsors: W. P. Pollock, Theodore Wannamaker and Elizabeth Sally Pollock. A. S. Thomas, Rector

On September 1911 At residence of Mr. W. P. Pollock in
Cheraw I baptized the following children of Wesley L. and
May Pegues

```
                                    ( Mrs. R. O. House
Erma    born Oct. 22, 1905   sponsors ( Erma Lide
                                    ( B. Frank Pegues
```

```
William Wesley  born Mch 27, 1906  Sponsors (Minnie P Evans
                                          ( B Frank Pegues
```

```
Cornelius Kollock born Nov. 18, 1908 Sponsors(Coney Pegues
                                             ( Nan Evans
```

```
Boordman Lide born July 10, 1910  Sponsors(Boordman Lide,Jr.
                                          (Minnie P Evans
                   A. S. Thomas, Rector
```

On June 25, 1911, at St. David's Church I baptized Florence
Lillie (born May 14, 1911) daughter of Robert & Lillie
Hereford. Sponsors: A. S. Thomas, Emily J. Thomas, Mrs. J.
D. Plyler.   A. S. Thomas, Rector

94   On September 3, 1911 at St. David's Church I baptized Agnes
Evans (born May 4, 1911) daughter of William and Agnes
Hickson Sponsors: W. R. Godfrey, Elizabeth (Mrs. W. R.) God-
frey, Agnes McLean.   A. S. Thomas, Rector

On May 12, 1912 at St. David's Church, I baptized Betsy
Jane daughter of Peter and Mattie C. Cassidy. Sponsors
                   A. S. Thomas, Rector

On May 19, 1912 at St. David's Church I baptized Virginia
Emack daughter of J. Walker and Mary Duvall, Sponsors: H.
M. Duvall, Miss Dora Emack.   A. S. Thomas, Rector

On July 7th 1912 at St. Davids Church I baptized Thomas
McIver (born March 30, 1912) son of William H. and Helen
Wannamaker. Sponsors: Edward McIver, Theodore Wannamaker,
Mabel McIver.   A. S. Thomas, Rector

On July 22, 1912 at residence of F. W. Vetoe at McBee, S.
C., I baptized Edward Alvin (born Aug. 14, 1910) son of Mr.
and Mrs. Edward Clifford Edgeworth. Sponsors; the father
and Mrs. F. W. Vetoe.   A. S. Thomas, Rector

On November 24, 1912 at St. Davids church I baptized the
following children of Thomas L. and Nannie Wood:
```
  Edgar McKinley   born Jan. 16, 1901
  Ivy Francis      "   Sept. 7, 1903
  Marvin Wilsey    "   Feb. 24, 1905
  Mary Lee         "   April 2, 1908
          Sponsors for( Albert S. Thomas
            all four ( Mrs. W. R. (Elizabeth) Godfrey
                     ( Alexine Harrall
          A. S. Thomas, Rector
```

95　On January 19, 1913 at St. David's Church I baptized

Charley F Haley born June 1, 1878
　　　　　Witnesses: H. L. Powe, W. R. Godfrey
And the following children of said Charley F and Shadie
Haley
Charley Boyd (born Sept. 3, 1905) Sponsors(H. L. Powe
　　　　　　　　　　　　　　　　　(Alexine Harrall
Virginia Beatrice (born March 25, 1907)
　　　　　　　　　　Sponsors　(H. L. Powe
　　　　　　　　　　　　　　　(Etta Powe
Edward Stanton (born Sept. 5, 1908)
　　　　　　　　　　Sponsors(W. R. Godfrey
　　　　　　　　　　　　　(Mrs. W. R. (Eliz.)God-
　　　　　　A. S. Thomas, Rector　　　　　　frey

On April 13, 1913 at St. David's Church I baptized William
Robbins (born Oct. 13, 1912) son of William and Agnes
Hickson. Sponsors: William Hickson, Mrs. D. J. Holcomb,
and W. R. Godfrey. 　　　A. S. Thomas, Rector

On April 13, 1913 at St. David's Church I baptized Blanche
Wythe daughter of G. W. and Blanche Martin born Sept. 27,
1912. Sponsors, the parents and Mrs. William (Agnes) Hickson. 　　　　　　　　A. S. Thomas, Rector

On April 27, 1913 at St. David's Church I baptized Albert
Sidney (born March 8, 1913) son of Albert Sidney and Emily
Jordan Thomas. Sponsors: Walter Couturier Thomas, A. S.
Thomas (his father) and Hattie Jordan Carrison.
　　　　　　　　　　　A. S. Thomas, Rector

On September 7, 1913, at St. David's Church I baptized Cora
Page (born June 29, 1913) daughter of William and Cora
Godfrey. Sponsors: S. G. Godfrey, Mrs. Dolly Goodwyn, Miss
Claude Godfrey. 　　　　　A. S. Thomas, Rector

On September 14, 1913, at St. David's Church I bpatized
following children of Laura Gainey and J. A. Hill.
　　　Martha Henrietta　born Nov. 20, 1909
　　　Laura Gainey　　　"　April 15, 1911
　　　Maude Ardilla　　　"　June 30, 1913
Sponsors of all three: Lydia Maude Kirkley, Lulu Harrington,
Fannie Duvall, and their father J. A. Hill.
　　　　　　　　　　　A. S. Thomas, Rector

96　On November 2, 1913, at St. David's Church, I baptized Mar-
shall Kent (born May 26, 1913) son of E. J. and Lola Waddill
Sponsors the father and Lulu Harrington
　　　　　　　　　　　A. S. Thomas, Rector

On December 14, 1913 at St. David's church, I baptized
Thomas Watterman Ford (born July 6, 1913) son of Thomas
and Selena F. Robeson. Sponsors: Catherine Vaux Ford, Thomas Ford, James Reese Ford. 　　A. S. Thomas, Rector

On April 22, 1914, at St. David's Church I baptized Mary
Emack daughter of Gideon Walker and Mary Duvall (born Dec.
18, 1913) Sponsors: William E. Duvall, Ruth Duvall, Margaret
Duvall. 　　　　　　　A. S. Thomas, Rector

On July 22, 1914, at St. David's Church, I baptized Lydia
Mabel (born Oct. 19, 1913) daughter of Peter and Mattie C.

Cassedy. Sponsors: Her father and Miss Mat E. Duvall and
Mrs. M. W. Duvall.   A. S. Thomas, Rector

On Sept. 23, 1914 at St. David's Church I baptized Thomas
David (born Feb. 1, 1914) son of Thomas L. and Nannie Woods.
Sponsors H. P. Duvall, H. L. Powe, Miss Etta Powe
                              A. S. Thomas, Rector

On Nov. 8, 1914, at St. David's Church I baptized Howard
Mareen (born May 20, 1914) son of Howard Mareen and Margaret
Duvall. Sponsors: (W. E. Duvall
                   (Mrs. H. D. Malloy
                   (Parents
                              A. S. Thomas, Rector

97   On Nov 25, 1914 at home (ill) in Cheraw I baptized William
      Andrew Hill born Nov. 22, 1914.
                              A. S. Thomas, Rector

Walter Smith (colored) 22 years old at home Dr. Richardson
(colored) on Jan 10, 1915. Witnesses Dr. Richardson & wife
                              A. S. Thomas

William Godfrey on May 31, 1914 at St. David's Church born
Jan. 1, 1914 son of S. Harrington & Cora Godfrey.
Sponsors (Wm Godfrey   Mrs. M. E. Thrower
         (W. R. Godfrey   Mrs. Meta Willite
         (Mrs. H. E. Godfrey
                              A. S. Thomas

At same time and place Samuel Gillespie Godfrey, son of
S. S. & Lucile Godfrey, born Feb. 5, 1914.
Sponsors (Wm., W. R. and Mrs. H. E. Godfrey
         (and Mrs. M. E. Thrower
                              A. S. Thomas

At. St. David's on Feb. 14, 1915
Theodore Oscar Peavy born Aug. 25, 1909
Carl Peavy   "   "   Oct. 13, 1911
William Douglas "   "   Dec. 18, 1913
    sons of Peter T. and Belle Hope Peavy
Sponsors (Rev. & Mrs. A. S. Thomas
         (Mrs. Ralph H. Johnson
                    A. S. Thomas

At St. Davids on April 11 1915 Grace McCulloh Powe born
Dec. 31, 1914, daughter of Mr. & Mrs. Thomas Erasmus Powe
Sponsors (H. L. Powe
         (Etta Powe
         (Roberta McCulloch
                    A. S. Thomas

98   At home at Marburg near Cheraw on April 16, 1915
      James Thomas Stanton born Aug. 6, 1967
      & his children (wife Florence Wickes)
      Bernice Theola   born Mch 5, 1911
      James Thomas (Jr.) " July 25, 1912
      Ruby Emmeline   " Nov 1, 1913
                    A. S. Thomas

At St. David's on June 2, 1915 Esther Ellerbe Godfrey
daughter S. S. & Lucile Godfrey born Feb. 19, 1915

[apparently sponsors to preceding] H. P. Duvall, Jr.
                                   Hattie Emily Godfre
                            Mrs. Marion (Charles) Prince
            A. S. Thomas

At St. David's on Oct 10, 1915, Naomi McPherson Pegues
daughter Sanais & Naomi Pegues born Jan 9, 1915
                    Sponsor (Ruth Roberts
                            (Marie Campbell
                            (Holmes Simons
   At same time & place received (having previously been
baptized) their son Rufus Marcellus Pegues born May 13,
1913.   (Lucy Pegues McClellan
         Sponsors (Hilliard Pegues
                  (Dr. Creighton Mitchell
                    A. S Thomas

At St. Davids, March 5, 1916, Mary Elizabeth Dameron born
Oct. 1, 1915 daughter of Lester R. & Julia N. (Monson)
Dameron   (Father
         Sponsors (Mrs. W. N. Monson
                  (Miss Emma Monson
                    A. S. Thomas

99   At St. David's on April 19, 1916, Ruth Pearl Martin born
     Jan. 14, 1916 daughter of Mr. & Mrs. G. W. Martin
                      (G. W. Martin (father)
            Sponsors (Mrs. Blanch Martin (mother)
                      (Mildred Wells
                        A. S. Thomas

Note hereafter all baptisms here recorded were held at the
new St. David's Church unless otherwise specified.

On July 23, 1916 Mary Devonald Pegues born Dec. 21, 1915
daughter of Frank B. and Hannah Pegues
                        W. R. Godfrey
                        Mrs. W. C. (Mary) Wilson
                        Mrs. A. S. (Emily) Thomas
                          A. S. Thomas

On June 4, 1916 John Kinghorn McIver born April 28, 1916
son Henry & Bessie K. McIver
                  (Edward McIver
         Sponsors (J. L. Craig
                  (Mabel McIver
                    A. S. Thomas
      First baptism in new church

On June 7, 1916, John Arthur Kittrell born April 23, 1912
son Lottie (Powe) Kittrell
            Sponsors (John H. Powe
                     (Roland Powe
                     (& Mother
                       A. S. Thomas

On Sept. 24, 1916, in Presbyterian Church at McBee Charles
Edward Prescott born June 14, 1916 son of Wm. Charles & Sallie Robertson Prescott
            Sponsors (Frank Wilhelm Wetor
                     (Annie Jennie Robertson
                     (& father
                       A. S. Thomas

                        87

100   At home (ill) in Cheraw Nov 9, 1916 Margaret Emily Hill
       daughter of Laura Gainey & J. A. Hill born Oct. 30, 1916
                                                A. S. Thomas

On Nov. 29, 1916   Cassidy

                                        A. S. Thomas

On Mch 2, 1917 Emma Issabelle Baker born Jan. 20, 1909
daughter of Mr. & Mrs. H. L. Baker
                        H. L. Powe
                        Miss M. E. Duvall
                        A. Laurie Harrall
                                        A. S. Thomas

At same time
    Mary Levier Graham born May 9, 1905
                        (known as Mary Melton)
daughter of Jos. & Anna Graham
            Sponsors   H. L. Pow
                       Mrs. W. R. Godfrey
                       A. S. Thomas

On April 1, 1917 William Evans Duvall born Nov. 14, 1916
son of W. E. & Ruth Duvall
                        (Ernest Duvall
            Sponsors   (Eliza Duvall
                       (Parents   A. S. Thomas

On April 4, 1917, Lucile Burroughs Godfrey born Sep 1, 1916
daughter of S. S. & Lucile Godfrey
                        Robert Thrower
                        Jenet MacFarlan
                        Eleanor Godfrey
                        Effie Edgerton
                                        A. S. Thomas

On May 10, 1917, Frances Dockery Waddill born Mch 6 1917
daughter Cornelius K & Frances Dockery Waddill
            Sponsors H. C. Dockery
                     Elizabeth Waddill
                     John L. Everett
        by Bishop W. A. Guerry
                                        A. S. Thomas

101   On May 13, 1917, Robert James Duvall born Jan. 16, 1917,
       son H. E. & Mildred Duvall
                        Sponsors (W. E. Duvall
                                 (Helen Wannamaker
                                  A. S. Thomas

On June 6, 1917, Emily Jordan Thomas born March 7, 1917,
daughter of A. S. and Emily Jordan Thomas
                        H. G. Camson
                        Mrs. (H. G.) Margaret Jordan Camson
                        Caroline Eliz. Thomas
                        A. S. Thomas

On Jan. 27, 1918, at home Rebecca Duvall McIver born Jan.
10, 1908   of Henry & Bessie K. McIver
            Sponsors   Norman Kinghorn
                     Miss Mary   "
                     " Susie McIver   A. S. Thomas

                            88

On March 10, 1918 Margaret Wilson Duvall daughter of Howard
Mareen and   born Jan. 16, 1918
                              Sponsors Mr. & Mrs. L. M. Evans
                                  Parents
                                      A. S. Thomas

On March 22, 1918 in Columbia by Rev. K. G. Finlay Margaret
Louise Huntley born Feb. 16, 1918 daughter of P. B. & Lillian
W. Huntley   Sponsors: Mrs. H. E. Wells
                          Margaret McGregor
                          E. C. McGregor
                                  A. S. Thomas

On April 3, 1918, Caroline Pemberton Morris born Jan. 6,
1918 daughter of J. J. and Alexine J. Morris
        Sponsors Mr & Mrs T P Harrall
                                      A. S. Thomas

102   On April 3, 1918
        Alda Pauline Haley   born Mch 26, 1913
        Wilber Drew Haley   "   Aug 26, 1915
        children of C. F. & Shadie Haley
     Sponsors of former   father & Mrs. P. B. Huntley
        "   " latter   "   " Miss A. L. Harrall
                          A. S. Thomas, Rector

On September 15, 1918   John Emack born Aug. 4, 1918, son
of G. W. and Mary Duvall Sponsors Ernest H. and Mildred
McCabe Duvall   A. S. Thomas, Rector of
                                  Good Shepherd, Columbia

On July 12, 1919 John Richardson born July 14, 1917, son
of H. L. and Ethel H. Horton Sponsors: L. C. Piree, J. H.
Coles, Mrs. W. J. Swink and Mrs. J. H. Coles
                          A. S. Thomas, Rector

On July 12, 1919 Jane Yancey born June 20, 1915 daughter
Mr. & Mrs. L. C. Piree   Sponsors: J. H. Coles, Mr. H. R.
Horton, Mrs. W. G. Swink, Mrs. J. H. Coles
                          A. S. Thomas, Rector

On March 23, 1919 Ermine Everett born Feb. 25, 1919
daughter of Cornelius K. and Francis Dockery Waddill
        Sponsors: Bessie Everett, Sarah Lilly Dockery,
                H. P. Duvall, Jr.   A. S. Thomas, Rector

On Nov. 2, 1919 Philip Rossignol born May 22, 1919 son of
P. R. & Mildred Wells Lochicotte of Waverly, S. C.
        Sponsors: J. J. Hazard, A. A. Springs, Mrs. E. C.
                McGregor, Miss Daisy McGregor
                                  A. S. Thomas, Rector

On June 13, 1920 Ellen Kollock born Mch 17, 1920 daughter
of C. K. & Francis Waddill Sponsors: E. H. Duvall, Mrs.
James (Annie) Dillingham, Mrs. Grimes Heyward.
                              A. S. Thomas, Rector

103   On June 27, 1920. Adeline Cooper, born Oct. 20, 1919,
      daughter of S. G. and Lucile Godfrey Sponsors: Wm. Godfrey,
      Claude Godfrey, Mrs. Marion (Godfrey) Boyd.
                              A. S. Thomas, Rector

On Nov. 10, 1920 Helen born July 9, 1920 daughter of
William H. & Helen Wannamaker. Sponsors Parents
A. S. Thomas, Rector

On February 13, 1921
Blanche McKelvie born Oct. 1, 1911 and
Harvey Bethea   "   Sept. 23, 1913
    children of Mr. & Mrs. B. McK. Lemon
Sponsors of Blanche Fred Edmunds
                     Mrs. G. W. (Blanche) Martin
                     Miss Fannie Duvall
         of Harvey   H. L. Powe, Fred Edmunds, Fannie Duvall
                     A. S. Thomas, Rector

On February 23, 1921 Thomas Howerton Vanderford born July
16, 1916.   Sponsors: Alexander Harrall and his wife the
                  mother of Thomas
                     A. S. Thomas, Rector

On September 4, 1921
    James Alexander b. May 30, 1908
    Rosa Evans   b. Mch 9, 1916
    Louisa McIntosh
        children of James A. & Louisa Spruill
        Sponsors Parents & Mrs. Edwin (Rosa) Dargan
                     A. S. Thomas, Rector

On September 18, 1921
Connie Lee Huggins born Nov. 16, 1918
Redmond Millard "   "   June 15, 1914
Pauline   "   "   Aug. 15, 1921
        Sponsors H. L. Powe
                 Etta Powe
                 Fannie Duvall
                     A. S. Thomas, Rector

104 On Sept. 18, 1921 Henry Walker born July 19, 1921 son of
Henry Walker and Bessie K. McIver
                 Sponsors H. L. Powe
                           Mrs. W. H. Wannamaker
                 A. S. Thomas, Rector

On Sept. 18, 1921 Edward Lilliott born Feb. 27, 1921, son
of Wm. and Agnes Hickson. Sponsors, Mrs. Wm. Hickon Sr. &
Parents   A. S. Thomas, Rector

On Sept. 18, 1921 William Edward born Aug. 15, 1921
    William & & Elizabeth (Waddill)McLauchlin
        Sponsors Neill McLauchlin
                  Mr. & Mrs. C. K. Waddill
                     A. S. Thomas, Rector

On Mar. 6, 1922 Annie MacRae, daughter of p. Justine Morris
and Alexine (Harrall) Morris born at Cheraw, S. C., Sept.
26, 1921.   Sponsors. Polly Harrall, Mrs. J. J. Morris and
J. J. Morris   J. S. Hartzell

On Sept. 28, 1922, I baptized Mary Agnes, born Nov. 25, 1918
in Darlington Co., and Easter Pauline born Apr. 30, 1922, in
Cheraw children of Peter and Mattie Servance Cassidy
                     J. S. Hartzell

105   On June 11, 1922 Sarah Duvall Justice daughter of John W. and Ellen K. Justice born January 3, 1922. Sponsors: Mrs. H. P. Duvall, Mrs. H. G. Osteen and E. W. Duvall.

                    A. S. Thomas
                    Rector St. Michael's Church

On April 8, 1923 John Thomas Grant born December 1, 1922 son of Mary Melton Grant and Stephen H. Grant. Sponsors: E. W. Duvall, H. L. Powe & Fannie B. Duvall
                    A. S. Thomas
                    Rector St. Michael's Church

On April 9, 1923, James Wilson Duvall born February 21, 1922, son of Howard Mareen Duvall and Margaret Malloy Duvall. Sponsors, G. Walker Duvall, Louise Meiklejohn Malloy and parents.   A S. Thomas
                    Rector St. Michael's Church

March ( ) 1912 Preston Brooks Huntley baptised at St. David's Church by Rev. A. S. Thomas Rector
Born Dec. 21, 1911 at Cheraw S. C.
Sponsors Anna R. Wells, E. M. Wells, John R. Wells
                  Entered by G. M. Hobart
                    3-28-'39

[pp. 106-199 blank]

200   Confirmations
       1823
May 9th This Church was visited by the Right Revd. Bishop Bowen who delivered a Sermon & confirmed the following persons Mrs. Pritchard & her two daughters Mary & Margaret Pritchard, Mrs. Harrington, Mrs. Kollock, Mrs. Wilson, Mrs. Mebane, Mrs. Rutland & Mr. James A. Harrington

1825
April 17th This Church was visited by the Right Revd. Bishop Bowen who preached in the morning & confirmed Mrs. Hawes & administered the Eucharist.
In the afternoon Divine Service was again held.

1827
Nov 4 This Church was visited by the Right Revd. N. Bowen D. D. Bishop of So Ca who preached & confirmed the following persons Mrs. Wm. Chapman, Mrs. James Townes, Mrs. R. E. Collins, Mrs. C. H. Powe, Miss E. A. Maynard, Miss H. K. Pritchard & Joseph J. Ling.

1829
Nov 8 This Church was visited by the Right Revd. N. Bowen D. D. Bishop of So Ca. who confirmed the following persons Genl & Mrs. E. Powe, Miss Mary C. Powe, Miss Rebecca Collins, Erasmus A. Powe, Erasmus P. Ellerbe, Alex W. Ellerbe & a colored man named Randel.

1832
Nov 11th This Church was visited by the Right Revd. N. Bowen D. D. Bishop of So Ca who preached & confirmed the following persons Mrs. Susan Dodge, Mrs. Sarah Turner, Mrs. C. Billingsly, Mrs. Sally C. Williams, Mrs. Maria H. Marshall, Mrs. Sarah McCollough, Miss M. J. Hawes, Miss Elizabeth S. Pritchard, Miss Josephine C. Pritchard, Miss Elizabeth Witherspoon & John B Billingsly. Kate, Charity,

Beck, Wisdom (servts. of Jno. Ellerbe),Charlotte (servt. of Genl. Powe) & Tom (servt. of Richard Maynard)

201 1834
This Church was visited by the Right Revd. N. Bowen D D Bishop of So Ca who confirmed the following persons Mrs. E. E. Pegues, Miss Rebecca A. Pegues, Mrs. Ann E. Drake, Mr. O. H. Kollock & Mr. Cranmore Wallace.
Harriet, Stephen (servts. of Col. Ervin) & Mark (servant of Mrs. Harrington)

1837
April 23 This Church was visited by the Right Revd. N. Bowen D D Bishop of So Ca who preached and confirmed the following persons Mrs. Mary A. Hopton, Mrs. Catherine B. Ellerbe, Mrs. Ann Francis, Miss Sarah Collins, Miss Mary Collins, Miss Frances Stinemetz, Wm.H. Robbins & John J. Marshall & Rodger D. Parke.

1838
Decr 9th This Church was visited by the Right Revd. N. Bowen D D Bishop of So Ca who preached and confirmed the following persons James Gillespie Senr., Christopher B. Pegues, Francis G Pegues, Nicholas B Pegues & Christopher Pegues. This was the last visit of Bishop Bowen

1841
April 25th This Church was visited by the Right Revd. C. Gadsden D D Bishop of So Ca who preached & Confirmed the following persons Miss Martha Rogers (of Marlborough) old Jim (servt. of G. H. Dunlap) & Mark (servt. of Mrs. Harrington)

1843
July 6 This church was visited by the Rt. Rev. C. E. Gadsden D D Bp of S. C. who preached & confirmed the following persons:
Mrs. Charlotte W. Gregg   Mr. Alexander Gregg
Miss Ellen H. Hart   Mr. William Godfrey
 "   Virginia Stinemetz   Dr. Abner Hopton
Mr. E. H. Downing   Dr. Thos. E. Powe

202 1848
April 28th This Church was visited by the Right Rev. Christopher E. Gadsden, Bishop of So Carolina, who confirmed the following persons having preached & made an address at the same time to the candidates Mrs. Sarah Westervelt, Mrs. Elizabeth Waddell, Mrs. Elizabeth Kelynn(?)
Frank, a servant of Mrs. Esther Powe & Frank, servant of William Godfrey

1850
June 14 Right Rev. C. E. Gadsden visited St. Davids Church, & confirmed the following persons, Caroline H. McIver, Dicey Edwards, James Hewitt, James Goodwyn (and in private) Duncan Stafford.

1854
April 30 This Church was visited by Right Rev. Thomas F. Davis, Bishop of the Diocese who confirmed the following persons. Mrs. Rebecca J. Harrington, Mrs. Massey Rushing, Mrs. Laura A. Harrall, Miss Mary Jane Gale, Mrs. Sarah R. Duvall, miss Martha Jane Goodwyn, Mrs. Jane Harn (of N. C.)

Mr. H. W. Harrington, Mrs. Mary Stafford, Mr. J. P. Harrall,
Mrs. Margaret Smith, Mr. J. D. Pickard, Mrs. Catherine Gale,
Mr. H. Westervelt, Mrs. Sarah Goodwyn, Sam, servant of Rev.
A. Gregg and Spencer, servant of Dr. T. E. Powe.

203   1855
May 27 This church was visited by Right Rev. Thomas F. Davis D. D. Bishop of South Carolina who confirmed the following persons. Mrs. Sophia Goodwyn, Mrs. Phebe Hewitt, Mary
Ann Stafford, Mary Drake, Charlton Drake, David Goodwyn,
John Middleton, William Patrick & Mary Annette & Louisa servants of Dr. T. E. Powe.
    The Bishop having preached & afterwards making(?) an
address.

1856
June 1 This church was visited by Right Rev. Thomas F. Davis who confirmed the following persons viz. Mrs. Mary Pervis,
Miss Claudia Godfrey, Miss Francis Gale, Douglass Westervelt,
and Mrs. Charlotte Cannon & Thomas C.Evans, of Darlington.

1857
June 7 This Church was visited by Right Rev. Thomas F. Da-
vis Bishop of South Carolina who confirmed the following
persons. viz. A. Miller, Francis Marion McIver, James
Harrington Powe, Alexander Gregg, Mrs. Harriet Gainey, Mrs.
Alice A. Wilson, Miss Henrietta K. Robbins, Miss Josephine
E. Robbins, Miss Margaret Raddy, Miss Elizabeth Raddy &
Sally, servant of Rev. A. Gregg.

204   1859
May 29 This Church was visited by the Right Rev. T. F. Da-
vis Bishop of the Diocese who confirmed the following persons
in the afternoon viz. James Tanzey*, Jacob Gainey, Emma
A. Bryan, Harriet Mills Brock & Fanny Turner.
* Removed in 1859.

1861
May 29   This Church was visited by the Rt. Rev. Thomas
Wednesday   F. Davis, Bishop of the Diocese, who confirmed
                the following persons in the afternoon viz.
                Edmund G. Waddill, John Edwards and Harriet
                Elizabeth Powe.

1862 June 8th
    This Church was visited this day (Whitsunday) by the Rt.
Rev. Thos. F. Davis, Bishop of the diocese who confirmed
the following persons in the afternoon Henry Duval, E. T.
Gailliard, Isaac Westervelt, Mary R. Brown, Louisa Wester-
velt, Anna Westervelt, Carrie Desel, Jennie Crock, Mary S.
Bryan, Rebecca Reddy and Anna Harrall.

Tues 10th Bishop Davis held confirmation again in this
          Church on Tuesday in Whitsun Week and confirmed
the following persons after morning service. John W. Harrington, Eliza W. Harrington, Mrs. La Roche & Ida Jenkins
(the last two from Wadmalaw Island.)

1863
June 14th
    This Church was visited by the Rt. Rev. Thos. F. Davis
Bishop of the Diocese who confirmed the following persons
in the morning viz. Mrs. Bowne, Miss Susan DeSaussure, Miss

205 Wilding DeSaussure, Carrie DeSaussure of Charleston, Rosa
. Jenkins of Edisto, Maria & Frances Gooding, Wm. Robbins
Godfrey, Gilbert Williams, Edgar Harrall, Jake, servant of
Jno K. McIver of Society Hill & Mary servant of Dr. Powe.

1864
June 19th. This Church was visited this day (4th Sun. aft.
Trinity) by the Rt. Rev. Thos. F. Davis, Bp. of the Diocese
who confirmed the following persons at morning service,
Kate A. Leman, Anna Gaillard (refugees from Charleston)
Mary Jenkins, refugee from Wadmalaw Isld., Sallie Duval &
Rose, colored woman belonging to Dr. T. E. Powe.
  On the same day Bp. Davis visited Grace Chapel near Cheraw
in the afternoon and confirmed Mrs. Atkinson & her daughter.

1865
July 9th This Church was visited this day by the Rt. Rev.
Thos. F. Davis, Bishop of the Diocese who confirmed the
following persons during morning service, Mrs. S. Nisbit,
Mrs. Cambridge, Mrs. Laura M. Prince, Mrs. E. D. Hearsey,
Miss Kate Gooch, Miss Walter, Miss Robertson, Mrs. Henry
Calder, Wm. A. Benton, Geo. W. Brown, Thos. Screven, Miss
Screven, S. Gillispie Godfrey, Grattan Hagner, Murdock D.
Mathison.

Bishop Davis visited Grace Chapel, Chesterfield Dist. on
the same day and confirmed Mrs. Blanche Leverett, refugee
from Wadmalaw.

1867
July 21st The Rt. Revd. Thos. F. Davis Bishop of the Diocese visited this church and confirmed the following persons
during morning service. Miss E. J. Harrington, Jno. H.
Powe, W. J. Westervelt.

206 1870
Jany 16th This Church was visited this day (2nd Sunday
after the Epiphany) by the Rt. Revd. Thos F. Davis Bp. of
the Diocese who confirmed the following persons at Morning
Service viz. Miss Ellen S. Kollock, Miss Mary D. Harrall,
Mr. Wm. L. Reid, Mrs. Viola E. Reid, Mrs. Allan E. Cash,
Mrs. Ann E. Drake, Miss Martha E. Duvall, Mr. Saml. J. Gil-
lespie, Mrs. Elisabeth Poston.

Nov. 27th This Church was visited this day (1st Sunday in
Advent) by the Rt. Revd. Thos. F. Davis Bishop of the Dio-
cese who confirmed the following persons at Morning Service
viz. Miss Mary H. McIver, Mr. John H. Harrall, Mrs. Emme
Peele, Mr. John Beaty, Miss Ann Eliza Beaty, Miss Mary Jane
Beaty.

1872 March 20th The Bishop of the Diocese the Rt. Revd. W.
W. Howe D. D. visited Grace Chapel and confirmed the follow-
ing Mrs. Rachel Atkinson & her daughters Sarah Catherine,
Rachel and Melissa

1872 March 24th The Rt. Revd. W. B. W. Howe D. D. Bishop of
the Diocese confirmed the following at St. David's during
Morning Prayer Mrs. Mary Monson, Miss Emily P. Gooch & Miss
M. Florence Gooch.

1873 June 25th The Rt. Revd. W. B. W. Howe D. D. Bishop of
the Diocese confirmed the following at Grace Chapel during

Evening Prayer Mrs. Eliza F. Ellerbe and Mrs. Sarah L. Brunson.

207   June 29th Fest. St. Peter The Rt. Rev. W. B. W. Howe D. D. Bishop of the Diocese confirmed the following in St. David's at Morning Service viz. Miss Mary Emma Tarrh, Miss Emma Monson, Miss L. Pauline Harrall, Clarence W. Wells, Lemuel D. Harrall.

1874 July 5th 5 Sunday after Trinity The Rt. Revd. W. B. W. Howe D. D. confirmed the following in St. David's at Morning Service viz Mr. Franklin Turner, Miss Mary Louisa Reddy, Miss Lucy Elizabeth Waddill, Miss Susan Rebecca Duvall.

1876 Jany 19th The Rt Revd. W. B. W. Howe D. D. Bishop of the Diocese confirmed at Grace Chapel during Evening Prayer Frances Farmer.

Jany 23rd The Rt. Revd. W. B. W. Howe D. D. Bishop of the Diocese confirmed in St. David's at Morning Prayer Miss Charlotte Powe Harrington, Miss Harriett Eleanor Harrington, Miss Clara Edna Graves, Mrs. Eleanor Harrington Malloy.

1879 Jany 5th The Rt. Rev. W. B. W. Howe D. D. Bishop of the Diocese confirmed in St. David's at Morning Prayer G. W. Duvall, Miss Margaret E. Godfrey, Miss Henrietta K. Powe, Miss Elizabeth W. Duvall.
On the same day in private F. M. West.

208   1880
May 2nd The Rt. Rev. W. B. W. Howe D. D. Bishop of the Diocese confirmed the following at Morning Prayer, Mr. Henry W. Harrington, Miss Sallie W. Gillespie, Miss Eliza L. Gillespie, Miss Annie H. Kollock, Miss Gertrude Waddill, Miss Henrietta C. Gayle

1881 July 10th The Rt. Revd. W. B. W. Howe D. D. Bishop of the Diocese confirmed the following at Morning Prayer, Marun W. Duvall and Mrs. Margaret D. Duvall.

1882 July 19th The Rt. Rev. W. D. W. Howe D. D. Bishop of the Diocese confirmed the following at Evening Prayer Edmund J. Waddill and Thomas P. Harrall.

1883 Dec. 16th The Rt. Revd. W. B. W. Howe D. D. Bishop of the Diocese confirmed at Morning Prayer Joseph J. Dunlap, of Wadesboro, No Ca., and at Evening Prayer Miss Nellie Louise Avery, Edward M. Avery, Henry W. Harrall and Wm. H. Robbins Powe.

1885 February 1st The Rt. Rev. W. B. Howe D. D. Bishop of the Diocese confirmed in St. David's at Morning Prayer Miss Charlotte H. McIver, Thomas P. Godfrey.

1886 July 4th The Rt. Rev. W. B. W. Howe D. D. Bishop of the Diocese confirmed in St. David's at Morn. Prayer Miss Margaret R. Wells, Fredrick A. Farmer.

209   1887
Dec. 4th The Rt. Rev. W. B. W. Howe, D. D. Bp. of the Diocese confirmed in St. David's at Evening Prayer Miss Isabella Ferguson, Miss Nannie Seay Pollock, James L. Gillespie,

Frank S. Gillespie, Edward M. Wells.

1888 Dec. 2. The Rt. Rev. W. B. W. Howe D. D. Bp of the
Diocese confirmed in St. David's at Morning Prayer Miss
Sydney L. Gillespie, Miss Alice Monson, Mr. Frank S. Gilles-
pie, Walter Harral, William H. McNair, Herbert C. Wells,
Walter H. Monson, Thomas E. Powe.

1891 March 22nd (2nd Sunday in Lent) St. David's Church
was visited this day by the Rt. Rev. W. B. W. Howe. D. D.
Bp. of the Diocese who confirmed the following persons at
Morning Service Miss Claudia Elizabeth Godfrey, Miss Mary
Lilian Wells, Mrs. Louis Ganey.

1892 Jan 24th By Rt. Rev. W. B. W. Howe, D. D.
Claudia, E. Powe, Gertrude C. Perkins, Carrie H. Powe, Emily
L. Powe

210 1894
June 1st This Church was visited this day by the Rt. Rev.
Ellison Capers, D. D. Assistant Bishop of the Diocese who
delivered a sermon and confirmed the following persons at
Evening service: Edmund Walker Duvall, Ichabod Futrell,
Mrs. Ichabod Futrell, Joseph Blaine Wells, Marion Gillespie
Godfrey, Annie Laurie McLean Wells, Laura Jane Gayney,
Dorothea DeWit McLean, Agnes Evans McLean, Mary Alline Gayle,
Charlotte Wilson Powe.

1895
May 19th St. David's Church was visited this day by the Rt.
Rev. Ellison Capers, D. D. Bishop of the Diocese who con-
firmed at 6 O. C. p. m. Tempie Harrington (colored) The
Bishop preached in the morning and also at night.

211 1896
Decr 13 7:30 P. M. Rt. Rev. Ellison Capers
1. Louis Gainey
2. Wm. Gainey
3. Etta Gainey
4. Gillespie Godfrey
5. R. C. Watts
6. Wm. McLean
7. G. Walter Duvall
8. Ernest Duvall
9. Henry Powe
10. Florence Powe
11. Fannie Duvall
12. Edith Duvall
13. Lulu Harrington
14. Reed(?) Harrington
15. Mildred Wells
16. Hattie T. Dabbs
17. Harry Harrall
18. Shady Stanton
19. May Reid
20. Mrs. James W. Dabbs

212 By Rt. Rev. Bishop Capers, D. D. May 3rd 1899
1. Hattie Godfrey
2. Laura Harrall
3. Harrington Godfrey
4. Alexander Harrall
5. Maggie Duvall

        6. William Duvall
        7. Courtney Watts
        8. Gus Watts
        9. Ernest Harrall
       10. Ella Harrall
       11. Bessie McCall
       12. Maude Gainey
       13. James Powe
       14. Mrs.   Hicks on May 6th

       August 2 1900 by Bishop Capers
       John Fletcher Grant   C. W. Boyd, Rector
       Rosanna Hewitt

       January 25th 1901
       Confirmed by Bishop Ellison Capers
       Mr. E. M. Wells
       Mrs. Hattie K. Eddings

213   January 12th 1902
       Confirmed by The Rt. Rev. Ellison Capers and presented by
       the rector Rev. C. W. Boyd the following
       William Godfrey, Cora High Godfrey, Alice Elizabeth Harrall,
       Elizabeth Turner Waddill, Annie Kollock Harrington, Eliza-
       beth Cannon Watts, Ann Eliza Duvall, Roland Davie Powe.

       Jan   1903
       Confirmed by the Rt. Rev. Ellison Capers and presented by
       the rector Rev. C. W. Boyd
       Mr. & Mrs. Cable Franklin Pendleton
       Tizzie Ola Pendleton
       Mrs.F. A. T. Brooks
       Catherine Elizabeth Powe
       Ellen Kollock Duvall

214   March 14th 1904
       Confirmed by the Rt. Rev. Ellison Capers and presented by
       the rector Rev. C. W. Boyd
       In St. Davids Church
       Edward McIver
       B. F. Pegues
       Daniel W. Evans
       Wm. Hickson
       T. S. Evans Jr.
       Elizabeth Evans
       At her home near Cheraw   Blanche A. Martin.

       Feb. 26th 1905
       Confirmed by Bishop Robt. Strange in place of Bp. Capers
       the following
       Lucinda Cassidy, Allie W.Cassidy, Peter T. Cassidy, Chas. E.
       Wesbster, Elizabeth E. Webseter, Henry McIver, Minnie
       Elizabeth Evans, Nancy Keit Evans, Phyllis Hickson.

215   March 11th 1906
       Confirmed by Bishop Ellison Capers and presented by Rev.
       C. W. Boyd
       Mr. Henry J. Thurman   Miss Sarah Estelle Thomas
        " J. J. Finley
       Mrs. Nell Pegues Thurman
        "   Dolly Aurelia
       Miss Mary Emma Monson
        "   Julia Monson

March 10th 1907
Confirmed by Bishop Ellison Capers and presented by the rec-
tor Rev. C. W. Boyd
Mrs. Irene Harrington Duvall (1)
  "   Mildred McCabe Duvall (2)
Miss Susie McIver   (3)
  "   Margaret Dewitt Evans (4)
  "   Charlotte   Harrall   (5)
  "   Alexine Harrall   (6)
  "   Anna Gleim Coachman (7)
Mr. Josiah Evans

   Jan 12th 1908
Confirmed by Bishop W. A. Guerry and presented by Rev. C.
W. Boyd Mrs.   Smith

216   Confirmed by Bishop W. A. Guerry presented by A. S. Thomas,
      Rector on Oct. 18, 1908
      Wesley L. Pegues   Lee H. Carraway
      Mary Pegues (his wife)   W. P. Pollock
      Hilliard Pegues   Bessie Pollock (his wife)
      Elbert Pegues   Frank Evans
      James A. Spruill
      Louisa Elizabeth Spruill (his wife)

      Confirmed by Bishop W. A. Guerry presented by A. S. Thomas,
      Rector on Jan. 2, 1910
      Doris Hartzell
      Edmund Waddill   A. S. Thomas

      Confirmec by Bishop W. A. Guerry, presented by A. S. Thomas,
      Rector Dec. 3, 1911
      Turner Waddill
      Suda Jack Walters
      Ralph Hiram Johnson
      Herbert Monson
      Godfrey Thrower
      Gertrude Waddill Hartzell
      Junie Harrall
      Edmund Hickson
      Lola Waddill   9   A. S. Thomas

      By same on Jan 19, 1913
      Clifton Medlin
      Carrie Godfrey
      William Thrower
      Charles Fox Haley
      M. C. Cassedy   5   A. S. Thomas

      By same on Jan 20, 1913 at McBee, S. C.
      Edward Clifford Edgeworth   First conf. ever
      Marie Edgeworth   held in McBee
      Mary Gray Robertson   3   A. S. Thomas

      By same on Jan. 11, 1914
      Clarence K. Gillespie
      Mamie (Mrs. C. J.) Williamson
      Edgar McKinley Wood
      Thomas Monson   4   A. S. Thomas

217   By same on Jan 17, 1915
      Thomas L. Wood
      Nannie Wood

George Hartzell
William Waters
Crusor Cassedy   5   A. S. Thomas

By same on Nov 7, 1915
Bessie Kinghorn McIver
Lucile B. Godfrey
Fannie Dockery Waddill
Nancy Page Godfrey
Harriet Powe Godfrey   5   A. S. Thomas

By same on Nov 8 1915 at McBee Pres. Church
Sallie Robertson Prescott
Richard Lovell Edgeworth   A. S. Thomas

By same on April 8, 1917 Easter Day
Louie M. Berry
Ivy Frances Wood
Marion Martin
Serena Cousey Evans
Thomas Macey Evans
Mary Lever Graham   (Mary Melton) Grant
Hughes Schoolfield (of Mullins) 7   A. S. Thomas

By same on Jan 13, 1918
Emma Gertrude Roper
Harrington Thrower   2   A. S. Thomas

By same on Feb. 1, 1920
Boyd McKelvey Lemon   Charley Boyd Haley
H. P. Duvall, Jr.   Evans Martin
Margaret Duvall   Sarah Pegues
Earnest Duvall   William Piree
Pauline Harrall   Wade Waddill
                                    A. S. Thomas, Rector

By same on Jan. 23, 1921
Thomas Robeson   Margaret Godfrey
Cyrene Duvall   Mary Lee Wood
Mildred Duvall   Emma Bell Baker
Virginia Beatrice Haley   Mrs. Alex (Vivian) Harrall
                                    A. S. Thomas, Rector

By same on Sept. 10, 1921
     Mrs. Howard Mareen (Margaret) Duvall
   and on Sept. 11, 1921
John Lewis Hill
Thomas Powel Harrall
Mareen W. Duvall
William Hickson
Junies Alexander Spruill
Eleanor Humes Duvall   A. S. Thomas

218   Ordinations
      1845
      May   This Church was visited by the Rt. Rev. E. E. Gads-
            den D. D. Bishop of So Car. who admitted to the
      Holy Order of Deacons E. H. Downing, a candidate for orders
      in this Diocese and residing in Cheraw, the Rev. Henry
      Elwell, Rector, presenting the candidate.

1846
June 10th This Church was visited by the Rt. Rev. Christopher Edwards Gadsden, D. D. Bishop of the Diocese of South
Carolina, who admitted to the Holy Order of Deacons Alexander Gregg, a candidate for orders in this Diocese. The Rev.
Alex. W. Marshall, Rector of St. Johns Chapel, Charleston,
presenting the candidate.

1855
May 17 This Church was visited by Right Rev. T. F. Davis
D. D. Bishop of the Diocese of S. C. who admitted to the
Holy Order of Priests: Rev. Augustus A. More, the Rev. Mr.
Hume presenting the candidate & the Rev. D. M. A. Curtis
preaching the ordination sermon.

219 1860. On Sunday Jan. 22d, The Rt. Revd. Alexander Gregg,
D. D. (who had been consecrated Bishop of the Diocese of
Texas, in the Monumental Church, Richmond, Virginia, on
Thursday, Oct. 13, 1859) acting with the consent of Bp.
Davis, of South Carolina, admitted to the Holy order of
Priests, the Revd. J. Hamilton Quinby, who was presented by
the Revd. Lucien C. Lance, Morning Prayer by the Rev. John
S. Kidney of Society Hill; & the Sermon by the Revd. Robert
B. Croes of the Diocese of New York. (Mr. Quinby soon af-
terward accompanied Bp. Gregg to Texas.) R. B. C.

1866
July 15th This church was visited by the Rt. Rev. Thos. F.
Davis D. D., Bishop of the Diocese of South Carolina, who
admitted to the Holy order of Deacons P. D. Hay, a candidate
for orders in this Diocese. The Rev. Augusutus A. More
of Mars Bluff, presenting the candidate and the Rev.W. B.
W. Howe of St. Phillip's Chh. Charleston, preaching the
ordination Sermon.

1868
Nov. 22nd This Church was visited by the Rt. Revd. Thos F.
David D. D. Bishop of the Diocese of South Carolina, who
admitted to the Holy Order of Priests, the Revd. Jno. W.
Motte, Minister of St. David's, who was presented by the
Rev. P. D. Hay, Rector of Trinity Church, Society Hill,
Morning Prayer by the Revd. P. D. Hay, & the sermon by the
Bishop.

220 Marriages

1841
Aprl 21 By the Rev. Edwin Gear (of No Ca) At the residence
of Oliver H. Kollock,Alexander Gregg of Cheraw & Charlotte
Wilson, daughter of Oliver H. and Sarah J. Kollock.

221 1826
Jany 3rd At Society Hill by the Revd. George W. Hathaway
James Gillespie of Marlborough to Sarah Olivia, daughter
of M B L Hawes of Society Hill.

At the residence of James A. Harrington by the Rev. George
W. Hathaway Dr. Thomas E. Powe of Cheraw to Charlotte H.
daughter of Jas. A. & E. W. Harrington of Marlborough.

1829 by the Rev. A. W. Marshall
Jan. 22nd At Society Hill, John J. Marshall to Maria Hawes
        daughter of M. B. L. Hawes, all of Society Hill.

June 18th At Society Hill, Thomas H. Edwards to Margaret
Marshall daughter of the late Adam Marshall, all of Society
Hill.

1831
Jany 30 At the residence of Genl Powe, John Ellerbe to
Mary C. daughter of Erasmus & Esther Powe, all of the vici-
nity of Cheraw.

1832
March 29 In Cheraw John Morrison to Ann Vannorden, all of
Cheraw.

June 28th In Cheraw William H. Robbins to Henrietta Kelsal
daughter of Joseph & Claudia Pritchard all of Cheraw.

Sept. 8 In Cheraw Eli Lassiter to Rebecca Jones.

Nov 16 In Cheraw James DuBose of Darlington to Harriet
daughter of C. B. & C. C. Pegues of Cheraw.

1833
Jany 17th In Cheraw James Lassiter to Sarah Johnson

222 1833
April 24th by the Rev. A. W. Marshall, Wm. H. Wells to
Jane daughter of Capt. McNair.

Nov 6. In Cheraw Abner Hopton to Mary Ann daughter of John
& Mary Stinemetz, all of Cheraw.

1834
Nov 12th Near Society Hill J. J. Westervelt to Sarah L
daughter of Esther Douglas.

1836
Feby 2nd In Cheraw Alexander W. Ellerbe to Catherine B.
daughter of C. B. & E. E. Pegues all of Cheraw

May 5th Solomon Wilks to Caroline daughter of Mrs. Thomas
about 6 miles from Cheraw.

May 31st At the Church Hiram Hutchinson to Rebecca daughter
of Rebecca Collins.

Sept 22nd about 6 miles from Cheraw William Wallace to Miss
Effy McDuffie

Octo 2 In Cheraw Edward Bowne to Mrs. Effy McQueen

1837
Feby 15th In Cheraw William Godfrey to Elizabeth S., daughter of Joseph & Claudia Pritchard

March 19 In Cheraw Samuel Parr to Elizabeth Harris

May 29 John Turnage to Miss Elvira Wallace at her residence

Aug 27 In Cheraw Ebenezer Hewitt to Miss Mary Ann Taylor.

1838
Nov 8th In Cheraw William H. Wingate to Harriet daughter
of John Morrison all of Cheraw

1839
April 9th   In Cheraw, Thomas A. Bryan to Frances daughter of John & Mary Stinemetz, all of Cheraw

223   1841   April 12th   For the record of this marriage see p. 220

1843
Septr 30   By Rev. A. E. Ford, Bennet (servant of Mr. Bownes) to Binale (servant of Miss Julia Hawes)

1844   By the Revd. H. Elwell

April 18th   In Cheraw William H. Tomlinson to Sarah Collins daughter of Rebecca Collins, all of Cheraw

May 9th   In Cheraw, Edmund J. Waddill to Elizabeth K. daughter of Franklin and Sarah Turner, all of Cheraw.

June 11th   Wm. Godfrey to Miss Margaret B. Pritchard, at the Bank; all of Cheraw.

August 11th   Hardy Shaw, a free colored man, to Charlotte servant of Mrs. Mary Stinemetz, at St. David's Church, Cheraw.

Septr. 5th   Angus Taylor to Esther Gainy, at my own residence.

Octr. 17th   James Middleton to Elizabeth Davis, at my own residence.

Novr 4th   At the house of John McCollough Esq: in Chesterfield District, David R. Williams, a free colored man to Rose, servant of John McCollough Esq: also, Anthony, servant of John F. Wilson Esq. to Louisa, servant of Mrs. Sarah E. Wheeler.

224   1845
On the night of Saturday Feby 1st at the house of Dr. Thomas E. Powe, Samuel, servant of David S. Harllee, to Jane, servant of Dr. Thomas E. Powe.

On the night of Saturday, April 5th, at the house of Mr. Lacoste, Edward servant of Mr. Wadsworth, to Lucy, servant of Mr. Lacoste.

            By the Revd. Alexander Gregg

1847
Jany 10th   At St. Davids Church after dismission of the congregation in the afternoon, Collins, servant of John H. McIver, to Edy, servant of Alexander Gregg.

Aug. 26th   At the residence of John McMillan, in Chesterfield District, James McIntosh to Sarah, daughter of John and   McMillan.

1848
Jany 13th   At the residence of James Allin in Cheraw, Sydney Douglass, of Chesterfield District, to Eliza Allen, eldest daughter of James Allen, of Cheraw.

Feby 28th   At the residence of Rev. A. Gregg, in Cheraw, Peter Ingram to Eliza Thomas, all of Chesterfield District.

225   1848
       Apl 6th At the residence of her Father, David Turnage to
       Caroline McCall, all of Chesterfield District.

       May 16th At Darlington Court House, John F. Ervin to Mary
       Ervin, all of that place.

       May 23 At her Brother's residence, Warren Davis, to Miss
       Marion Pickard, all of Cheraw.

       Septr 10th At residence of Rev. A. Gregg, in the country,
       Frank, servant of Wm. Godfrey, to Jane, servant of Rev. A.
       Gregg.

       Septr. 16th At plantation of Dr. Thomas E. Powe, Calvan to
       Maria, his servants.

       Novr. 21st At residence of Rev. A. Gregg in Cheraw, Riley
       Driggers and Elizabeth Bone, all of Chesterfield District.

       Decr 7th At residence of Rev. A. Gregg in Cheraw, William
       Mumford and Clarissa Knight, free coloured persons, of
       this place.

       1849
       Jany 11th At the residence of Rev. A. Gregg in Cheraw, John
       Croly and Jane Poston, all of Chesterfield District.

       March 10th At the residence of Rev. A. Gregg, in Cheraw,
       Jack, servant of Dr. T. E. Powe, to Harriet, servant of
       A. P. Lacoste.

226   April 1 At the residence of Rev. A. Gregg in Cheraw, Thomas
       Saunders to Easter Purvis, both of this district.

       June 7th At the residence of her Father, Caroline H. Powe
       and Henry McIver, all of Cheraw.

          28th At St. David's Church, Milford G. Tarrh and
       Virginia Stinemetz, all of Cheraw.

       Aug. 23 At my own residence in the country, Elisha and
       Elizabeth Poston, all of this district.

       1850
       Jany 3 At the residence of James Eddins, Thomas Hewitt and
       Effy Kiti, all of this District.

          " 12 At the plantation of Dr. Thomas E. Powe, George and
       Alsy, servants of Dr. Powe.

       Febry 25. At my own residence Pinckney Cranford and Mary
       Saunders, all of this District.

       March 2 At the residence of her master in Cheraw, Harriet
       servant of W. L. T. Prince, and Cork, servant of Mrs. Jane
       Campbell

       Apl 18th At my residence in Cheraw, James Purvis and Nancy
       Cranford, all of this District.

       1851
       Feby 27 At my residence in Cheraw, Samuel Thompson and

                                103

Sarah Watson, all of this District.

227 June 1 At the church after evening service, Jerry and Annet servants of Mr. H. Tomlinson & Dr. T. E. Powe.

29 At the residence of J. J. Ervin at Darlington C. H. William J. Harris of Cabarrus County, N. C. and Jane Ervin of the former place.

Decr. 3. At the residence of Mrs. Brockington, in Darlington District, Thomas Wainwright & Ada Bacot of said District.

21 At my own residence, Lafayette L. Peltier and Mary Jane Jonnikin(?), all of this District.

1852
Feby 7 At the residence of Dr. T. E. Powe, Daniel servant of Mrs. Esther Powe & Mary, servant of Dr. Powe.

" 12 At my residence Thomas Gulledge and Sarah Bone, both of this District.

Nov. 10 At the residence of T. E. B. Pegues in Cheraw, Nicholas Pegues of Alabama and Mary Saunders, of Cheraw.

1853
Jany 2 At my residence after return from church in evening Jim Watson and Elizabeth Hatcher, free cold. people of this place.

Feb. 27 At my own residence George Deas & Mary Watson, both of this District.

228 1853
March 13 At her Father's residence in Cheraw, Nathan Newby and Jemima Beard, both of this place.

" 24 At the residence of John Parr, Lewis Freeman & Marr Parr, both of this District.

May 1 At the church after dismissal of congregation in afternoon, Joshua, servant of H. W. Harrington and Rachael servant of Mrs. Esther Powe.

" 26 At the residence of M. G. Tarrh in Cheraw, Cornelia servant of R. Killen, and Eli, servant of John Evans Sr.

" 28 At the residence of W. Godfrey, Ellen his servant and Dave, servant of H. M. Tomlinson.

June 25 At my summer residence, Cesar and Julia, my servants.

Aug 28. At the house of James Poulson, Jacob Huggins and Eliza Poulson, daughter of the former.

Nov. 12. At the residence of Mr. T. E. B. Pegues, Jack, servant of J. W. Leak, and Dema, servant of Mr. Pegues.

1854
Jany 10 At residence of Jesse Sweat in this District, Jackson Poulson and Nicey Eddings.

229   Jany 14 At the residence of Dr. Thomas E. Powe, Noel and
       Rose, his servants.

       May 2 At the residence of James Goodwyn near Cheraw,
       Samuel Taylor and Martha Jane Goodwyn.

       July 2 At the residence of Nancy Parr, in this District,
       Jesse Sweat and Nancy Parr

       Novr. 4 At the residence of Wm. H. Tomlinson, in Cheraw,
       Mike, servant of James Drake, and Harriet, servant of Wm.
       H. Tomlinson.

       Decr. 10. At my residence John Howard and Harriet Cole,
       both of this District.

       1855
       Feby 2 At my residence of G. W. Grider and Rebecca Strick-
       lin, of this town.

       Aug. At my residence in Cheraw, Thomas Bright and Emiline
       White, of this town.

       Novr. 28 At the residence of Mrs. Ann Drake, in Cheraw,
       Robert A. Kendall, and Charlotte P. Drake

       1856
       Feby 2 At the residence of Henry McIver, Eliza, servant
       of S. Keeler, and Tamar, servant of H. McIver.

       Apr. 6 At my own residence at night, Plenty and Julia, my
       servants.

230   June 5 At the residence of Mr. E. L. Adams, in Charleston,
       John J. McIver and Julia R. Gregg, both of Darlington Dis-
       trict.

       May(?) 18 At the residence of Jacob Gainey in this Dis-
       trict, William Roller and Ruthy Parker.

       Aug. 2 At my residence, Calvin, servant of O. H. Kollock
       and Sally, my servant.

       Octr. 18. At the residence of H. W. Harrington, in Marl-
       boro, Eli, servant of James Gillespie, & Clara, servant
       of H. W. Harrington.

       Decr. 2. At the residence of Duncan Stafford, in this
       place, Samuel McLauglin, of Darlington C. H. and Louisa
       Stafford, daughter of the former.

       1857
       July 26 At the residence of James Hewitt, William Graves
       and Mary G. Lassiter, both of this District.

       Aug. 15 At the residence of Alex McQueen in this District,
       Frederick & Grace, his servants.

       "   20 At the residence of Wm Hewitt, in this District,
       Eli Howell and Ann Elizabeth Wallace.

Septr 17 At the residence of her Father, Jas. H. Irby, at Laurens C. H., John W. Harrington of Marlboro Dist. & Eliza Irby of the former place.

231 Aug 3 At the residence of the family in Cheraw, Ebenezer Wells and Margaret Reddy.

" 10 At the Church, Francis M. M'Iver and Henrietta K. Robbins.

Septr. 11 At my residence, George,servant of W. L. T. Prince and Ann, my servant.

Novr. 21. At the Church, after evening service, Frank, servant of Henrietta Saunders, & Nelly, my servant

" 27 At the residence of F. Turner, in Cheraw, Edward servant of A. M'Iver and Jenny, servant of F. Turner.

Decr 25 At the Church, after Service, Alick, servant of J. W. Harrington, and Charlotte, servant of O. H. Kollock.

" " At the residence of Mrs. Bright in Cheraw, Toni, servant of J. A. Moore, & Caroline servant of Mrs. Bright.

1859
Jany 6 At the residence of William M'Call in this town, Ralph Braddock and Sarah Jane Loyd.

Feby 5 At the residence of H. W. Harrington in Marlboro, Caleb and Maria, his servants.

" 6 At the residence of Stephen Brock, in this District, Isaiah(?) Smith of this Dist. & Diana Jarrol of N. C.

232 1859
Feby 4 At the Post Office in this town, John Bran(?) and Mary Sweat, both of this District.

March 17th At the residence of Jacob Gainey,near Cheraw Samuel J. Parker and Hannah Lee.

" " At the residence of James Eddins, in this District, William T.Goodwyn and Effy Bone.

June 14 At the residence of M. F. Ellerbe, in Cheraw, M. H. Duvall & Mary Jane Ellerbe.

July 31. At the residence of her Father in this District, John Goodwyn & Mary Hicks.

Sept. 15 At the residence of Jacob Gainey, near Cheraw, James C. Lee and Hawley Parker, both of this District.

1860
May 24th At the residence of her mother, Edward T. Gaillard of Charleston, to Mary A. Drake of Cheraw, married by Rev. Mr. Corbett Presbyterian minister of Cheraw.

1861.
August 1 At St. David's Church, by the Rev. Mr. Kidney, of Society Hill, W. Allen Benton to Fannie M. Turner, both of Cheraw.

233   Marriages by Rev. R. T. Brown.

Nov. 17th At the Church St. David's Hill & Dinah, servants
of Mrs. Drake, of this place.

Dec. 26th At the residence of Mr. J. H. McIver, Guy, servant of Dr. McRae and Selina servant of Mr. & Mrs. McIver.

1862
February 20th At "Westmoreland," Col. A. Macfarlan's country
residence near this place, Mr. C. H. Leverett, to Blanche,
daughter of Major R. H. Jenkins, refugees from Wadmalaw
Island, So. Ca.

March 18th At the residence of the bride's Mother near
Cheraw, Lieut. Jas. H. Powe of the Confederate Army, and
Josephine E. second daughter of the late Wm. H. Robbins.

June 28th At the residence of Mr. W. H. Godfrey (Saturday
evening) Leopold and Laura, servants of Mr. Godfrey.

July 27 At St. David's Church, before afternoon service,
Roger, servant of Dr. C. Kollock, and Cheny servant girl
of Mr. R. A. Kendall-- of Cheraw.
Also, at the same time & place, Abraham and Sappho, servants
of Dr. Thos. E. Powe, of this district.

October 16th (In absence of the Rector) by the Rev. J. H.
Quinby, Mr. L. L. Pelletier and Mary Jane Talbot, of Cheraw.

1863
June 9th At. St. David's Church, at 8½ p. m. Mr. Samuel R.
Brown to Miss Nannie B. Williams, daughter of Mr. H. H.
Williams, refugees from Charleston.

234   1863
September 15th. At the "Homestead" the residence of the
bride's father, near Cheraw, Lieut. S. Gillespie Godfrey
and Harriet Elizabeth, daughter of Thos. E. Powe, all of
Chesterfield District.

November 19th At the residence of the Bride's Father,
Cheraw, William D. Styron, of No Ca: and Esther Louisa,
daughter of John Irving & Sarah Westervelt of Cheraw.

Decr. 23d At the residence of Mrs. Lawrence Prince, Marlboro District, George Hersey of Marlboro, and Bettie Gooch
daughter of J. H. Gooch, of Weldon, North Carolina.

1864
May 12th At the residence of Mr. Geo: Walker, Cheraw, James
servant of Mrs.   of Charleston and Louisa servant of
Mrs. Desel, refugee from Charleston.

August 2nd At the residence of the Bride's Father, Cheraw,
D. R. W. McIver, Adj.t 21st S. C. Regt. & Eliza F., daughter
of Chas. DeSaussure of Charleston.

1865
February 9th At the residence of the Bride's Father, Cheraw,
Dr. John K. McLean, Surgeon C. S. A. and Claudia Elizabeth
daughter of Wm. Godfrey, all of Chesterfield District.

Feby. 25th At the "Homestead" near Cheraw, Van and Martha
servants of Dr. Thos E. Powe.

235 July 3rd At St. David's Rectory, Cheraw, John Wilkenson
and Anna Polson of Chesterfield Distirct.

27th At St. Davids Ch. Cheraw, at 7½ p. m. P. Dawes Hay
and Mary Jane Pinckney, daughter of the late R. Q. Pinckney,
all of Charleston Dist.

October 12th At the residence of Dr. C. Holbert, Cheraw,
Mitchell Coachman and Nancy Reid colored persons.

Decr. 25th At the residence of Dr. Thos E.Powe, near
Cheraw, Perry and Mary (coloured).

1866
July 17th At the residence of the Bride's mother in Cheraw,
by Rt. Rev. Thos F. Davis D. D. Emma E. Bryan to C. Edward
Jarret of Darlington Dist.

1867 By Revd. Jno. W. Motte, Minister of the parish,
Dec 5th   At the residence of the Bride's father, Hugh W.
          Scott of Sumter So Ca. & Anna C. eldest daughter
          of Jas. P. Harrall.

1868
Feby 9th At the "African M. E. Church" John Parks (cold).
& Lissa Pegues (cold.)

Feby 9th At the "African M. E. Church" Fletcher Powe (cold.)
to Isabella Fairy (cold.)

236 1868
Feby 24th At the residence of Mrs. Louise M. Prince, Marlboro' Dist. Jas McN. Alford M. D. & Mrs. Bettie D. Hearsey
all of Marlboro' District.

April 13th At her residence Marlboro' Dist., Capt. A. A.
Pollock & Mrs. Rebecca J. Harrington all of Marlboro' Dist.

June 23rd At the residence of her parents Lucy Arthur (cold.)
to William Stewart (cold.)

July 22nd At the residence of Mrs. Sarah Goodwyn Cheraw,
Edna Ann Ballard of Anson Co. No Ca. to Robert C. Goodman
of Cheraw So Ca.

Nov. 5th At the residence of the Bride's Mother James
Eddings to Maria M., daughter of Mrs. Sarah Goodwyn

1869 By Revd. Jno W. Motte Rector of the parish.

Jany 2nd At the residence of the Bride's Mother Orangeburg
Dist. So Ca. Wm. L. Reid Jr. of Cheraw and Miss Viola E.
daughter of W. & M. Glover of Orangeburg Dist. So Ca.

April 28th At the residence of Mrs. Louisa M. Prince, Marlboro Co. Agustus L. Evans of Cheraw and Miss Kate daughter
of J. H. Gooch of Marlboro Co. So. Ca.

237 June 9th At St. David's Church Cheraw by the Revd. P. D.
Hay, Revd. Jno W. Motte and Mary S. Bryan of Cheraw.

July 4th At the Bank Boykin Witherspoon (cold.) and Harriet
Johnson (cold.)

Sept 16th At the residence of the Bride's Mother, John Eddings and S. Frances Goodwyn, daughter of Mrs. Sarah Goodwyn.

Oct. 21st At my residence in Cheraw James F. Terry and Mrs.
Catherine Ann ____ all of Chesterfield District.

Dec. 7th At St. David's Church Cheraw Henry P. Duvall and
Sarah J. daughter of Edmund J. and Elizabeth K. Waddill,
all of Cheraw.

Dec. 22nd At my residence William Craig (cold.) and Caroline
Williams (cold.) [over William in a different hand is written
"Abram"]

Dec. 28th At the residence of Mr. W. L. Reid in Cheraw Tom
Teal (cold.) and Laura Davis (cold.)

1870
Feby 10th At my residence Tom Bennett (cold.) and Linsy
Jane Hinton (cold.) all from North Carolina.

July 24th At my residence Daniel Ford (cold.) and Ann Chapman (cold.) all of Chesterfield County.

August 7th At my residence Elijah Davis and Marry Dees all
of Chesterfield County

238 Aug. 22nd At my residence Drum Bowne (cold.) and Rosi
Prince (Cold.) all of Cheraw

Dec. 22nd At the plantation of Dr. Thos. E. Powe Edmund
Harrington (cold.) and Bickie Powe (cold). of Chesterfield
Co.

Dec. 28th Fest. Holy Innocents At St. David's Church Edwin
F. Malloy and Miss Eleanor H. McIver daughter of Capt. Henry
McIver, all of Cheraw

1871
Oct. 26 At the plantation of Dr. Thos E. Powe, Richardson
Powe (cold.) and Jane Dergan (cold.)

Nov 2nd At the residence of Madison Levi (cold), John
Maxnell (cold.) and Mary Chapman (cold.)

1872
Jany 4th At my residence Moses Chapman (cold.) and Suky
Braboy (cold.)

April 6th At the residence of Mrs. Louisa M. Prince Cheraw
John H. Powe and Miss Emily P. daughter of J. H. Gooch of
Cheraw So Ca.

1873
January 14th At the residence of Mrs. Louisa M. Prince
Cheraw, J. Clarence McLeod and Miss M. Florence Gooch, of
Cheraw So Ca.

December 2nd At. St. David's Church James D. Harden of
Ashville N. C. and Miss Mary H. McIver, second daughter of

Capt. Henry McIver of Cheraw.

239   Dec. 17th At the residence of the Bride's step father,
Capt. A. A. Pollock of Chesterfield Co., Henry J. Rogers
Jr. of Marlboro' Co. and Miss E. J. Harrington, eldest
daughter of Henry W. and Rebecca J. Harrington.

1875 June 3rd At the residence of the Bride's step-father
Ned Ford (cold.) of Chesterfield Co., James Simons (cold.)
and Lily.

1877 Aug. 7th At St. David's Church Daniel H. Reid and
Mary D. daughter of J. P. & Laura R. Harrall all of Cheraw.

Dec. 11th At St. David's Church, Henry W. Harrington and
Lucy Elizabeth, daughter of E. S. & E. K. Waddill, all of
Cheraw.

1878 Jany 30th At the residence of the Bride's father,
Thomas P. McIver and Susan R., daughter of G. W. & Sarah
R. Duvall, all of Cheraw, S. C.

1879 April 30th At the residence of Mrs. Mary Maxwell,
cold. Emerson Hagger cold. & C. Anna Powe, cold. of Cheraw.

Oct. 15th At the residence of the Bride's step father Capt.
A. A. Pollock, of Chesterfield Co., Lemuel D. Harrall of
Cheraw S. C. and Miss Charlotte P. daughter of Henry W. and
Rebecca J. Harrington.

Nov. 27th At St. David's Church, Franklin A. Waddill,
M. D. of Little's Mills N. C. and Ellen Shaw, eldest daughter
of Cornelius and M. H. Kollock of Cheraw So. Ca.

240   Dec. 24th At. St. David's Church, Pickens M. Brown (cold.)
and Anna Bryan (cold.)

1880 June 23rd At the residence of the Bride's Father, James
C. McNair of Cheraw So Ca. and Margerie B. daughter of Hon.
Thos S. and Caroline Ashe of Wadesboro No. Ca.

1881 Nov. 2nd At the residence of the Bride's Father,
Richard C. Watts of Laurens C. H. So. Ca. and Alleine Eunice
daughter of Col. E. B. C. and Allen Cash of Cash's Depot
So. Ca.

1882 Dec. 6th At the residence of the Bride's Father, John
W. Mills and Sarah T. Burns, daughter of James B. and Lydia
A. Burns., all of Wadesboro, N. C.

Dec. 7th At the residence of the Bride's Mother, Dougald
McDougald of Cumberland Co., N. C. and Mattie H. daughter
of Robert T. and Eliza M. Hall of Marlboro Co., So. Ca.

Dec. 14th In the St. David's Church, Walter N. Munson and
Henrietta O. daughter of Mrs. Mary J. Brown, all of Cheraw
S. C.

1883 Dec. 24th At the residence of the Bride's step-father
Nancy E. McAllister (cold.) and James L. Murphy cold. of
Charleston, So. Ca.

241 1884
March 5th At the residence of Mrs. S. H. Hisbet, Cheraw,
Charles H. McAllister (cold.) and Carrie Leake (cold.)

Nov. 19th In St. David's Church, Richard H. Pegues and Sarah
E. Duvall daughter of Gideon W. and Sarah R. Duvall, all of
Cheraw, S. C.

1886 Jany 14th At Home, George T. Radcliffe of Charleston
S. Ca. and Elisabeth I. daughter of Prichard P. and Elisabeth Q. Reddy.

1887 Nov 10th At Home Bennettsville, So Ca., John M. Jackson and Elisabeth W. Duvall, daughter of Marun H. H. and
Mary Irene Duvall.

1880 Aug. 2nd In St. David's Church, Harbert E. Wells of
Cheraw, S. C. and Annie M. Cordell of Cheraw S. C. daughter
of Nathaniel N. and S. E. Cordelle.

1890 March 5th In St. David's Church by Rev. Jno W. Motte
Rector St. Andrew Darien, Ga. Miss Annie H. Kollock daughter
of Dr. C. and Mrs. M.H. Kollock of Cheraw S. C. and James
Dillingham of Charleston, S. C.

242 Oct. 15th At St. David's Rectory, Solomon Tuttle and Emeline
Lang, A. A. McDonough officiating.

1891 Oct. 29th At St. David's Rectory, George McCall and
Amelia Reed (colored) A. A. McDonough officiating.

Nov 12th In St. David's Church, E. Waddill Pegues and
Nannie Pollock, daughter of Capt. A. A. and Mrs. Pollock of
Cheraw, S. C. A. A. McDonough officiating.

1892 May 12th At the residence of the Bride's Parents,
Earnest Allison Palmer and Virginia S. Pollock daughter of
Capt. and Mrs. A. A. Pollock of Cheraw, So. Ca. A. A. Mc-
Donough officiating

Oct. 5th In St. David's Church, William Thos. Thrower and
Margaret Elizabeth Godfrey daughter of S. G. and Hattie E.
Godfrey of Cheraw So Ca.

1895 June 20th In St. Davids Church, by Rev. Jno. W. Motte
Rector Ch. Epiphany Upper St. John's Berkely Co., So. Ca.,
Rev. Jacob S. Hartzell of Mt. Pleasant So. Ca. and Mrs.
Gertrude Waddill, daughter of Edmund J. & Elisabeth K.
Waddill.

243 1896 April 16 in St. David's Church Judge R. C. Watts and
Miss Lottie McIver daughter of Judge Henry McIver, all of
Cheraw, S. C. (Rev.) Thomas P. Baker, Minister.

1896 December In St. David's Ch. W. Henry Harrall and
Myrtle Walke, all of Cheraw, S. C.   Thomas P. Baker, Minister.

1896 Christmas Eve. James Auld Harrington and Sarah Wilde
Gillespie, daughter of Francis and Sidney Gillespie all of
Marlboro Co., S. C. This marriage was celebrated at the
residence of bride's parents in Marlboro Co., S. C.
                         Thomas P. Baker, minister

1897 In June, I married James Hicks & Easter Elizabeth Talton at the Rectory in Cheraw, S. C. all of Chesterfield Co., S. C.   T. P. Baker

244   On the 18th of June 96, I united in marriage at St. David's Rectory, Thomas Smith & Rebecca Brown, colored persons.
                                              Thomas P. Baker

1898 Married in St. Davids Church on the afternoon of July 28 '98 by the Rev. J. W. Motte, Elizabeth Waddill Duvall of Cheraw S. C. and Herbert Graham Osteen of Sumter, S. C.

1900 Married in St. Davids church Augus (sic) 2, 1900, Daisy McLean Wells to Eugene Charles McGregor. Rt. Rev. Ellison Capers officiating and Rev. C. W. Boyd assisting.

1901 Married at the home of the bride's parents Aug. 21st 1901 Charlotte Wilson Powe to Arthur Kittrell by the Rector C. W. Boyd.

245   Married in St. Davids church on the 1st day of January 1903 Marion Gillespie Godfrey to Rev. C. W. Boyd, rector of the parish, by the Rt. Revd. Ellison Capers.

On 1st June 1904 at St. Davids Church I united in matrimony William Gist Duncan of Columbia S. C. and Eleanor(?) McIver Harden of Cheraw, S. C.   C. W. Boyd, rector

On the 29th Oct. 1904 at their home I united in matrimony Charles Haley and Shady Estelle Stanton.   C. W. Boyd

On the 30th day of November 1905 I united in matrimony Henry Jordan Thurman and Nell Pegues Evans at St. Davids Church.
                                              C. W. Boyd, Rector

On the 25th day of April 1906 at St. Davids church I united in matrimony William H. Hickson Jr. and Agnes Evans McLean.
                                              C. W. Boyd, rector

On the 3d of July 1906 John Mitchell Witsell and Edith Duvall were united in matrimony at St. Davids church the Rev. W. P. Witsell officiating, assisted by the rector Rev. C. W. Boyd.

246   On the 24th Sept 1907 at the house of the bride's parents I united in matrimony John Hill and Laura Jane Gainey.
                                              C. W. Boyd, rector

Married in St. David's church on the 30th day of April 1908
Walter Miller Stevens   Witnesses
       and   Mary McEachern
Hannah Wilson Malloy   Hannah P. W. Malloy
                     Harold Thomas, Rector of St. John's
                     church, Florence, S. C. officiating

On the 31st day of December 1907 at St. David's Church I united in Holy Matrimony Preston B. Huntley and Lillian Wells.   A. S. Thomas, Rector

On the 27 day of April 1910 at St. David's Church I united in Holy Matrimony William Wannamaker and Helen McIver.
                                              A. S. Thomas, Rector

112

On April 10, 1912 Timothy Terrell Brooks and Carrie Ella
Pollock at residence W. P. Pollock   A. S. Thomas

On Oct. 9, 1912, Charles Lemuel Prince Jr. and Marian Hickson at St. Davids   A. S. Thomas

On June 18, 1913 Henry George Carrison Jr. and Phyllis Dudley
Hickson at St. Davids.   A. S. Thomas

On July 22, 1914, John L. Evans, and Marie Sparks at the
rectory.   A. S. Thomas

247 On Sep. 7, 1914, William Evander Bailey and Elizabeth Summer-
ford at rectory both of Mars Bluff neighborhood.
                                           A. S. Thomas

On Dec. 19, 1914, Lester Robinson Dameron and Julia Nomah
Monson at St. Davids   A. S. Thomas

On March 30, 1915, Edgar E. Davis of Greensboro N. C. and
Viola Edna Henderson of Eldorado N. C. at Rectory.
                                           A. S. Thomas

On April 21, 1915, Walter Brooks Smith & Celestine Cornelia
Marshall at residence of latter Cheraw (colored)
                                           A. S. Thomas

On Sept. 18, 1915, Thomas Bingham Spencer and Nan Keitt
Evans at St. Davids   A. S. Thomas

On May 25, 1916, John Edgar McDonald & Marie Edgeworth of
McBee at St. Davids   A. S. Thomas

On Feb. 14, 1917, James Justin Morris and Jane Alexine
Harrall at home of latter.   A. S. Thomas

On April 12, 1917, William Prestiss Walker and Charlotte
Harrington Harrall at St. Davids (new church from this on-
ward).   A. S. Thomas

On April 30, 1917, Philip R. Lachicotte and Mildred ORoddey
Wells at St. David's.   A. S. Thomas

On Feb. 10, 1918, Donald B. Page and Katherine Eliz. Powe
at home of latter.   A. S. Thomas

248 Alfonso Sturbird and Bertha Smith at Rectory Cheraw
March 10, 1920 Witnesses Mrs. Wm. Waldrop
                     "   Harry Winn
                           A. S. Thomas, Rector

William Edward McLaughlin age 33
Elizabeth Turner Waddill age 31
on June 15, 1920 at St. David's A. S. Thomas Rector

John W. Justice age 28
Ellen K. Duvall age 30 on Oct. 20, 1920 at St. David's
                           A. S. Thomas

Thomas L. McDuffie   23
Bessie May Teal   18
Nov. 27, 1920 at Rectory.   A. S. Thomas

[pp. 249-258 are blank.]

259   Burials of Soldiers from the Cheraw Hospitals
     1865
     Feby
       12th Mr. P. Jackson S. C. St. David's Church Yard
       17th W. S. Culbertson "   Soldiers Burial Ground
       18th A Soldier   "   "   "
       20th   "   "   "   "

260   Burials
     1829   By Rev. A. W. Marshall
     March 31st At St. David's Church old Mrs. McCall aged 84 years
     Sept. 2nd A son of Mrs. McMillan   " 15 months
     " 7th Mary Rebecca daughter of Joseph Townes
     Sept 19   At the Family Ground Ground   ) about
               Mrs. Martha Ellerbe wife of John Ellerbe) 33 years
     " 27th   At the Family Burying Ground)
               John son of John Ellerbe   )   2 weeks
     Octo 3   At St. David's Church Virginia Hopkins)
            eldest daughter of Joseph Townes   ) 3 years
     Nov. 15 At the Church, Dr. John G. Lance

     1830
     April 21st At the Church Rebecca wife of)   aged 36 years
               Joseph Townes   )

     May 23rd at the Church a Mrs. Parker
     July 10th Martha youngest daughter of)
               L. S. & Ann Drake   )
     Octo 6th The Infant Son of A. P. Lacoste

     1831
     Sept 29th At the Family Burying Ground   )
               Genl. Erasmus Powe service at the church)
     Octo 15th At the church (service at the house))
               Helena daughter of Franklin Turner)
     " 11th A Mr. Gainey service at the house
     " 16th A Mrs. Clarke (widow) service at the house

     1832
     May 16th At the Family Burying Ground)
           Mary C. wife of John Ellerbe) aged 30 years

     June 9th At the above burying ground   )
           Elizabeth wife of James R. Ervin)
     July   at the Church a Mr. McQuaige
     Sept   "   "   " the infant child of a Mr. _____

261 1833
     May 30 At St. David's Church Jane McCrady)
           daughter of John Morrison   ) aged 5 months

     July   at the Church John Day
     Aug 10th In Marlborough Alexander K. Ellerbe
     " 22nd Julia daughter of F. Turner at the Church
     Sept. 29th At the Church Mr. Clement L. Prince
     Octr. 11th At the Church an Infant child of Mr. Scrovell

     1834
     March At the Family Burying Ground in Marlboro)
     22nd   Mr. James A. Harrington, in his 49th year)

Octo. 20th   At St. David Church, Mr. Solomon McColl

1835
April 9th   At the church Mrs. Muirhead wife)
            of Alexander Muirhead   )
July   At the church Francis McCall

1836
June 28th   At the Family Burying Ground near)
            Cheraw   Col. James R. Ervin
July 6th   Mr. John Lee
Aug   At the F B Ground in Marlborough)
        Erasmus son of Dr. T. E. Powe   )
Sept 14th   At the Church Mr. John Charles
Octo 2nd   At the Church Augustus ser of)
            A P Lacoste   )

1837
Jany 1st   At the Church a Mr. Deweston
Sept 17th   At the Church   James son of)
            John & Mary Stinemetz   )
Octo 1st   At the Church Alexander Powe

1839
March 14th   At the church Archibald Strickland
Nov 13th   At the Church Mrs. Claudia K. Pritchard

262   1840
May 25th   At St. David's Church   John S Stinemetz
Octo 19th   At the Church a poor Woman daughter)
            of Mrs. King, named Tabitta(?)   )
Decr 26   At Sneedsborough No Ca   )
            Mrs Herbert Pearson   aged)   73 years

A. D.
1841   By Rev. J. W. Miles
Sept. 11th   At Burial place on Mrs. Harrington's planta-
              tion; a female servant (baptised by Rev. A.
              W. Marshall)

1842
July 13th   At St. David's Church yard: Chandler Robbins; aet.
            9 months.
Oct. 28th   At St. David's Church-yard: Mrs. Elizabeth God-
            frey: aet 23 yrs 8 Mo.

1843
March 27th At St. David's Church yard: William H. Robbins:
            aet 45 yrs.

1843   By Rev. A. E. Ford
Sept 12   At the Burial place on Mrs. Harrington's plantation
          Eleanor Esther Powe daughter of Thos: E. & C. H.
          Powe

Septr 13 At the same place Mrs. Eleanor W. Harrington,
          widow of James A. Harrington in the 51st year of
          her age

263   1844   By the Revd Henry Elwell Rector.

115

Feby 12th   In the Church Yard of St. David's Church James,
infant child of Dr. A. & Mary Ann Hopton, who survived
his birth only a few hours.

Feby 21st   In the Church Yard of St. David's Church, Mary
Ann Hopton, wife of Dr. A. Hopton, aged Twenty-Nine Year.

July 2d   On Mr Kollock's plantation an aged Negro, named
Abraham

August 26th   On Mr. Harrington's plantation a negro girl,
about seven year of age named Louisa.

Octr. 29th   In the Church Yard of St. David's, Mrs. Edwards,
wife of John E. Edwards.

1845
Feby 8th   Mrs. Rebecca Edwards, in the Church-Yard of St.
David's Church

July 16th   Miss Ellen Stinemetz, in the Church Yard of St.
Davids, aged 34 years & 5 months.

By Rev. Alexr. Gregg

1847
July 13th   On Dr. Thomas E. Powes plantation a Negro Woman
named Chany, a member of the Methodist church.

Novr 22   On the plantation of John W. Harrington in Marlboro
District a negro woman named Becky a slave of Henry W.
Harrington & a member of the Methodist Church.

264   Decr 5th   At the family residence in Marlboro District, Mr.
John B. Billingsly, aged sixty five years

1848
Feby 2   At the residence of Dr. Thomas E Powe in Cheraw,
read the burial service over Indy, a negro child belonging
to Dr. Powe.

March 2   At the residence of his Father in Cheraw   James
Richardson aged 11 years.

"   16th   At the residence of her Father in Marlboro District
Mary A., daughter of Oliver H. and Sarah J. Kollock aged
fourteen years and nine months.

"   26th   At the Negro burying ground on John W. Harringtons
plantation in Marl. District Adam, servant of Henry W. Harrington, aged forty nine years.

"   27th   At the plantation of Dr. T. E. Powe, in Chesterfield District, Sarah, servant of Dr. Powe, aged about seventy years & a member of the Methodist Church.

Aprl 30th   At the plantation of Dr. Thos E. Powe in Chesterfield District, Hagar, servant of Dr. Powe, aged about 40
years.

May 14th   In St. Davids Church yard, a Mrs. South, aged
45 years.

265   May 6th At the plantation of Mrs. Esther Powe, near Cheraw, Frank, her servant, aged 45 years.

June 17th At the plantation of Dr. Thos E. Powe, near Cheraw, Polly, his servant, aged about 70 years, a member of the Methodist church.

Septr 10th At the residence of the Parents, in Cheraw, Sarah Ann, daughter of James and Ann Jane Molfus, aged three years.

" 13th At same place, James Riley, son of James and Ann Jane Molfus, aged thirteen years.

Octr. 5th At the family residence, in the outskirts of Cheraw, Lemuel Edwards, aged about 35 years.

Octr. 10th At the Episcopal church in Wadesboro, N. C., Mrs. Mana Burguin, aged 62 years, an exemplary member of the church.

Octr. 20th At the residence of John More in Cheraw, David More, aged 25 years.

Octr. 21. At St. Davids church, John Godfrey aged about 45 years.

266   October 22 At his residence and in the Presbyterian Church yard, Cheraw, John Taylor aged eighty years.

(by Rev. M. A. Curtis)

Novr 2 At their residence, Attalinda, Infant daughter of Alexander and C W Gregg.

by Rev. A. Gregg, Rector

Novr. 8th In the church yard of St. David's William M'Quage aged 25 years.

Novr. 13th In the yard of St. Davids church, John M'Intosh, aged about 45 years.

" 19th At the residence on his Mother in Cheraw, Angus M'Intosh, aged 15 years.

Decr. 6th At the residence of Wm Godfrey in Cheraw, his servant Maria, aged about 30 years, a member of the Methodist Church.

" 10th At St. Davids church, an infant daughter of Sydney & Eliza Douglass, aged 24 hours.

1849
Jany 22 In the church yard of St. Davids Church, Abigail Edwards aged about 30 years.

March 3 At the residence of B. Campin(?), in Cheraw, & the church yard of St. Davids church, Stephen Hays, aged 75 years.

" 27th In the church yard of St. Davids church, Elizabeth Davis Middleton, aged about 45 years.

267   May 18 on the plantation of J. W. Harrington his servant
Judy, aged about 45 years

Aug 17th At the house of the Mother, Julius King, infant
son of Sarah Stafford.

Octr 28 In the church yard of St. Davids Margaret Arne(?)
infant daughter of D. L. and Mary Jane M'Kay, aged a few
hours.

1850
Febry 1st At the residence of Duncan Stafford and in the
church yard of St. Davids Sarah Stafford, aged 30 years.

March 18th At the residence of Duncan Stafford and in the
church yard of St. Davids church, John Stafford aged 73
years.

May 23rd At the family residence & at the grave Mrs. Catharine Billingsly, aged 70 years.

June 8th At the family residence in Cheraw, L S Drake, aged
about 50 years.

Aug 14 At the church, Fanny Blythe, daughter of D. L. and
Mary Jane M'Kay, aged 5 years.

1851
Jany 9th At the family residence & in the yard of St. Davids
Mrs. Munson, aged   years.

Aug. 21 At the family residence & at the grave in the yard
of the Baptist Church at Society Hill, Mary Laurens, Infant
daughter of L & M S Adams aged 2 years.

268   Oct 20 At the church, Infant child of D L & Mary Jane
M'Kay.

   " 23 At the family residence and the family burying ground
in Marlboro, William Alexander, son of Dr. Thomas E. & C. W.
Powe, aged 4 years.

1852
Jany 6 At the plantation of Dr. T. E. Powe, Milly, an aged
servant of Dr. Powe.

Feby 12 At the residence of her husband in Cheraw, Lucy Ann,
wife of William Bailey, aged 25 years.

   " 15 At the plantation of Dr. T. E. Powe, Rachael,
his servant aged about forty years.

May 7th At the residence of O. H. Kollock, in Marlboro,
Lucy, his servant, aged about 75 years.

Octr 28 At the Ellerbe burial ground, in Chesterfield District, Aurelia Douglass, wife of Ellerbe Douglass, aged
seventeen years.

1852
Jany 13 At Mrs. Esther Powe's, Sue an aged servant of Mrs.
Powe

April 26 At the residence of her brother in Cheraw & in
the year of St. Davids, Mary Jane Smith aged twenty nine
years

269 May 18 At the Church, Charlotte Eliza, daughter of T. E. B.
& Charlotte Peuges, aged about 4 years.

Septr 6 At the Church Dicey Edwards aged about 70 years.

" 16 At the family residence and the grave, at the Ellerbe burial ground, Mrs. Esther Powe, aged 81 years.

Octr 29 At the family residence in Cheraw, Wilson Gilchrist
son of Rev. J. C. & Malinda Coil, aged between 3 & 4 years.

Novr 10 At the residence of the Master, near Cheraw, Mary
Jane, child of Annette, servants of Dr. T. E. Powe, aged
one year.

1854
Feby 2 At the residence of Mr. Napier, John Sheorn, aged
13 years.

" 27 At the church, Capt. George Coates, of Charleston,
aged 35 years 9 months.

March 23. At my own residence, Betsey Pinn, a free colored
woman, aged 80 years.

Apr. 13 At the family residence in Cheraw & at the grave at
St. Davids Church yard, Ann L. Campbell aged   years.

June 18th At the church & grave inMarlboro, Wilson, son of
Alexr & C W Gregg, aged 18 months, 16 days (by Rev M W
Curtis).

270 July 3d At the family residence & the grave near Cheraw
Charlotte Rosanna, daughter of T. E. & C. H. Powe, aged one
year.

" 8th At the residence of the Parents in Cheraw, & at the
grave, in the yard of St. David's church, John, infant son
of Mr. & Mrs. Harney(?).

Aug. 16 At the church & grave, an infant son of Cornelius
and Henrietta Kollock aged 8 hours.

Septr 6 At the family residence, Orange Grove, and grave,
in the family burial ground, near Cheraw, Erasmus A. Powe,
aged 40 years

Octr. 7 At the family residence in this District, Harriet
Thompson wife of James Thompson, aged 45 years.

" 20 At the church & grave, Julia, daughter of Edmund J.
and Elizabeth Waddell, aged 9 years.

        At the same time and place, Everal, son of Thomas
E. B. and Charlotte J. Pegues, aged 7 years 8 months and 16
days.

Novrm 10 At Wadesboro, N. C., Mr. N. Boggan, aged 49 years.

119

Novm 23 At the home in Cheraw & in the yard of St. Davids
church Josiah Edwards, aged 35 years.

271   Decr 13 At the Ellerbe burial ground (red hill) Sarah Jane
daughter of Sydney and Eliza Douglass, aged three years.

" 19 At the same place, Allen, daughter of Sydney and
Eliza Douglass, aged about 5 years.

1855
Feby 4   At the church & grave, Henry C. Turner, aged 30
years.

" 18 At the Presbyterian Church & in the yard of St.
Davids, John Evans, aged   years.

July 4. At the family residence in Chesterfield District,
and at the grave, James Hewitt Sr., aged 70 years

Nov 29 At the residence of Thomas Shiver in Cheraw & at
the grave, in St. Davids church yard, Daniel Irick, aged 32
years.

Dec 2 At the residence of Wm Godfrey, Solomon, servant of
Miss J. Pritchard, & one of the Sextons of St. Davids church,
aged 28 years.

1856
Jany 1 At the residence of Edward Bowne(?), in Cheraw,
Mary, aged 55, servant of a Mr. Bailey of Columbia.

" 19 At the house of the Mother, and at the grave in St.
Davids church yard, Alexander, son of Sally McIntosh, aged
18 years.

272   June 13 At my own residence & at the grave, Sue, infant
child of Julia, my servant, aged 24 hours.

Aug 4 At the residence of John Taylor in this District,
Caroline, infant daughter of Caroline Taylor, deceased.

" 5 At the residence of the Parents in Cheraw, & at the
grave in St. Davids church yard, Thomas Cherry, aged 4 years.

" 16 At the residence of Wm M'Call(?), in Cheraw, & at
St. Davids church yard, Jesse Cherry, aged 4 years.

Septr. 8 At the residence of the Parents in Cheraw, & in
the Yard of St. Davids church, James, infant son of Benjamin & Jane Brock, aged 1 year.

"   23 At the church & the grave, Mrs. Mary Jane wife of
D. L. McKay, aged 43 years.

"   28 At the residence of Britton Patrick in this District, and at the grave, Mary Cole, aged 45 years.

Decr 2 At the family residence in Cheraw, and at the grave,
in St. Davids Church Yard, Mrs. Lavinia Swain, aged about
80 years

" 8 At the house of the Parents near Cheraw, Benjamin
Thomas, infant son of William and Harriet Waddell, aged

three months

273   Decr 17 At her dwelling in Cheraw, and in the yard of St. Davids Church, Sally M'Intosh, aged about 42 years.

1857
Jany 4 In the afternoon, at the Ellerbe burial ground Mary, daughter of E. B. C. & Allan Cash, aged 7 years

"   8 At the residence of O. H. Kollock, in Marlboro, & at the burial ground of J. W. Harrington, Sue, servant of O. H. Kollock, aged about 90 years

June 17 At St. Davids Church (in the morning) & at the grave, in the yard, Mary Wilson, daughter of Cornelius & Mary Henrietta Kollock, aged 15 months and 5 days.

"   At same place (in afternoon) Mrs. Ellen F. M'Intosh wife of Benjamin M'Intosh, aged 37.

July 20 At the residence of her Father on Gopher(?) Hill Chesterfield District, Frances Taylor, aged 19 years.

" 23 At the residence of Mrs. Boan(?), in this District, John Boan, aged about 65 years.

Aug 3 At the residence of the Parents in Cheraw, and at the grave, in the country, Lura Ann, infant daughter of William & Martha Clark, aged 6 months.

Septr 3 At the residence of the Parents, in Cheraw & the grave, in St. Davids Church yard, Alice Eliza, daughter of Mr. & Mrs. E. L. Brim, aged 3 yr & 8 ms.

274   Oct 2 At the family residence in Marlboro & the grave, Mrs. Sarah J. Kollock, aged 62 years, 4 ms & 15 days.

" 18 At her residence in Cheraw, & the grave in St. Davids Church yard, Nancy M'Call, aged about 55 years.

Novr 3 At the grave in St. Davids church yard, James Allen, aged about 60 years.

Decr 11 At the Church & grave in St. Davids church yard, Benjamin M'Intosh.

" 14 At the family residence, in this District, Daniel Campbell, aged about 55 years.

" 16 At the residence of the Mother in this town, John Hays, aged 16 years.

1858
Jany 19 At the residence of the family in Cheraw, and the grave in the Methodist Church yard, John Rushing, aged 63 years.

" 21 At the grave, in this District, Eli Wallace, aged about 50 years.

" 22 At the church & the grave in the yard, James Maynard, son of the late James(?) Maynard, aged 15 years.

Feby 19 At the Church & the grave, in Church Yard, Samuel
son of Lemuel & Sarah Edwards deceased, aged about seven
years.

275 March 17 At the church & grave, Lydia Atkins, aged about
65 years.

June 9 At the residence of the family in Cheraw, Barbara,
wife of Hiram Lunsford, aged about 30 years.

Aug 9 At the Church and the grave, John D. Pickard, aged
43 years.

Septr. 28 At the residence of the Parents in this District
and at the grave, Simeon son of D. & Mary J. Chapman, aged
thirteen years.

Oct. 1 At my own residence in the Country, Cato, child of
Cato & Laura, aged two years.

Nov. 30 At the Church & grave, Elizabeth M'Coll, aged 68
years.

1859
Feby 26 At the residence of Mrs. Cannon, in Cheraw, and the
grave, in St. Davids church yard, Henry Williams, aged about
35 years.

June 23d At the church & grave, Mrs. Charlotte H. Powe, in
the 50th year of her age.

Aug. 26 At the grave, on Mr. O. H. Kollock's plantation in
Marlboro, William servant of Mr. Kollock, aged 28 years.

1860
Sept. by the Rev. Mr. Corbet, Presbyterian minister of this
place, Henrietta Cornelia, infant daughter of Dr. C. Kollock
and Henrietta his wife.

276 1861
Novr 22nd At St. Davids Church, Margaret Hawes, daughter
of Cornelius & M. H. Kollock, aged 3 years & 2 months.

" 30th At Dr. C. Kollock's, & at the Colored Burial
ground in Cheraw, a colored infant child, aged about six
weeks.

Dec. 24th At St. Davids Church, & in the church yard,
Alexander Gregg jr., eldest son of Rt. Rev. Alex. Gregg of
Texas, who died at Dumfries Va. in 4th Texas Regt., Decr.
13th & was brought on to this place for burial in St. David's
Church yard.

1862
March 1st At St. Davids Church & in the Church yard, William
Pegues, infant son of Henry W. & Rebecca Harrington aged
fifteen months.

June 1st At St. David's church & church yard, Annie Elizabeth Augusta, infant daughter of Mr. & Mrs. E. M. Wells, aged
fourteen months & 7 days.

July 13th At Mr. W. H. Godfrey's, Ella Frances, servant

child of Miss Josephine Pritchards, aged six years.

July 26th At St. Davids Church & at the family burial
ground in Marlboro', Mr. Oliver H. Kollock, aged 72 years
& 2 months.

August 19th At. Mr. William Godfrey's residence, Cheraw,
at 9 O clk A. M. Luke, servant child of Miss Josephine
Pritchard's, aged three years.

277 Novr 21st At St. Davids Church yard, Mrs. Louisa McLaughlin of Darlington C. H., formerly of this district, aged
20 years.

1863
Jany 11th At. Mr. W. Godfrey's Quarters, Mark, infant
child of Frank, servant of Mr C. & Jane servant ot Mr. J.
J. McIver, of Society Hill, aged 4 months.

June 1st At the colored Burial ground near Cheraw, a servant woman belonging to Mrs. Simmons (a refugee from Charleston) aged 62 years.

June 2nd At. St. David's Church & churchyard Robert Peyton,
son of Rev. R. T. & Marion R. Brown, aged 7 years & 8 months
(services performed by the Rev. J. S. Kidney of Society Hill)

June 27th At "Westmoreland" near Cheraw, Chesterfield
District, William Jenkins, aged 22 months, son of Mr. & Mrs.
Jos. La Roche, refugees from Wadmalaw Island buried in St.
David's Church yard.

August 26th At St. David's Church & Yard, Eliza Irby, infant daughter of John W. & Eliza W. Harrington of Marlboro'
District born September 8th 1862, died August 25th 1863

Sept. 13th At. St. David's church & yard, Miss Annie Graham
daughter of Mrs. Elizabeth Graham, of Cheraw, formerly of
Ireland.

19th At the residence of his parents in Cheraw, and
at St. David's Church yard, James son of William McAll
aged 10 years & 7 months.

278 1863 September 28th at St. David's Church yard, an infant
daughter of G. Maxwell & S. W. Hendrix of Florence, aged 22
days.

October 13th At St. Davids Church yard, William Wallace,
aged 32 years, son of Franklin & Sarah Turner of Cheraw he
was a private in the Chesterfield Guards, 8th S. C. Regt.,
served from the beginning of the war. after passing safely
through many severe battles, was mortally wounded in the
skirmish near Chattanooga died after a few days suffering,
this body was brought home for interment.

Nov. 30th At St. David's Church yard, Harman Westervelt,
aged 27 years, Eldest son of John J. & Sarah Westervelt of
Cheraw, he died of the effects of an accidental gun-shot
wound recd. near Florence on the 26th ult.

1864
May 2nd At St. David's Church, Mrs. Sarah P. Dove, refugee

from Charleston   aged 73   the body was taken to Charleston for burial.

    18th   At St. Davids Church & Churchyard Mrs. Sarah L. Westervelt aged 45 years, wife of J. J. Westervelt of Cheraw.

August
2nd   At St. Davids Ch. & Ch. yard Mrs. Mary Stevens refugee from Charleston   aged 91 years & 8 months.   The deceased was born in Florida during the reign of George III while very young she went to Nova Scotia & after a few years removed to Charleston where she resided 80 years when she came to this place as a refugee

279   1865
March 13th   At St. David's Church-Yard, Louisa Brock aged 13 years, daughter of Mr.   Brock & his wife, of Cheraw

April 5th   Near Cheraw & at St. David's Church-Yard by the Rev. W. O. Prentiss of Charleston, Henrietta Amanda, aged 12 months, daughter of Emanuel Witsell & Mary his wife, refugees from St. Bartholomew's Parish.

April 15th   At St. David's Church & Church-Yard, Pennill F. Coombe, O. S. Co. C. Lucas Battallion, 1st S. C. Heavy Artillery; (The decd. was a native of Kent Co., Md., he entered the C. S. A. at the beginning of the war, with two brothers & a relative. The three later were killed by a shell, during the last attack in Morris Island, & he himself was wounded by the same shell. In a deep decline he was brot to the Cheraw Hospital at the evacuation of Charleston, & was removed to the house of Rev. R. T. Brown, here he breathed his last in peace.)

April 22nd   At the residence of Jos. F. Walker, Cheraw, Catherine Sanders, a free-colored refugee woman from Charleston.

April 25th   At St. David's Church-Yard, Mrs.Sophia Gooding, wife of David Gooding of Chesterfield District.

April 27th   At St. David's Church & Church-yard, Mrs. Mary Huger, aged   years, wife of Majr. Cleland Huger, of Charleston.

May 8th   At the residence of Mr. M. Matheson, Cheraw, Edward Brentford, colored mans servant of Chs. Seebring of Charleston.

280   May 13th   At St. David's Church & Church-yard, Sarah Ellen aged 9 weeks, infant daughter of Majr. J. H. Serevent & Ellen W.his wife, refugees from Beaufort District.

    " 19th   At the residence of Geo. H. Ingraham, Cheraw, a coloured infant, only a few hours old.

    " 20th   At St. David's Churchyard, Joanna, aged four years and nine months, daughter of John and Mary Jane Patrick, of Chesterfield Dist.

    " 26th   On the rail Road Cars near Cheraw, Eugene, aged 10 days, infant of   Smart &   his wife, refugees from

124

Charleston.

29th At St. David's Church & Church-Yard, Miss Susan D. Armstrong, aged 35, daughter of Mrs. S. F. Armstrong, refugees from Charleston.

31st At the Bank in Cheraw, Henry, aged 12 years, servant of Rev. W. O. Prentiss, refugees from the Coast.

June 4th At St. David's Church & Church-Yard, Elizabeth Gaillard Matheson, aged 18 years, daughter of M. P. Matheson, refugees from Charleston.

14th At. St. David's Church & Church-yard, Mrs. Catherine C. Jenkins, aged 71 yrs. & 8 months, refugee from Charleston.

281 June 15th At, St. David's Church & Church-Yard, Henry W. Harrington jr., aged 38 yrs, of Marlboro' District.

July 4th At the residence of Chancellor Dunkin, Cheraw, Sarah Harlston, aged 10 months, infant daughter of Alfred & Eliza Dunkin, from Waccamaw.

" 9th At the residence of M. D. Matheson, Cheraw, a coloured infant.

" 20th At St. David's Church & Church-yard (by the Rev. W. O. Prentiss) Mrs. Mary D. Walker, aged 34 years, wife of Geo. Walker of Charleston.

Septr 26th At St. David's Church & Church-Yard, Aurelia Josephine, daughter of J. J. Westervelt, Cheraw, aged 4 years.

Octr. 5th At. St. David's Church Yard, Edwin infant of James & Laura Harrall, aged 1 month.

1866
Jany 7th At. St. David's Church and Church-Yard, Mr. Jno. Bickly, of Charleston, aged 75 yrs.

Jany 20th At. the residence of Jas. McCall, Cheraw, Rosier Cannon, aged 19 yrs.

" 21st At St. David's Church & Church Yard, Mr. Geo: W. Walker, of Charleston, aged 40 years.

Feby 8th At. the Residence of Mr. Gideon Duvall, Mrs. Martha Powe, aged 74 yrs, 9 months, of Chesterfield District.

282 April 3rd At St. David's Church and burial-ground Caroline Harriet, aged ten months, infant daughter of Henry & Caroline McIver.

May 11th At. St. David's Church and Church-Yard, Mary Patterson, aged nine months, & twenty-eight days, infant daughter of Cornelius & Henrietta Kollock.

May 13th At the residence of Mrs. L. W. Prince & at the family burial ground in Marlboro District, George R. Hearsey, aged thirty-four years.

125

May 28th At his residence in Cheraw, and at St. David's
Church-yard, James Goodwin aged 57 yrs 6 month, of Chesterfield Dist.

1866   By Rev. P. D. Hay
August 14th
     At St. Davids Church and Church Yard Henry McIver aged
twelve years and eleven days eldest son of Caroline H. and
Henry McIver of Cheraw S. C.

Sept. 2nd At. St. David's Chh. & Chh. yard Mary Salina
Infant daughter of E. M. and Margaret Wells of Cheraw S. C.

*

1867
February 12th At. St. David's Chh & Chh yard Charlotte
Harrington infant of Harriet E. and S. S. Godfrey of Cheraw
S. C.

283

*1866
Oct. 2nd At. St. Davids Church & Church yard, Capt. Thomas
E. Powe, who died at Gettysburg Pa., July 22nd 1863.

          By Revd. Jno W. Motte Minister of the Parish

1867
August 29th At. St. David's Church and Church Yard David
R. W. McIver of Cheraw Aged _____

August 30th At St. David's Church yard (The services being
performed at the grave) Thomas Wilson, aged fifteen (15)
days infant son of E. M. & Margaret Wells.

Sept 2rd At St. David's Church Yard (The services being
performed at the grave) Claudia Helen, aged nineteen (19)
days infant daughter of E. M. & Margaret Wells.

Dec. 31st At. St. David's Church and Church Yard Claudia
Porcher, aged two months and fourteen days, infant daughter
of S. Gillespie and Harriet E.Godfrey.

1868
Feby 3rd At. St. David's Church Yard An infant son of
Samuel and Laura Goodwyn aged two months and eighteen days.

March 8th At. St. Davids Church and Church Yard, Mrs. Mary
Stinemetz aged seventynine years and four months and nineteen days.

May 9th At. St. Davids Church Yard, William Henry son of
Wm. B. and P. Smith aged two years.

July 14th At. St. David's Church and Church Yard, William
Harris aged 50 years.

284   Sept 16th An infant son of Roger & Cheney Kollock (cold.)
      aged _____

      Sept 28th At. the plantation of Dr. T. E. Powe, Daniel Powe
      (cold.) aged _____

126

Oct. 23rd At. St. David's Church Yard, Martin Surles aged

1869
Sept. 10th Aaron Jackson Powe, son of Aaron and Jane Powe
(cold.) aged Eleven years.

Sept. 22nd At. St. David's Church & Church Yard Mrs. Effie
Bowne, wife of Mr. Ed. Bowne, Aged 72 Years.

Nov. 10th At the residence of Dr. C. Kollock Cheraw, Milley
an aged servant of the family. The body was interred at the
plantation burying ground.

1870 Feby 2nd At. the residence of Capt. Heny. McIver,
Cheraw, The Burrial service was performed on the remains
of Maria (cold.) Aged 68 years.

March 26th At the residence of Mr. F. S. Eaton, an infant
daughter of F. H. & A. Eaton, Aged 24 Hours.

April 11th At the residence of his parents an infant daughter of Revd. Jno W. & M. S. Motte.

Sept 2nd At. St. David's Church Yard, Mrs.   Newell of
Fayetteville No Ca.,Aged 70 yrs.

285 1871
March 31st Louisa (cold.) Aged ____ At the Coloured Burial
          Ground in Cheraw

April 13th At the family burial ground Red Hill Mrs. Elizabeth Ellerbe, widow of the late Crawford Ellerbe

June 9th At St. David's Church and Church Yard Rosa Henrietta, infant daughter of Col. Jno. W. and Eliza W. Harrington.

Sept. 25th At. St. David's Church and Church Yard, Mrs.
Georgina Scoffin, wife of Mr. John Scoffin, of Liverpool,
England.

Dec. 24th At. St. David's Church Yard, Miss Caroline
Munger of Kershaw County.

1872 April 9th At the family burial ground Red Hill, Erwin,
infant son of Erwin & Sarah Brunson.

Sept. 13th At St. David's Church and Church Yard, Tallula
Sherwood, infant daughter of Jno W. and Eliza W. Harrington.

1873 March 2nd At St. David's Church, an infant daughter of
Dr. J. K. and Claudia E. McLean of Cheraw.

March 4th At. St. David's Church and Church Yard, Mrs.
Claudia Elisabeth McLean, wife of Dr. Jno K. McLean, of
Cheraw

July 31st At. St. David's Church and Church Yard, Mrs.
Elisabeth K. Waddill, wife of Erd. J. Waddill of Cheraw.

286 1873 Aug 19th In St. David's Church Yard, Charles Walter
Ernest aged 3 yrs, 2 mos. 16 days, infant son of John D.
and Sarah J. Pickard

Aug 26th At the family Burial Ground in Marlboro', Mrs.
Rebecca A.Williams, from Marlboro Co. widow of Judge Williams, M. D.

Sept 24th In St. David's Church Yard, Rosa aged 2 yrs,
daughter of Robert T. and Eliza Hall of Richmond Co., N. C.

Oct. 31st At the family Burial Ground Red Hill, Benjamin
Franklin Ellerbe of Chesterfield Co.

1874 April 25th At St. David's Church Yard, Edward Bowne
of Cheraw So Ca. aged _____.

April 28th At St. David's Church and Church Yard, Miss
Lucetta Greenup of Cheraw So. Ca.

July 9th At St. David's Church Yard, Willie son of W. H.
and Miley(?) Monson.

July 18th At St. David's Church and Church Yard, John Wilson eldest son of Col. Jno W. and E. W. Harrington.

Aug 7th   At St. David's Church & Church Yard Martha LeNair
second daughter of Jas. F. and Ann E. Drake.

287 Aug. 10th At St. David's Church and Church Yard Edmund
Chapman infant son of Jas. F. and Ann E. Drake.

Aug. 21st At St. David's Church Yard William Henry infant
son of Col. Jno W. and Eliza W. Harrington.

Aug. 25th At St. David's Church and CHurch Yard Harriet
Eleanor infant daughter of S. G. and H. E. Godfrey aged 1
month.

Sept 29th At St. David's Church and Church Yard Emma T.
wife of A. T. Peele of Trinity parish, Southport England.

Oct. 18th At St. David's Church Yard, Samuel Gainey infant
son of Samuel & Laura Goodwyn

Dec. 4th At. St. David's Church and Church Yard, Ellen
wife of John Beaty, formerly of Haverhill, Mass.

Dec. 10th At St. David's Church and Church Yard Emily
Florence infant daughter of Emily P. and John H. Powe.

1875 April 11th At St. David's Church and Church Yard Archie
Beaty from Havenhill, Mass. Aged 86 yrs.

July 14th At the family Burial Ground in Marlboro' Co., Hon:
Charles Irby of Marlboro' Co: Aged 51 yrs.

Sept 21st At the residence of Dr. C. Kollock Cheraw Roger
(cold.) son of Aleck and Charlotte Temple.

288 Novem 4th At St. David's Church Yard, Robert infant son of
Revd. Jno W. and Mary Motte.

1876 Feby 13th At St. David's Church & Church Yard Mrs. Ann
E. Drake of Cheraw   Aged 71 years.

Aug 11th At St. David's Church and Church Yard, Arthur Fredric son of Wm. H. & Mary Monson aged 2 yrs 7 months.

Aug. 12th At St. David's Church and Church Yard, Margaret B. wife of Wm. Godfrey Aged 68 yrs.

Sept 18th At St. David's Church Yard Mary Etta daughter of Louis and Henrietta K. Gainey Aged 3 yrs.

Sept. 29th At the burial ground of Red Hill, Zachariah E. Powe Aged 76 yrs. 6 mos.

Oct. 16th At St. David's Church and Church Yard Franklin Turner Aged 80 yrs.

1877 Feby 25th By Rev. E. T. Buist Presbyterian minister
     At the family Burial Ground in Marlboro' Co. Genl James Gillespie Warden of St. David's Aged 82

May 6th At St. David's Church & Church Yard Douglas Nisbet native of Kirkardnight Scotland Aged 58 years.

May 24th At St. David's & Church Yard John Evans, infant son of Dr. Jno K. and Agnes B. McLean.   Born

289 July 28th At St. David's Church and Church Yard Henry Laurence Britton, son of E. M. & Margaret Wells Aged 3 yrs

July 29th At St. David's Church and Church Yard, James Patton of New York city Aged 45 yrs.

Oct. 4th In St. David's Church Yard Charlotte, wife of Jno F. Edwards of Chesterfield Co.

Nov. 20th At St. David's Church and Church Yard Sarah Rebecca aged 13 years daughter of Rebecca and Henry W. Harrington.

1878
Jany 7th In St. David's Church Yard Sarah, wife of ____ Spears of Chesterfield Co.

April 14th In St. David's Church Yard Mrs. Henrietta K. McIver.

Nov. 15th In St. David's Church, Yard, Rebecca Gainey of Chesterfield Co. Aged 60 yrs.

Nov. 18th In St. David's Church Yard, Hattie May, daughter of Louis & Henrietta H. Gainey Aged 13 mos.

1879
June 24th At St. David's Church and Church Yard, Edmund Waddill son of H. W. & Lucy E. Harrington, aged 6 mos.

July 11th At St. David's Church and Church Yard, Viola E wife of Wm. L. Reid, Aged ___

290 July 13th At St. David's Church and Church Yard William L. Reid Aged ___

Aug. 15th At St. David's Church and Church Yard, Dr. Thos. E. Powe Born Feby 23rd 1800

Dec. 20th At St. David's Church and Church Yard, Mrs.
Sarah Turner Aged 81 years

1880 Feby 1st At St. David's Church Yard, Mrs. Jane Taylor
Aged 40 years

March 23rd At the family Burial in Marlboro Co., Oliver H.
Gillespie M. D. Aged 48 years

April 20th At St. David's Church and Church Yard, Mrs.
Allan Eunice aged 51 years wife of Col. E. B. C. Cash of
Chesterfield Co.

June 9th At St. David's Church and Church Yard Capt. M. G.
Tarrh, aged 55 years

June 15th At St. David's Church and Church Yard, Meta
Inglis born Nov. 23rd 1878 daughter of James D. and Mary
H. Hardin.

Oct. 13th At St. David's Church and Church Yard Mrs. Eliza
Ellerbe aged   years, widow of Benj. Franklin Ellerbe of
Chesterfield Co.

1881 Jany 15th At the Coloured Cemetery Robert Thomas aged
4 mos and 4 days son of Pickins M. and Anna Brown.

291   Dec. 19th At St. David's Church and Church Yard Mrs.
Charlotte W. Gregg Born Jany 29th 1822 wife of Rt. Revd.
Alexander Gregg D. D. Bishop of Texas   1880

1881 May 11th At St. David's Church and Church Yard Maj.
Robert T. Hall of Marlboro' Co., Aged 63 years.

Sept. 11th At St. David's Church Yard, Duvall born Sept.
10th 1881 son of Thos P. and Susan R. McIver.

Oct. 16th At St. David's Church Yard, Mary Pauline aged
1 year 10 mos. daughter of ___ and McQueen Linton.

Oct. 28th At St. David's Church and Church Yard, Mrs. Mary
Jane Duvall aged 42 years

1882 Jany 1st At St. David's Church and Church Yard Matilda
Born June _____ 1879 daughter of James and A. Tunstall.

Feby 11th At the colored cemetery Pickins M. Brown Born
April 19th 1861

Feby 14th At the family burial ground "Red Hill" Martha
Aged 42 years wife of Zachariah Ellerbe of Chesterfield Co.

March 4th At St. David's Church and Church Yard Margerie
B.   Born   wife of James E. McNair.

292   June 4th At St. David's Church and Church Yard Col. Jno W.
Harrington Born Feby 28th 1824

June 13th In St. David's Church Yard Daniel H. Reid

July 4th In St. David's Church Yard, Edward Roscoe Born
June 13th 1880 son of W. H. and Mary Monson.

Aug 10th   At St. David's Church and Church Yard Susanna
Caroline Aged 4 years daughter of A. Catherine and T. Franklin Sherrill.

Aug. 11th   At St. David's Church Yard, Jessie Graham Born
April 8th 1882 daughter of Saml M. C. & Mary E. Moore

Sept 6th   At St. David's Church and Church Yard Mary Ann
Aged   wife of Harris Stanton

Nov. 26th   In St. David's Church Yard Mrs. Elizabeth Graham
of County Antrim Irland

Nov 28th   In St. David's Church and Church Yard Gideon W.
Duvall

1883 May 14th   In St. David's Church and Church Yard Laura
Born Feby 20th 1881   daughter of Daniel H. and Mary D. Reid

293   May 20th   From Pres. Ch. in St. David's Church Yard William
Aged 21 Months   son of Wm. C. and Ella J. McCreight

May 22nd   In St. David's Church Yard Arthur Vanderbilt Aged
2 years   son of John J. and Emma Liles

Aug 17th   At African Methodist Ch. and Grave Yard   Roger
Kollock (cold.) Aged 48 years

Nov 20th   In St. David's Church Yard, Louisa J. B.   Aged
38 years wife of Isaac S. Huntley

Dec. 10th   In St. David's Church Yard, Nellie Ingraham Aged
1 year   daughter of Samuel & Martha Ingram

1884 Jany 22nd   At St. David's Church and Church Yard Edmund James Waddill Aged 62 years

Jany 27th   In St. David's Church and Church Yard Robert
Alexander Born Feby 28th 1867 son of A. A. and   Pollock

Aug. 19th   At St. David's Church and Church Yard Richard P
Reddy born Nov   1808 in Dundack, County Droghead, Ireland.

Sept 17th   In St. David's Church Yard, Norwood   Born Oct
1883 son of Madison F. and Adele Ellerbee

294   Sept 21st   At St. David's Church and Church Yard Clarence
W. Wells Born June 17th 1859

1885 Jany 29th   In St. David's Church Yard, Jacob Jackson
Born March 20th 1883 son of Louis and Henrietta Gainey

March 7th   At Christ Church Mars Bluff Rev. Edwin C. Steele
aged 34 years

May 3rd In the Coloured Burial Ground   aged 8 mos daughter
of Jane Woods, cold.

May 29th   In St. David's Church and Church Yard, William
Godfrey Born Jany 29th 1802

1886 March 6th In St. David's Ch. and Ch. Yard Mrs. Sarah
H. Nibset

131

Aug 17th In St. David's Ch and Ch. Yard James Edward McNair
Born Oct 4th 1846

Aug. 24th In St. David's Ch Yard   daughter of John J.
and Emma LIles

Oct. 21st In St. David's Ch. and Ch. Yard Alexander Gregg
Born Dec. 20th 1880 son of Ellen S. and F. A. Waddill M.
D.

295   Nov 6th In St. David's Ch. and Ch. Yard Elise F. W. Prophet daughter of Rev. E. T. Walker Dio. So. Ca. wife of
Richmond D. Prophet

Dec. 28th In St. David's Ch. and Ch. Yard Gertrude Born
Nov. 13th 1886 daughter of H. W. and Lucy E. Harrington

1887 Jany 3rd In St. David's Ch. Yard,Mrs. Elizabeth Ellen
Preston

Jany 9th In the family burial ground Marlboro' Co. Samuel
J. Gillespie Aged   services were performed by Rev. Do.
Shipp, Methodist Ch.

July 14th In St. David's Ch Yard, Charles G. Purves(?)
aged 76 years

1888 Jany 2nd At the Red Hill Burial Ground Mrs. Mary
Purvis widow of Charles G. Purvis. Aged 71

Feby 7 In St. David's Ch. & Ch. Yard Mrs. Catherine Gayle
Aged 80

April 28 In St. David's Ch. & Ch. Yard Miss Mary Crawford
Ellerbe Aged   daughter Dr. Crawford & Elizabeth Ellerbe

May 14 In St. David's Ch. & Ch. Yard, Henry William Harrington Aged 33 years of Chesterfield Co., So. Ca.

296   May 25 In Baptist Ch. Yard Society Hill, S. C. Miss M.
Julia Hawes aged 74 years daughter of Dr. Clever & Mary
Hawes of Society Hill

June 19th In St. David's Ch. Yard An Infant daughter of
Lemuel D. & Charlotte P. Harrall

Sept. 12 In St. David's Ch & Ch Yard Annie   aged 17 years
daughter of W. H. & M. Monson

Dec. 20th In St. David's Ch & Ch Yard Thomas W. Powe aged
78 years

1890
Jan 3rd In St. David's Church & Church Yard Mrs. Mary Jane
Browne Born Dec. 29th 1836 Rev. Chas. C. Quin Rector of
Calvary Church of Wadesboro, N. C.

March 27th In St. David's Church & Ch yard William H.
McNair Born Jan. 25th 1849   Rev. A. A. McDonough, officiating

June 5th in St. David's Ch. & Ch yard Mrs. Atkinson.

1891
March 8th In St. David's Ch & Ch yard (re-interment) C. K.
Gregg Born

297   May 26th In St. David's Ch and Ch Yard William Motte Aged
nearly two years   Son of Walter N. and Henrietta C. Munson

1892
March 25th In St. David's Ch. and Ch. Yard Miss Josephine
C. Whitehard Aged

1893   In Memoriam

The Rt. Rev. Alexander Gregg, D. D. LL. D. was Rector of
St. David's Church, Cheraw, South Carolina, from 1846 to
1859. Was elected Bishop of Texas in 1859 and consecrated
in Richmond, Virginia, where the General Convention met in
that year.
Having done noble work in that Diocese for the Church of
God he fell asleep after a lingering illness July 10th 1893.
Was buried in St. David's Church yard July 16th 1893. A
beautiful memorial address was made in the Church after
Morning Prayer by the Rt. Rev. George H. Kinsolving, who
succeeds Bishop Gregg as Diocesan of Texas. Bishop Kinsolving, and Rev. J. B. Cheshire, Bishop-Elect of North Carolina, officiated at the burial.

298   1893
August 11th In St. David's Church and Church-Yard, Thomas
Powe Gregory, Aged 24 Years and six months.

1894
May 15th In St. David's Church and Ch. yard William Thomas
8 months and 12 days old Son of Mr. and Mrs. William Thomas
Thrower.

Oct. 7th In St. David's Church and Ch yard, Jacob Ganey
Aged about 80 years. Rev. C. C. Quin of Wadesboro, N. C.
officiated the rector being in Europe at the time

1894 Nov 19th In St. David's Church and Church yard, Dora-
thea De Witt aged 16 yrs and 10 months daughter of Dr. J.
K. and Mrs. Agnes B. McLean.   Rev. Dr. Evans of Trinity
Church, Columbia, S. C. officiating.

1895 Feby 13th In St. Davids Church and Church yard Mrs.
Mary Stafford Aged upwards of 80 years

Dec 17th In St. David's Church & Church yard Mrs. Sarah R.
Duvall, widow of Gideon W. Duvall aged 71 years. Rev. R.
W. Barnwell Ass't minister of Grace Church, Charleston, S.
C. officiating.

1895 April In St. Davids Church yard Alice Monson aged
about 22 Rev. A. A. McDonough officiating

299   Name   Goodwin a male infant
Died   July 15 1896
Age   About 4 months
Buried   St. Davids
Minister   Thos P. Baker

133

```
Name      Emma Dabbs
Died      Oct. 21 1896 at Cheraw, S. C.
Age       Born May 5th 1896  Age 5½ months
Buried    October 22 1896   St Davids
Minister  Thomas P. Baker

1897
Name      Mary H. Hardin
Died      Feby 7 1897 in Charleston So. Ca.
Age       Born 1852
Bui'd     February 8th  4 P. M. St. Davids
Minister  Thomas P. Baker

Name      Cornelius Kollock, M. D.
Died      Aug 17  1:20 A. M. 1897
Age       Seventy two Yrs (72) 8 months
Buried    Aug. 17   5:30 P. M.
Minister  Thomas P. Baker
          Dr. Kollock had been for many years a vestryman
of St. Davids, & at the time of his death was Senior Warden.
                                              T. P. B.
```

300
```
Name      S. Gillespie Godfrey
Died      Sept. 3d 1:30 A. M. 1897
Age       Was born Decr. 28th 1839
Buried    October 1st 12 o'c. M. 1897
Minister  Thomas P. Baker
          Mr. Godfrey was for many yrs a vestryman of St.
Davids & at his death was Jr. Warden He was lay reader for
24 years.
```

```
1898
Name      Mrs. Robbins
Died      March 16 1898
Age       about 80
Buried    March 18 1898 St. David's yard
Minister  Thomas P. Baker

Name      Carrie McIver Godfrey
Died      March 17 1898
Age       25 yrs
Buried    March 19th 1898   St. Davids yard
Minister  Thomas P. Baker

Name      Alex A. Pollock
Died      June 30 1898
Age       67 yrs
Buried    July 1 1898 St Davids yard
Minister  Thomas P. Baker
```

301
```
Name      James H. Powe, M. D.
died      Aug 1st 1 o'c. a. m. 1898
Age       63
buried    Aug 3rd in St. David's yard
Minister  Thomas P. Baker
    Dr. Powe at the time of his death was the supt. of St.
David's S. School.
```

```
Name      William Gainey
Died      Nov 15th 1898
Age       21 years
Buried    Nov.
Minister  Thos. P. Baker
```

1900
Name   Henrietta S. Kollock, widow of the late Dr. C.
        Kollock
Died   Sunday A. M. January 14th 1900
Age   72 years & 11 months
Buried In St. David's yard Jany 15 1900 by the Rector of
        St. David's Church   Thomas P. Baker

302   In Darlington June 2, I assisted the Rev. R. W. Barnwell at
        the burial of Theodora Wagner Woods, wife of Edward Woods
        Age about 33   Thomas P. Baker

        Allen Benton Wells died July 21st 1900 and buried St. Davids
        Church yard by Rev. H. M. Jarvis July 22nd

        1901
        Eliza May Hall buried in St. Davids church yard Mch 9th 1901
        by the Rector C. W. Boyd

        July 19th 1901 Pauline Harrall aged   was buried in St.
        Davids Churchyard   C. W. Boyd   R.

        Aug 5th 1901 Francis Samuel Gillespie was buried in family
        cemetery in Marlboro County   C. W. Boyd   R.

        Aug 25th 1901 Eleanor H. Malloy was buried in St. Davids
        churchyard   C. W. Boyd   R.

303   Jan 5th 1902 Mrs. Martha Roscoe buried from St. Davids
        Church by the rector C. W. Boyd

        Caroline Harrington McIver wife of Henry McIver was buried
        from St. Davids Church on the 10th Jan 1902 aged 73 years
        Funeral services by the rector C. W. Boyd

        Jan 27th 1902 Margaret Evans Duvall eldest daughter of
        Marine Duvall was buried from St. Davids Church by the
        rector C. W. Boyd Deceased was in her 16th year

        Jan 28th 1902 Charlie Stanton son of Harris Stanton buried
        from St. Davids church by the rector Deceased was in his
        13th year   C. W. Boyd rector

        Feb. 11th 1902 Daniel Harrington son of W. T. and M. E.
        Thrower was buried from St. Davids church aged 4 months
        C. W. Boyd rector

        Burbank
        March 31st 1902 Florine Louise Wilson wife of Dr. T. F.
        Burbank was buried in St. Davids churchyard by the rector
        C. W. Boyd

304   Harrington
        Annie Kollock Harrington on the 16th June 1902 at St. Davids
        churchyard Funeral services by the rector C. W. Boyd

        Thrower
        On the 29th July 1902 Hariet Powe infant daughter of Mr. and
        Mrs. W. T. Thrower was buried from St. Davids Church by the
        rector C. W. Boyd

Bigham
On the 28th Aug. 1902 Mrs. Caroline Harriet Bigham was buried at Davids (sic) Churchyard, Dr. F. H. Waddill reading the service he being lay reader for the parish. C. W. Boyd

Powe
On 24th Sept 1902 Charlotte Powe colored was buried from St. Davids church Funeral services by the rector C. W. Boyd

305   On the 13th January 1903 Judge Henry McIver was buried from St. Davids church. Funeral service by the rector. Deceased was born Sept. 25th 1826.

On the 15th May 1903 from St. Davids Church Fletcher Grant was buried services by the rector C. W. Boyd

On the 11th June 1903 David Goodwin was buried from St. Davids Church services by rector C. W. Boyd

On the 16th June 1903 I read funeral service over Daisy Etoil daughter of Mr. and Mrs. Eddings   C. W. Boyd

On the 26th Aug 1903 the infant daughter of A. and C. W. Kittrell was buried from St. Davids Church services by the rector

On the 10th of Jan. 1904 Fannie Turner wife of W. A. Benton was buried from St. Davids church   C. W. Boyd rector

On the 19th March 1904 Lucinda Croley was buried from St. Davids church   C. W. Boyd, rector

306   At St. Davids Church Aug. 14th 1904 Wm. Godfrey McLean was buried by the rector   C. W. Boyd

At St. Davids church Aug 23d 1904 Thos P. McIver was buried by the rector   C. W. Boyd

On Oct 26th 1904 I read the funeral service over Mr. Van Tyere(?) at his house and the cemetery   C. W. Boyd

On 23d May 1905 I officiated at the burial of Dr. T. A. Waddill at St. Davids church and churchyard   C. W. Boyd

On the 23d June 1905 Frances Pemberton Harrell daughter of Mr. and Mrs. T. P. Harrell was buried from St. Davids church by the rector.   C. W. Boyd

On the 10th July 1906, J. P. Harrall aged 88 years was buried from St. Davids church.   C. W. Boyd, rector

On the 12th Sept 1906, I buried from her home 8 miles below Cheraw, Melissa Atkinson aged about 46 years.
                    C. W. Boyd

307   On the 20th day of Dec. 1906 from St. Davids Church, Elizabeth Graham was buried. She died Dec. 28th aged about 77 years.   C. W. Boyd

On the 20th July 1907 Mrs. Ellen S. Waddill was buried from St. Davids Church   C. W. Boyd, rector

On the 15th August 1907 W. A. Benton was buried from St. Davids Church. The Rev. J. S. Hartzell officiating in the absence of the rector.   C. W. Boyd

On the 19th Oct 1907, Charlotte Harrington Powe was buried from St. David's Church   C. W. Boyd, rector

On the 12th of January 1908, Mrs. W. H. Monson was buried from St. Davids Church.   C. W. Boyd, rector

On the 18th of January 1908, Mrs. Laura A. wife of J. P. Harrall was buried from the church. The Rev.A. S. Thomas of Darlington officiating.   C. W. Boyd, rector

On the 14th Feb 1908, Jas Miles Croley was buried from the church.   C. W. Boyd, rector

308 On the 17th of Feb 1908, Mrs. Gertrude wife of Mr. Clarence Medlin was buried from the church.   C. W. Boyd, rector.

On the 8th of April 1908, Mr. E. M. Wells, aged about 77 years, was buried from the church.   C. W. Boyd, rector.

On the 19th of March 1909 Miss Mary Elizabeth Shaw, who died in Newark, N. Y., Mch 17, 1909, I buried from St. David's Church. She was born in Boston, Mass. September 20, 1817. A. S. Thomas, Rector.

On the 14th of October 1909, Benjamin Reeves Hickson (died 13th Oct.) I buried from the church an infant.
                              A. S. Thomas, Rector.

On the 20th day of July 1910   Mrs.   Atkinson I buried from her home near Cash's Depot interment at Bethel yard below Cash's.   A. S. Thomas

On May 10, 1911, Carrie Boyd died in Rock Hill, May 8, 1911, was buried in St. David's church yard.   A. S. Thomas

On May 15, 1911, (died same day) Lillie Watson Hereford in St. David's lot in new part of Cemetary.   A. S. Thomas

On   Maree in new part of Cemetary.   A. S. Thomas

On Sept. 11, 1912 (died on 10th) at McBee S. C. Anna (Mrs. L. D.) Robertson.   A. S. Thomas

309 On Aug 22, 1913, Robert Beale Hereford (died Aug 21, 1913) in St. Davids lot in new part cemetary beside his wife
                              A. S. Thomas

On Sept 11, 1913 (died on 10) Mrs. Allie Cassedy
                              A. S. Thomas

On   W. Dewitt Evans   died   A. S. Thomas.

On Dec. 24, 1913; Lemuel D. Harrall died Dec. 23, 1913.
                              A. S. Thomas

On July 23, 1914, Gideon Walker Duvall age 4 years 1 mo. 18 day. died July 22, 1914.   A. S. Thomas

On Oct. 24, 1914, Samuel Gillespie Godfrey died same date.
A. S. Thomas

On Nov. 25, 1914 (died on 24th) an infant (twin) of Laura Gainey & J. A. Hill.
A. S. Thomas

On 20 April 1915, Lewis Gainey died on 19 April 1915.
A. S. Thomas

On April 24, 1915, J. Thomas Stanton died April 23, 1915.
A. S. Thomas

On   July 1915   J. Thomas Stanton (son of above)
A. S. Thomas

On Jan. 22, 1916, Henrietta K. Gainey died Jan 21, 1916.
A. S. Thomas

310   Maude Ardella Hill on April 29, 1916, died April 28, 1916.
A. S. Thomas-

On July 4, 1916, John H. Wells, died on July 3, 1916
A. S. Thomas

On Jan 15, 1917, Mary Elizabeth Dameron died Jan 14, 1917
A. S. Thomas

On June 5, 1917, Josephine Elizabeth Powe died June 4, 1917.
A. S. Thomas

On Sept. 13, 1917 (died same day) Thomas L. Woods.
A. S. Thomas

On Jan   1918   Mrs. Margaret Wells died in Columbia
Jan   1918   A. S. Thomas

On Sept. 3, 1918 Mrs. J. C. Patrick at St. Davids died
Sept 1, 1918   A. S. Thomas

On April 19, 1918 John Powe   died April 18, 1918
A. S. Thomas

On Sept 14, 1918, Mrs. Rebecca F. Pollock died on Sept.
13, 1918.   A. S. Thomas

On Dec. 11, 1918 Mrs. H. P. (Irene) Duvall Jr. died on Dec.
10, 1918   A. S. Thomas

On Sept. (about 8th) 1919, George Brown

311   On September 26, 1919, Walter N. Monson died Sept. 25, 1919
A. S. Thomas

On   Mrs. Charles F. (Shadie) Haley died
A. S. Thomas

On December 30, 1920, Margaret Wilson Duvall died in
Columbia on Dec. 29, 1920.   A. S. Thomas

On Feb. 9, 1921, Mrs. S. G. (Hattie) Godfrey died Feb. 8,
1921.   A. S. Thomas

138

On April 25, 1921, Zella May Wood died April 24, 1921
                                          A. S. Thomas

On August 2, 1921 Eleanor Josephine Godfrey died on same
day.   A. S. Thomas

On October 19, 1921 by Mr. A. S. Thomas, Mrs. Mary Emack
Duvall, wife of G. W. Duvall, who died in Philadelphia, Pa.
on Oct. 17, 1921

On June 4, 1922 by Mr. O. T. Porcher of Bennettsville S. C.
(St. Davids having no Rector) Hon William Pegues Pollock
died June 3rd 1922.

On June 20, 1922 by Mr. A. S. Thomas, Judge Edward McIver
died June 19, 1922

312 On Oct. 1st 1922 by Mr. J. S. Hartzell,Easter Pauline
Cassidy aged 5 mos. daughter of Peter & Mattie Cassidy died
Sept 29, 1922.

On Nov. 10, 1922 by Mr. A. S. Thomas, Mrs.Henrietta Munson
wife of W. N. Munson died in Charleston, S. C. Nov 9, 1922

On Nov. 29, 1922 by Mr. A. S. Thomas, Wm. Robbins Godfrey,
Senior Warden of St. Davids died Nov. 28, 1922.

On January 24, 1923, by Rev. A. S. Thomas Anne McRae Morris
daughter of J. J. and Alevine Morris at home of Thomas P.
Harrall died Jan. 22, 1923.

[Pages 313-333 are blank.]

334 Communion Alms during the ministration of Revd. Jno W.
Motte (Deacon) Minister of St. Davids.
Revd. P. D. Hay (Presbyter) administering the Sacrament.

1867	Collected		1867 Disbursed		
July 14th	Bp. Gregg officiating	$7.55	July 26th Mr. Johnson		$3.00
Aug. 11th	Revd. P. D. Hay "	6.25	Aug 2nd Mrs. Stafford		2.25
			Sept 1st Subscrpt		
			to Courier(?)		2.25
Sept 8th	--------------------	3.85	Sept 12th Wine for		
			Communion		3.50
Oct 13th (Collection by ?)		2.35	Sept. 30th Mrs. Stafford		1.00
			"	Mrs. Goodwin	1.00
			Oct. 7th	" "	1.00
			" "	Mrs. Stafford	1.00
			" "	Quinine for the	
				Poor	.80
			" 28th	Mrs. Johnson	2.60
			Nov. 1st	" "	.60
			" 5th	Mrs. Stafford	1.00
Nov. 10th Revd. P. D. Hay officiating					
		5.00	Dec. 2nd	" "	2.00
Dec. 8th (collection by MOM?)		4.75	" "	Mrs. Goodwyn	2.00
			" 18th	" "	2.00
			" "	" Stafford	2.00
			1868		
			Jany 2nd Mrs. Sarah Stafford		
					1.50
1868 Jany 12th (collected by MOM?) 6.20			" 12th Mrs. Goodwyn		2.00

	[Jany] 12th Mrs. Stafford 2.00
	" " Mrs. Stafford (Sarah) 1.00
	" " Mrs. Croule .50
	" 21st Mrs. Stafford .70
Feby 9th (collected by M. O. M.) 3.95	Feby 10th Lucinda Crouly .50
	" 11th Mrs. Stafford 1.70
	" " Mrs. Goodwyn 1.75
March 8th (colltd. by MOM) 6.00	March 9th Mrs. Stafford 2.50
	" " Mrs. Goodwyn 2.50
	" 26th " " 1.00
Easter Day " " 9.05	April 13th Mrs. Gayle 2.00
	" 15th Mrs. Stafford 3.00
	" " Mrs. Goodwyn 3.00

335   Communion Alms

Collected	Disbursed
Brot forward 1.30	April 24th Lucinda Crouly .75
Trinity: Revd L. F. Gregg offtd. 5.13	June 15th Mrs. Stafford 2.00
	" " " Goodwyn 2.00
	" " a destitute infant 1.13
	" " Mrs. Gayle .55
July 12th (Revd. P. D. Hay offtg) 5.16	July 16th Mrs. Goodwyn 2.00
	" " Mrs. Stafford 2.00
	" 17th Lucinda Crowly .50
	" 23rd Mrs. Stafford 1.00
Aug. 2nd (Revd. L. F. Guerry offtg.) 3.80	Aug. 4th Mrs. Sarah Stafford .25
	" 6th Mrs. Mary Goodwin .50
	" " Mrs. Elisabeth .55
	" " Mrs. Stafford 1.25
Septr 13th (Revd. P. D. Hay offtg.) 2.40	" " Mrs. Goodwin 1.25
	Sept 16 " " 1.25
	" " Mrs. Stafford 1.20
Nov. 22nd (Ordination) 14.46	Nov. 22nd To the Bp. 14.46
1869	
Feby 7th 3.38	Feby 10 Mrs. Goodwyn 1.00
	" 12 Mrs. Gayle 1.00
	" 16th Mrs. Stafford 1.38
March 7th 7.88	March 8th Mrs. Goodwyn 3.00
	" " Mrs. Stafford 3.00
	" 15 Mrs. Gayle 1.25
March 28th Easter Day 5.40	" 30 " " 1.00
	April 6th Mrs. Stafford 2.00
	" 24th Mrs. Goodwyn 2.00
	" " Mrs. Goodwyn 1.00
April 23rd Collection for	
Advancemt. Socty 15.15	" 22 To Rev. P ----[?] 15.16
May 2nd 3.36	May 4th Mrs. Stafford 1.50
	" " Mrs. Goodwyn 1.50
June 6th 8.53	June 8th Mrs. Gayle 2.00
	" 27 Mrs. Goodwyn 3.00
	" 29th Mrs. Stafford 3.00
	July Mrs. Gayle 1.03
Total 46.79	46.79

338   Communicants of St. David's, Cheraw

The following were Communicants, at the departure for Texas
of Bishop Gregg, who was the last rector of the parish.

1860, Feb. 1   Oliver H. Kollock (dead) & Dr. Cor-
nelius Kollock, his son. Henry W. Harrington, & his wife
Rebecca, Wm. Godfrey & his wife, Margaret. Miss Josephine
C. Pritchard; Miss Claudia E. Godfrey. Miss Julia M. Hawes;
Mrs. Mary Steinmetz & her daughters, Mrs. Frances Bryan, &
Mrs. Virginia C. Tarrh. Mrs. Kensal Robbins & her daughter,
Miss Josephine E. R. Mrs. Margaret Wells & her sister Miss
Elizth. Reddy. Miss Harriet Brock (removed), Miss Fanny
Turner. Genl. James Gillespie, James Harral, & his wife
Laura. Mrs. Ann Drake & her daughters Miss Mary Drake & Mrs.
Charlotte Kendall. Mrs. Catherine Gale & her two daughters
Mary and Frances[stricken]. Mrs. Sarah, wife of Mr. Gideon
Duvall. Mrs. Mary Jane, wife of Mr. Marine Duvall. Mrs.
Mary Stafford. Mrs. Saphy, wife of David Goodwyn. Mrs. Sarah
wife of James Goodwyn & her daughters, Mrs. Martha Taylor.
Mrs. Mary Purvis[stricken]. Dr. Thomas E. Powe, & His daugh-
ter Mrs. Caroline McIver, & his son Dr. James H. Powe. Miss
Maria Inglis[stricken]. Miss Emma Bryan. Harman Westervelt
(dead) & his wife, Emily. Mr. John Irving Westervelt & his
wife Sarah (decd.). Francis M. McIver & his wife Henrietta.
Mr. Jacob Ganey & his wife Harriet.   Total 47
Coloured. Frank, Charlotte, Louisa, Mary & Spencer, servants
of Dr. Th. E. Powe. Frank, servant of Mr. W. Godfrey. Total
6.   Attest, Robt. B. Croes.

There were three white & one colored, communicants in Bp.
Gregg's family, who removed in Feb, 1860.

Removals. March 14, 1860, Miss Josephine C. Pritchard, April
16, '60, Miss Elizabeth Reddy.* [entire entry stricken]

* James Tauzey was a communicant who removed in 1859, before
Bp. Gregg's departure.

339   Communicants
Additions. Easter Sunday, April 8th, 1860.

Mrs. Elizabeth Waddill, Mrs. Eliza Williams Harrington & John
P. Edwards.   removed
Mrs. Marion R Brown moved into the parish   Oct. 1861
Miss Mary R. Brown added to communion   Feby 2nd 1862
Mrs. Turner   "   April 6 1862
Edward T. Gaillard & John W.Harrington   May 11th
Mary S. Bryan, Jennie Brock(removed) Henry Duval, Anna
Harrall, Rebecca Raddy, Annie Westervelt added July 6th
Louisa Westervelt (Cheraw) Misses Wilding & Susan DeSaussure
(Charleston)   Sept 7th
Mrs. E. Bowne added to communion Whitsunday 1863
Miss Ida Jenkins refugee   from Wadmelaw   June 7th
Miss Rosa Jenkins   "   Carrie DeSaussure Frances Goodwin
Wm Robbins Godfrey, Edgar Harrall.
Jane servt. of J. K. McIver & May servt. of Dr. T. E. Powe,
all added July 5th, 63.
1864
July 3d Sallie Waddell, Annie Gaillard, Chston., Kate A.
Lemar of Charleston, & Rose, colored woman of Dr. T. E. Powe.

1865
May   George Wilmer Brown, Army N. V.
July 2nd   Miss Simmons & Mrs. E. D. Hearsey
Augst 7th   M. D. Matheson, Grattan Hagser, Miss F. Walter
"   "   Mrs Laura Prince, Miss Kate Gooch, S. Gillespie
Godfrey, Wm Allen Benton.

                                     Total   39

340   1867   Communicants of St. David's Church

      July 14th   Cornelius Kollock, M. D.
      "   "   Wm Godfrey & wife Margaret & son Wm. R. Godfrey
      "   "   Miss Josephine C. Pritchard
      "   "   Mrs. Claudia E. McLean
      "   "   Miss Julia M. Hawes   rm. '68
      "   "   Mrs. Kensal Robbins
      "   "   Dr. Jas. H. Powe & wife Josephine
      "   "   Dr. T. E. Powe
      "   "   Mr. S. G. Godfrey & wife Harriet E.
      "   "   Mrs. Caroline McIver
      "   "   Genl. Jas. Gillespie
      "   "   Mrs. Frank Gillespie
      "   "   Mr. E. J. Waddell, wife Elisabeth & daughter
                     Sarah
      "   "   Mrs. Sarah Turner
      "   "   Col. Jno W. Harrington & wife Eliza W.
      "   "   Mrs. Rebecca Harrington
      "   "   Mrs. Mary Stinemetz (died March 6th 1868)
      "   "   Mrs. Virginia Tarrh
      "   "   Mrs. Frances Bryan & daughter Mary S.
      "   "   Mr. J. J. Westervelt & daughter Annie (R. Oct.
                                                    24th 1868)
      "   "   Mrs. Margaret Wells & her sisters Elisabeth &
                     Rebeca Reddy
      "   "   Mr. Jas. Harrall his wife Laura, daughter Anna &
                     son Edgar
      "   "   Mrs. Hagner & daughter Fannie & sister Miss Gaunup
      "   "   Mrs. Sarah Duvall daughter Sarah & son Henry
      "   "   Mr. Allen Benton & wife Fanny
      "   "   Mrs. Ann Drake
      "   "   Mrs. E. D. Hausey & sisters Mrs. Louisa Prince &
                     Miss Kate Gooch
      "   "   Mrs. E. Bowne
      "   "   Mrs. Catherine Gayle & daughter Mrs. Mary Gayle
      "   "   Mrs. Mary Stafford
      "   "   Mrs. Sophy Goodwyn
      "   "   Mr. Jacob Gainey & wife Harriet
      "   "   Mrs. Walker   Mrs. Purvis   Total 59
      "   "   Frank (coloured)

341   July 21st 1867   Miss Lizzie Harrington
      "   W. J. Westervelt (R. Aug. 1st 1868)
      "   Jno H. Powe
      1867 Dec. 13th   (Mr. John Beatty wife (added) from Haverton,
                        Mass) [this entry stricken]
      1869 Jany   Admitted Frances Goodwyn
      "   March 15th "   Mrs. W. R. Ried   from M. E. Church
                        Mrs. Stanton

342   Communicants reported to Council, May, 1900

      Mrs. James H. Powe   1   Charlotte Powe   3
      Etta Powe   2   Claudia Powe   4

                              142

Thos P. Baker   ) removed
Mrs. T. P. Baker)
Mrs. E. M. Wells 5
Lillian Wells 6
Maggie Wells Removed
Mildred Wells 7
Jos. B. Wells Removed
Mrs. S. G. Godfrey 8
Gillespie Godfrey 9
Harrington Godfrey 10
Claudia Godfrey 11
Marion Godfrey 12
Hattie Godfrey 13
Eleanor Godfrey 14
L. D. Harrall 15
Mrs. L. D, Harrall 16
Harry Harrall 17
Laura Harrall 18
Alex. Harrall 19
Fletcher Grant 20

Miss Hewett 21
Mrs. Agnes E. McLean 22
Agnes McLean 23
William McLean 24
Bessie McLean 25
Miss Mary Shaw   ) Removed
Mrs. James Dillingham)
Dr. Frank A. Waddill 26
Mrs. F. A. Waddill 27
Cornelius K. Waddill 28
Mrs. Rebekah Pollock 29
  Ella Pollock 30
Mrs. Waddill Pegues 31
Rev. H. M. Jarvis 32
  W. R. Godfrey 34
Mrs. W. R. Godfrey
Louis Gainey 36
Mrs. Lewis Gainey 37
Mrs. Kelsall Gainey 38
  Laura Gainey 39
  Etta Gainey 40
  Maude Gainey 41
  David Goodwin 42
  Shady Stanton 43

343   Communicants   cont'd   May 1900

M. W. Duvall 44
Mrs. M. W. Duvall 45
G. Walker Duvall 46
Howard Duvall 47
Ernest Duvall 48
Will Duvall 49
Maggie Duvall 50
Miss Mattie Duvall 51
Judge R. C. Watts 52
Mrs. R. C. Watts 53
Courtenay Watts 54
Gus Watts 55
Walter Mouson 56
Mrs. Mary Reid 58
  May Reid 59
  H. P. Duvall 60
Mrs. H. P. Duvall 61
E. Walker Duvall 62
Fannie Duvall 64
Edith Duvall 65
  James P. Harrall 66
Mrs. James P. Harrall 67
Pauline Harrall 68
Thomas P. Harrall 69
Ernest Harrall 70
Ella Harrall 71
  W. A. Benton 72
Mrs. W. A. Benton 73

John H. Powe 74
Mrs. John H. Powe 75
  Lettie Powe 76
  Henry Powe 77
  James Powe 78
  Florence Powe 79
Mrs. Warren Guy (Revm.
Mrs. Henry McIver 80
Mrs. Eleanor Malloy 81
  Nell Harden 82
Mrs. Leola Harrington 83
  Lulee Harrington 84
Mrs. Atkinson 86)
Miss Atkinson 87) Cash's, S.C.
  Frank Gillespie 88
Mrs. Frank Gillespie 89
Wm. Harrington 90
  Eliza Gillespie 91
  Sidney Gillespie 92
  Frank Gillespie 93
Miss Lizzie Graham 94
  Alyne Gayle 95

Tempie Harrington, cold. 96
Charlotte Powe, cold.   97

          Total
Males   Females
 34   70
          104

143

Mrs. James H. Powe   Mrs. S. G. Godfrey
Etta Powe   Gillespie Godfrey
Charlotte Powe   Harrington Godfrey
Claudia Powe   Claudia Godfrey
Mr. E. M. Wells   Marion Godfrey
Mrs. E. M. Wells   Eleanor Godfrey
   Lillian Wells   Hattie Godfrey
   Mildred Wells   Mr. T. D. Harrall
   John Wells   Mrs. T. D. Harrall
                                 Harry Harrall
                                 Alex. Harrall
                                 Laura Harrall

345   Communicants Reported May 1902

Mrs. James Powe   )
   Etta Powe   )
   Charlotte Powe) 5
   Claudia Powe   )
Mrs. Hattie Lynch)

Mr. E. M. Wells)
Mrs. E. M. Wells)
   Lilian Wells) 5
   Mildred Wells)
   John Wells   )

Mrs. S. G. Godfrey   )
   Gillespie Godfrey   )
   Harrington Godfrey   )
   Claudia Godfrey   ) 7̶ 6
   Marion Godfrey [stricken])
   Eleanor Godfrey   )
   Hattie Godfrey   )

Mr. L. D. Harrall)
Mrs. L. D. Harrall)   7 members
   Harry Harrall) 5
   Alex. Harrall)   Lottie Harrall
   Laurie Harrall)   James Harrall

Fletcher Grant) [both stricken]
Miss Hewitt   )

346   Mrs. Agnes McLean   )
          Bessie McLean   )
          Agnes McLean   ) 4
          William McLean   )

Dr. F. A. Waddill)
Mrs. Waddill   ) 4
   Cornelius   )
   Elizabeth   )

```
Mrs. Rebecca Pollock)
      Ella Pollock ) 3
Mrs. Waddill Pegues ) removed

Rev. H. M. Jarvis)   2
Mrs. H. M. Jarvis)  removed

Mr. W. R. Godfrey )
Mrs. W. R. Godfrey) 2

Mr. Wm. Godfrey)
Mrs Wm. Godfrey) 2 + 3 = 5

Mr. Louis Gainey    )
Mrs.  "   Gainey    )
Mrs. Kellsall Gainey)
      Laura Gainey  )  6
      Etta Gainey   )
      Maude Gainey  )

David Goodwin      dead
Shady Stanton
```

347
```
Mr. M. W. Duvall     )
Mrs. M. W. Duvall    )
  G. Walker Duvall   )
  Howard Duvall      )
  Ernest Duvall      )  8
  Elise Duvall       )
  Willie Duvall      )
Miss Mattie Duvall   )

Judge R. C. Watts )
  Mrs. Watts      ) 5 + 1 = 6
Courtney Watts    )
Gus Watts         )
Bessie Watts      )

Mrs. Mary Reid)
     May Reid ) 2

Mr. Thomas Harrall) 2 + 2
Mrs. Thos Harrall )

Mr. H. P. Duvall    )
Mrs H. P. Duvall    )
  E. Walker Duvall  )
  Heal Duvall       )  7
  Fannie Duvall     )
  Edith Duvall      )
  Ellen Duvall      )

Mr. J. P. Harrall  )
Mrs. J. P. Harrall )
   Bessie Harrall  )  5
   Ernest Harrall  )
   Ella Harrall    )

Mr. W. A. Benton   1
Mrs. W. A. Benton [stricken]
```

348 Mr. John H. Powe)   Bessie Powe
     Mrs. J. H. Powe)
         Henry Powe)
         James Powe)   7
       Roland Powe)
     Florence Powe)

     Miss Nell Harden   1

     Mrs. Lulu Harrington
         Lulu Harrington   3
         Ruth Harrington
         Annie Harrington died

     Mrs. Atkinson)   2
     Miss Atkinson)

     Mrs. Frank Gillespie
       Mrs. Harrington   4
     Eliza Gillespie
     Sidney Gillespie[stricken]
     Frank Gillespie

     Mrs Cobb)   1 + 4

     Tempie Harrington col'd.   1

     Charlotte Powe   col'd 1   died

     Males 35 Females 66 Total 101

     Add Miss Lizzie Graham
     Add Mrs Eddings
     Families 27

349 Rev. Mr. Hartsell
      Mrs. Hartsell
     Dorith Hartsell
     Gertrude   "   2 + 3
     George   "

     Mr. Pendleton)
     Mrs. Pendleton) 2

     Mr. Martin)2 + 1
     Mrs. Martin)

     W. T. Thrower   )
     Mrs. W. T. Thrower) 1 + 4

     Mrs. Emily Guy)
       Edwin Guy   ) 1 + 1

     Mr. Wm Hickson Sr.)
     Mrs. Hickson   ) 3 + 2
     Wm. Hickson Jr.   )

     Mrs. Wild Pegues
     Mrs. C. W. Boyd 1 + 1

350 Mr. Edward McIver   Mr. Saml Evans
     Mr. B. F. Pegues   Bess Evans
                             Thos Evans   Henry Howell

146

[Pages 351-375 are blank.]

376   Series of Church Services in St. David's

1864
May 15 Whitsunday   morning & afternoon
"   16th Monday in Whitsun Week morning
"   17th Tuesday   "   "   "
May 18th   Funeral Service
"   22nd Trinity Sunday morning & afternoon   communion
"   29th 1st Sunday aft. Trinity [morning & afternoon]
June 1st _____ Wednesday afternoon Service
"   5th 2d Sunday after Trinity morning & after. communion
                                        & catechism
"   8th   Wednesday Afternoon   service & Lecture
"   12th 3rd Sunday aft. Trinity morning rainy evening
"   15th Wednesday aftn. Service & Lecture.
"   19th Fourth Sunday aft. Trinity morning Bp. Davis
            preached & confirmed
"   "   same afternoon at Grace Chapel
"   26th Fifth Sunday aft. Trinity morning & afternoon
"   29th Wednesday afternoon service & lecture
July 3rd Sixth Sun. aft. Trininty morning communion aftn.
            Cat. & Baptism
"   6th   Wednesday afternoon service & lecture
"   10th 7th Sun. aft. Trinity   morning & afternoon
"   17th 8th "   "   "   "   "
"   24th 9th "   "   "   "   rainy
"   31st 10th "   "   "   "
Augst. 2nd   morning Infant Baptism   afternoon Funeral
"   7th 11th Sunday aft. Trininty morning commn. afternoon
                                        catechizing
"   12th " 13th & 14th Sundays Lay-reading morning
Septr. 4th 15th Sun. aft. Trininty morning communion aftn.
                                        catechism
"   7th Wednesday aftn. service & Lecture
[remainder of this page and of page 377 shows morning and
afternoon services on sundays and Wednesday services aftn.
service & Lecture, and give no pertinent information for
inclusion here.]

[Pages 378 and 379 are blank.]

380   Collections
1860, Jan. 22d Sunday. Delivered to Revd. R. B. Croes, by
Bishop Gregg $2.50
        Sunday Feb. 5   collected (Communion) $4.70
        ditto Feb. 19   do for Foreign Missions $19.25
        ditto March 4   (Communion collecn.) $5.58
        ditto Easter, April 8, Comn. Offerings for Missions
                                in Texas $45.00
        ditto May 6, Communion, Offerings for Missions in
                            S. Carolina $15.75
                            Total, $92.78

1861
Novr 3rd Sunday   Communion Offerings $5.50
Decr. 1st "   "   " $4.70
1862
Jany 5th   "   "   " $2.30
"   "   Collection for sufferers in
                            Charleston $25.00

147

```
Feby 2nd     Collection for Diocesan quota        $15.00
March 2nd    Communion Offerings                  $6.45
April 6th       "          "                      $8.00
May 11th     Convocation   "                      $18.08
June 1st     Communion     "                      $8.75
  "   8th    (Whitsunday)  "                       $7.00
1863
Easter Sunday   communion offerings               $25.45
April 9th   pd. Mrs. R. for distribution          $25.45
Whitsunday morning Communion offerings            $22.35
 May 25th   pd. Mrs. R. for distrubution          $22.35
  "   "   Offering for Sunday School for Texas     $54.01
June 7th   Communion offerings                    $16.25
         pd. above to Mrs. R. for distribution
June 14th  Collection at Bishop's visit for
                     Diocesan Missions            $5.55
  "  15th  pd. above to the Bishop
July 5th   Communion Offerings (distributed by    $24.65
                              Mrs. R.)
Augt 2nd    "          " (distributed by Mrs. R)  $26.05
  "  21st  Fast Day collection handed to Ladies
           S. A. Association for Charleston Hospitals $62.40
Septr 6th  Communion Offerings (distributed by Ladies)$35.55
Octr 4th      "          "           "        "     $32.35
Nov. 1st      "          "           "        "     $69.15
Dec. 6th      "          "           "        "     $70.80
  "  16th  Fast day offering --- for soldiers families $20.00
```

[the following two pages were not paginated in original]
```
381     1860 Payments   Sunday, Feb. 19, $2.00 Feb. 20, $2.50
April 9, 1860, Easter Monday, Sent $45.00 to Bp. Gregg for
Texas.  The money was received.
April 23d  paid $1.00  May 15, Paid to Dr. Thos E. Powe,
Delegate to the Diocesan Convn. $15.45 for Diocesan Missions
May 17 Appropriated for Sunday School Books, $.500.
Delivered to Mrs. Godfrey for distribution $1.68  R. B. Croes

1861
Novr 3d  Delivered to Dr. C. Kollock for distribution  $5.50
Decr. 4th Returned to me by  "    $1
  "    "   Distributed to Mrs. Sayle $2 to Mrs. Gooding $2
Mrs. Stafford $1.70 = $5.70
1862
Jany 5th  pd to Mr. Waddell Trasr. to be transmitted to
                     Charleston                    $25.00
  "  19th Gen. Gillespie pd. for Charleston transmitted $25.00
  "  Mr. Waddell $20 Dr. Powe $20 M. Godfrey $20    $60.00
Feb. 13th  pd. to Dr. Powe in Charleston for Convn. quota
                                                   $13.00
March 4th   distributed among three famillies      $5.00
  "  29th  pd for posts for pasonage fence          $1.00
May 1st gave to Mrs. Robbins for distribution      $10.00
June 10th pd Bp Davis offerings on Whitsunday       $7.00
July 2nd  pd. Rev. W. A. Patrick convocation collection
                                                   $20.00
  "   6th  Communion offerings                     $11.95
  "   7th  pd. Mrs. Robbins for distribution       $15.00
Augst 3rd    Communion offerings                    $6.70
Septr 7th     "          "                         $13.30
  "  10th   pd. Miss C. Godfrey for distribution   $14.00
  "  18th  Thanksgiving offering St. David's Ch.   $59.00
     19th   Forwarded same for S. C. Hospitals in Va. $59.00
```

```
October 5th   Communion offerings                        $10.80
    "     7th   pd. Mrs. Robbins for distribution          $10.70
Nov. 2nd       Communion offerings                        $20.75
    "  10th   pd. Mrs. R. for distribution               $10.00
    " 29th        "      "      "       "                  $5.00
        Revd. from 2 or 3 persons for S. Churchman         $3.00
             for 8th S. C. Regt.  forwarded for same       $5.00
Dec. 7th   Communion Offerings                            $15.70
     9th   pd. Mrs. R. for distribution                   $10.00
1863
Jany 4th       Communion Offerings                        $15.45
    "  6th   gave Mrs. R. check for distribution          $10.00
Feby 1st       Communion offerings                        $15.05
    "  8th   Collection for Convention Fund               $22.00
    "        pd. over same to M. W. Godfrey
     9th   distributed among three families $6.50
           pd, for Wood for Parochial School $2.00
    24th   pd. W. F. Wells for 1 Gal wine for Comn.        $8.00
March 1st   Communion Offerings                           $10.70
    "  5th Thanksgiving & Prayer Day                      $33.35
    " 13th   Forwarded same to Richmond to supply
             the Army with Bibles & Testaments
    " 18th   pd. Mrs. R. for distribution                 $10.00

382  1864
Jany 3rd   Communion offerings distributed by Mrs. R. $33.90
    " 24th   Mr. A. Benton gave for Soldiers families  $20.00
    " 27th   gave Mrs. Gayle & 3 others $5 each         $20.00
Feby 7th   Communion Offerings  distributed by Mrs. R $77.20
March 6th       "          "                           $56.25
    "  7th Collected by Rev. E. A. Bolles for C. S.
                       Bible Society                   $36.00
    29th Communion alms   Easter distributed           $58.45
April 8th   Fast Day Offering for Wayside Home at
                                       Florence        $88.00
May 1st    Communion Offerings  Distributed            $30.00
May 22nd      "          "   Trinity Sunday "          $38.05
June 5th      "          "   " 2nd Sunday              $31.50
July 3d       "          "   " 6th Sunday              $33.25
Augst 7th     "          "   " 11th  "                 $43.00
   "    "   the above distribute by Mrs. R.            $62.30
Septr 4th    Communion offerings   "     "             $83.
Octr 2nd         "              "
    "    "   $40 for Convention the bal. distribd.
    " 25th   forwarded to Widow's & orphans of Decd.
                       Clergy Fund                     $60.00
Nov. 6th   Communion alms   distributed by ladies      $75.00
Dec. 4th        "          "                           $81.00
1865
Jany 1st        "          "          "          "     $10.00
    " 22nd   Collection
             for Sexton $50 pd for Lock on door $5
Feby 5th   Communion offerings                         $84.00
March 19th      "          "                          $151.15
April 2nd       "          "                          $141.75

        ─────────────────────────────

For Communion Alms from July 14th 1867  see page 334

1867 Sept 30 Contribution by Note to Bp's Fund  by four
                         Communicants   $200.00
                END
                149
```

www.ingramcontent.com/pod-product-compliance
Lightning Source LLC
Chambersburg PA
CBHW021829020426
42334CB00014B/546